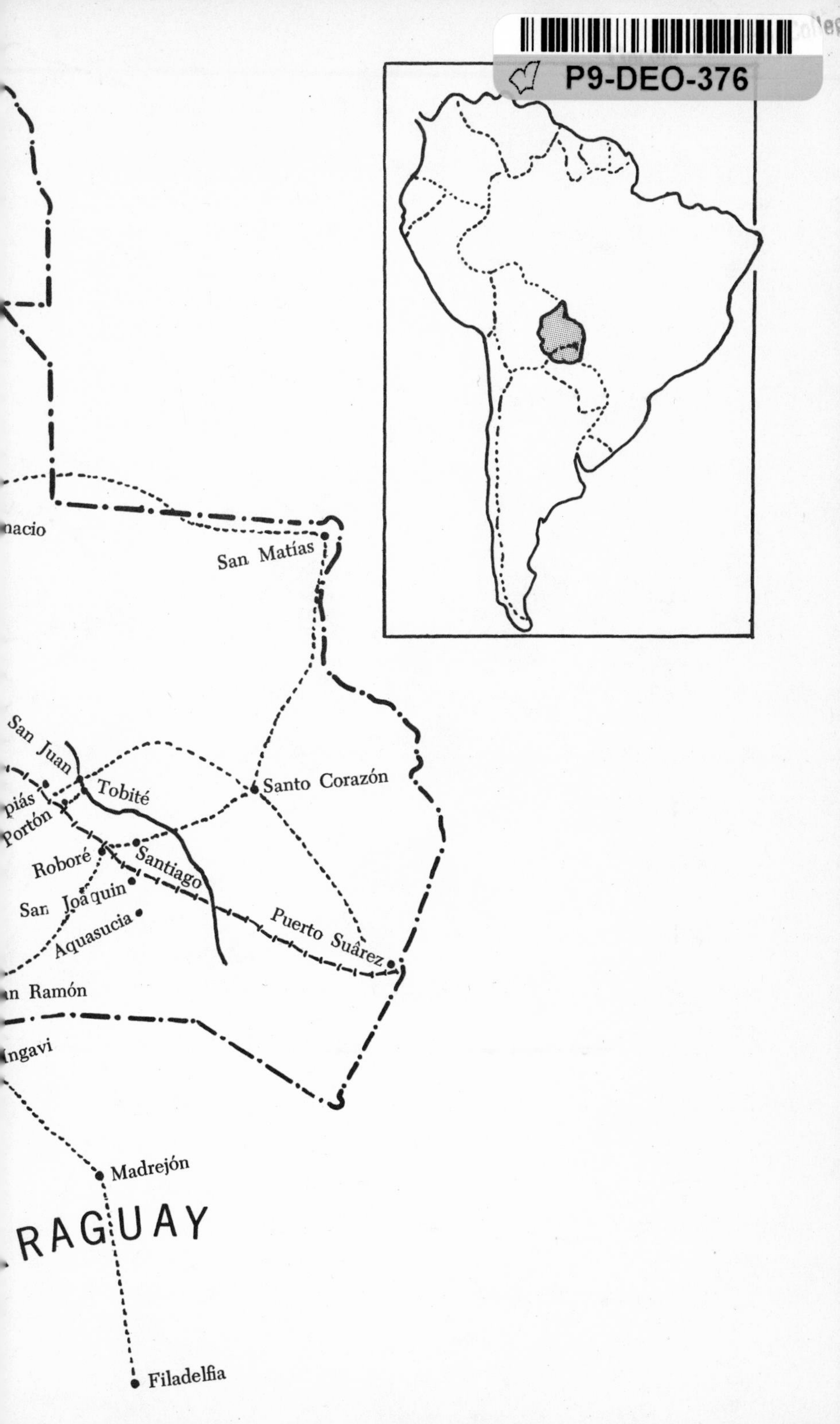
nacio
San Matías
San Juan
Tobité
Santo Corazón
piás
Portón
Roboré
Santiago
San Joaquin
Aquasucia
Puerto Suârez
n Ramón
ngavi
Madrejón
RAGUAY
Filadelfia

DEFEAT OF THE BIRD GOD

defeat of the bird god

"the story of
missionary bill pencille,
who risked his life to reach
the ayorés of bolivia"

c. peter wagner

foreword by paul s. rees

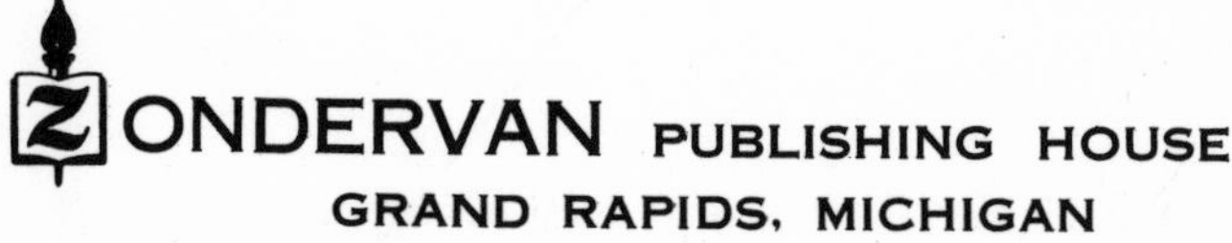

DEFEAT OF THE BIRD GOD

Library of Congress catalog card number: 67-11615

Printed in the United States of America

To my wife

DORIS

whose companionship has changed
missionary life
from a vocation
to an adventure
this book is affectionately dedicated

Foreword

In Saigon I passed the spot where, a few days earlier, a Buddhist monk had gone to his fiery death, self-destroyed.

In the following pages, in a Bolivian jungle setting, is the story of a Christian missionary in which, in place of a single, sensational act of self-immolation, there is the day-by-day offering of one's soul and body as "a living sacrifice" and the repeated hazarding of one's life for Christ's sake and the Gospel's.

Not that Bill Pencille would have it publicized in these terms, nor indeed that Peter Wagner, as author, has sentimentalized the tale in this fashion. Considering the raw materials that have gone into the making of this chronicle, there is extremely little of heroics. The authentic heroism that comes into view needs no rhetorical heightening.

How the good news of Christ reached Stone Age Indians in the middle of the twentieth century — this is the theme that is here unfolded. Neither the inaccessibility nor the hostility of the savage Ayorés was permitted to daunt or defeat the Pencilles and their comrades.

What follows makes absorbing reading: now because of the light it throws on the strange ways in which God guides His servants and now because of the incredible length to which He will go in proving their mettle; here because of the astonishing similarity between pride in savages and pride in sophisticates and there because of the incredible patience required in order to conquer with love the hearts of men made hard with hate.

The story scores. It has angles enough to give every reader a chance to make an application to himself, anguish enough to make pain wrench his spirit, achievement enough to send his gratitude soaring up to "the God of all grace."

A number of times, as I read the manuscript, I was reminded of that scene, many years ago, in which David Livingstone, back from Africa, was given the degree of Doctor of Laws by the University of Glasgow. In response to the honor conferred upon him Livingstone, bronzed by the equatorial sun and gaunt from many a bout with fever, announced his intention to return to the Africa he loved:

> I return with misgiving and with great gladness. For would you like me to tell you what supported me through all the years of exile among people whose language I could not understand, and whose attitude towards me was always uncertain and often hostile? It was this: "Lo, I am with you alway, even unto the end of the world!" On these words I staked everything, and they never failed!

So Bill Pencille found it in Bolivia. And so Peter Wagner — putting us all in his debt — has recorded it.

Paul S. Rees

Preface

The evangelization of the primitive Ayoré tribe, originally some 3,000 strong and spread throughout the vast Green Hell area of eastern Bolivia and northern Paraguay, has involved a large number of courageous missionaries, six of whom gave their lives that these savage and barbarous people might learn about Christ. Books could be written about many of the missionaries, representing the South America Indian Mission, New Tribes Mission, Mennonite Chuch, Latvian Baptists, and Evangelical Union of South America who have had a part in reaching the Ayorés. But of them all, one stands out most clearly as the "Apostle to the Ayorés." That is why, when I decided to write about this great missionary venture some years ago, I knew that the story must revolve around the person of Bill Pencille.

Many exciting episodes in this epic have had to be omitted: the several trips which George Haight made into the jungles around Santiago de Chiquitos in the 1930's, the martyrdom of five New Tribes missionaries in 1943, the establishment of the first permanent station at Tobité, the heroic work of Herschel Dunn in the Rincón del Tigre area, the frustrated attempts to penetrate Ayoré territory from the south by Leslie Harwood of the Evangelical Union of South America, the murder of Mennonite Cornelius Isaak in 1958 in Paraguay, the establishment of the camp at Yoquidai by John Depue, the sacrificial efforts of such missionaries as Joe Moreno, Jean Dye Johnson, Chuck Ramsey, and others.

Just a word about the martyrs. In 1943 Cecil and Robert Dye, David Bacon, George Hosbach, and Eldon Hunter arrived in Bolivia under the recently-formed New Tribes

Mission, and settled in the town of Roboré. These soldiers of the Cross were dedicated to reach the Ayoré tribe with the Gospel of Christ, come what may.

At that time the Indians were commonly known as *"bárbaros,"* Spanish for savages. Centuries previously, the Jesuits had called them "Zamucos," and they also have been known as "Yanaiguas" (Guaraní for "forest dwellers"), "Flecha Corta" ("short arrows"), "Moros" (in Paraguay), and "Tobas" (inaccurately in Julian Duguid's *Green Hell*). Any of these names struck terror into the hearts of the civilized folk who lived in the area.

The five men soon made friends with George Haight of the South America Indian Mission in Santiago de Chiquitos, twelve miles from Roboré. Haight was the only missionary at that time with Ayoré experience, having made two friendly contacts with them. As the discussion about reaching the tribe progressed, a conflict of principles developed. The New Tribes five had firmly decided not to carry firearms on their jungle expeditions. Haight, on the other hand, insisted that they should be armed, not only to provide wild game for food but also for protection if necessary. "If you don't take guns," the jungle veteran said, "you'll never come back alive." Cecil Dye, the group's leader, maintained that even if they died, it would serve to arouse complacent Christians at home and stimulate the prayer needed for a larger missionary outreach to lost tribes.

Both theories were allowed to reach their practical conclusions as subsequent events unfolded. The five were brutally murdered by savage war clubs in November, 1943. George Haight, who risked his life on two expeditions attempting to locate the lost men, was forced to engage the murderers in a jungle battle and shoot in self-defense.

The five martyrs turned out to be "seeds planted by God," as a recent author has described them, and the fruit began when the New Tribes made a permanent contact and established the Ayoré settlement of Tobité. One of the first outsiders to visit Tobité was Bill Pencille, who had then been in Bolivia four years and had learned Spanish. The visit strengthened his decision to give himself to the Ayoré work.

Bill and Harriet Pencille have four children, all born in Bolivia. When the family moved to the jungle camp of Zapocó in 1951 to live with the Ayorés, Dick was seven, Bruce four, and Jeanne just a year old. Stephen was born three years later. Zapocó was home to them, and they grew up among the Indians.

Until 1956 Harriet taught the children at home. But as Zapocó flourished, the pressure of work, especially with the Indian orphans and the complex Ayoré dictionary, made it necessary to send them to a nearby mission school. Each vacation, however, found them home in Zapocó among the Ayorés, and with their natural proficiency in the language, they won a large place in the hearts of the former savages and helped in their evangelization.

Today Bill and his family live in Rochester, Minnesota, where he is the area representative for the South America Indian Mission, and the pastor of the First Baptist Church.

Several missionaries gave themselves unselfishly to help prepare this book. Bill Pencille provided the bulk of the information and did excellent editorial work. The sections which so vividly depict the life and customs of the Ayorés are virtually his. George Haight was most gracious in opening his file of valuable historic documents concerning the Ayorés. Bill Hammond contributed much data, as did Frank Pickering who also helped considerably with editorial work. G. Hunter Norwood, Director of the South America Indian Mission, kindly gave his permission and encouragement to the production of the book. Finally, Harriet Pencille, Janet Briggs, and my wife, Doris, did a most praiseworthy job in the secretarial department.

C. PETER WAGNER

Cochabamba, Bolivia
January, 1967

The people . . . the book

The Ayoré are people like you and your neighbors — with physical, mental and above all spiritual hungers and needs. They do not always recognize or express these in the way you do. Thus, the difficulty of communication. One of the frustrations of the missionary-on-furlough is not being able to make people see his "field" as it really is. Pictures, descriptions, curios are all attempts to enlighten. Recent books on jungle missionary subjects have thrown more light. *Defeat of the Bird God* is a spotlight on another section of the uncivilized, wild Indians in South America.

G. Hunter Norwood
General Director
South America Indian Mission

Mission history contains few more exciting and soul-moving episodes than those experienced by Bill Pencille. No ordinary missionary, he was uniquely gifted for a task few men would dare to tackle. Living daily among savage, naked and murderous Indians in their jungle haunts, Pencille's real worth is revealed in courageous, sacrificial manhood seldom equalled these days. Intrepidly he trailed the Ayoré to gain his friendship, learn his language and present to him the claims of Christ.

Author Wagner, through his intimate friendship with Pencille and his first-hand knowledge of the mission field, presents a heart-moving story.

Joseph S. McCullough
General Director
Andes Evangelical Mission

Table of Contents

1.

Asoná Reigns Supreme

"Edocarate deji ta, quiiiii!"

The Indians in the jungle clearing fell suddenly silent at the cry. Everyone stopped what they were doing and stared into the darkening sky. Sure enough, Comai had been right! Hanging just above the treetops in the northeast horizon was the red star.* The sky to the west was still a blaze of color where the great ball of the sun had sunk from sight, and the darkness in the east had crept up the sky just far enough to outline *Edocarate* as she rose into view.

The old men, already gathering in their nightly council circle, stopped their elaborate pipe-lighting ceremonies. Women laid aside their weaving and were unusually silent. Young men and girls ceased their teasing banter. Even little children seemed to realize that this was somehow different from the hundred other sundowns they could remember. Comai felt proud that he had been the one to see *Edocarate* on her very first appearance this year in the evening sky.

The Indians seemed loath to speak, as though they were witnesses of some great and solemn portent. The very forest itself seemed stricken with awe. The familiar daytime calls of the birds and the chatter of the monkeys ceased, and the nightly cacophony of insects and birds had not yet begun. Only the crickets, almost irreverently, broke the silence — one here, and another there, like the first sounds of some mighty orchestra striving to bring itself into tune. Deguide, the witch doctor, was the first to speak:

---

*Arcturus, the red star in the constellation Boötes, which rises at sundown in the northeast in May, is the third brightest star in the southern sky at this time of year. It is visible for the entire night and continues so for several months, appearing a bit higher in the sky each evening.

"Now that *Edocarate* has shown herself in the evening sky, the whole world is closed up."

"True," agreed Natuine. "And it will remain closed for four moons. Until Asoná sings."

"These will be dangerous moons for the Ayorés! Mothers must watch their children most carefully." It was Deguide who spoke again, and he spoke as chief witch doctor, with all wisdom and authority.

The women carefully folded their weaving and laid it aside. Quietly they joined the circle of wise old men, sitting on the calves of their legs, their toes pointed inward as is the Ayoré custom. Even the young men and women seemed willing to forego, or at least postpone, the usual nightly play and pleasure, and were seated quietly in the shadows. Comai crept close to his mother's side to better hear what the men would say. He was only six — his mother now holds up all the fingers of her right hand and the thumb of the other to tell how many times the world has been closed up since he was born.

The old men had their pipes lighted now, and were inhaling great draughts of the tobacco smoke. They ceremoniously passed them from one to another, and when not actually smoking, were careful to hold the pipe to one side and at arm's length. Comai wondered if you would really die if some of the smoke from the pipe should accidentally blow into your face! Or if you would really become blind if you should smoke a pipe with only one airhole! But why think such thoughts? Of course, you would! All the wise men said so.

By now the men were trembling from the effects of the smoke. But Comai knew it wasn't really the smoke. Tobacco was named Sidi, and of course every Ayoré boy knew who Sidi was. Wasn't he the wisest, bravest, strongest Ayoré who ever lived? And when he left this world, didn't he turn all of these virtues over to the tobacco plant? And could not the Ayorés, even today, be imbued with all of this wisdom and courage simply by smoking the tobacco and swallowing the smoke? Of course they could! No one ever doubted that this was the way it was. The old men felt the need of this wisdom to face the new crisis brought about by the appearance of *Edocarate* in the sky. They were trembling all over now, a sure sign that Sidi was in them and about to speak.

Comai drew nearer to his mother's side. Her rough woven skirt hurt his skin. He wanted to hear what the men would say. He hadn't been old enough last time it happened to really pay attention, and he couldn't remember.

Deguide was speaking again in a strange, choked voice. "My children, Asoná has closed up the whole world from this night on! It won't rain. The jungle will become dry and burned. Many of the little birds and animals will no longer appear. At night, it will often be cold. Even Asoná will hide herself. She will sleep now for four moons. Then she will sing at the full moon, and the world will open again!"

There were murmurs of assent and understanding among the little group. Yes, this was the way it was — the way it always had been — and the way it always would be. Asoná opens the world. Asoná closes the world. The fate of the world and every Ayoré in it is in the hands of Asoná — the terrible Bird God!

After a few more swallows of smoke and a new infilling with the wisdom of Sidi, Deguide continued. "Now, you mothers will have to watch the children carefully. You know that Asoná sleeps all day under the leaves and sticks of the forest floor. She does not want to be awakened for four more moons. No child must be allowed to kick among the leaves or turn over old logs and refuse. And now you must be especially careful to keep your eyebrows and eyelashes plucked. Asoná does not like hair on the face. Do not do anything to displease Asoná, or she will be angry."

The young men and women cast meaningful glances at one another, as much as to say that this would be the easiest part of all that Asoná imposed upon them. It was not difficult to lay your head in the lap of someone you loved and feel the tender caress of affectionate hands as they pulled out your eyebrows and eyelashes! Self-conscious titters spread among the young people as they thought with pleasure of obeying Asoná in this matter!

Deguide was becoming more animated in his speech. His pipe had burned out and he refilled it. All of the wisdom of Sidi poured from his lips.

"My daughters," he counseled, "do not eat the egg of the

The safest place for a small boy is as close to his mother as he can get. *Doria* root is OK to eat if there's no honey or turtle (pp. 33-44).

An Ayoré jungle village is never very permanent and gets dirty fast.

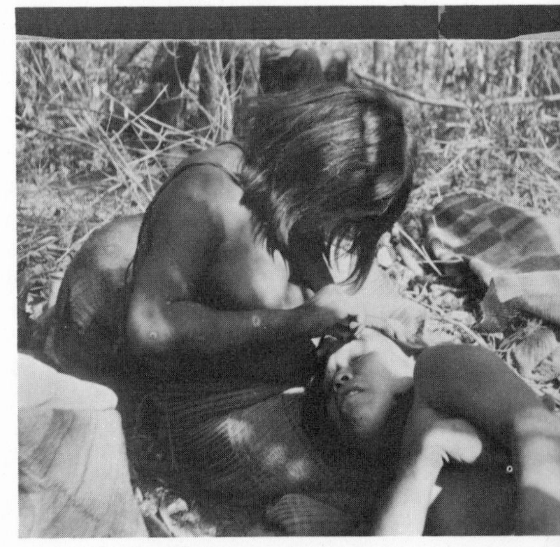

Facial hair on Ayorés offends the bird god. Ashes are rubbed on first as sort of a local anesthetic.

turtle. And you, my sons, must not touch the larvae of the honey bee. Take the best of care of your long hair. And it isn't too soon to begin spinning thread from the *doriaquedena* plant to make new belts for the men for the coming year."

Long after Deguide's pipe went out for the second time, the little group continued around the central fire. The chill of fall was in the air, and the heat of the flames felt good on their naked bodies. The flickering firelight with its alternate light and shadows made a strange, weird picture. Many of the men had completely blackened their bodies with charcoal at the first sign of the star, and were almost invisible even in the strongest glow of the fire. Most of the younger men and boys were so coated with dirt that they were scarcely more visible. The women and girls seated in the outer circle glanced with fear and apprehension at their little ones, now asleep at their knees. The center ring of men fell silent, and then in a slowly rising crescendo, not unlike the increasing tempo of a storm as it rages through the treetops of the jungle, all began to talk at once, addressing no one in particular. Everyone recalled the countless times when Asoná had revenged some oversight or slight. And she always got revenge — there was never any escape. Tensions seemed to be relieved by talking about it . . .

"Remember the time Goane dropped the honey gourd he was bringing as an offering to Asoná? Then he grew thin and died, and not even the witch doctors could help him!" — "Yes, and when Igarede frightened the bird as a little boy, and then the tree limb fell on him when he was a man." — "Surely, Asoná has a long memory."

Now everyone was talking animatedly. "Noraine ate bee larvae, and look what happened!" — "Uapede ate turtle eggs and had twins!" — "Ojidaquide let his beard grow and . . ." — "Sirine drank water during the fast of the full moon and . . ."

Comai's head had sunk down onto his mother's lap, and she slowly slid it to the ground. There was no other bed. Stretching herself out on the cool, soft earth beside him, she covered him with half of her own skirt. *Edocarate* had climbed into midheaven by the time quiet descended upon the little clearing. Even the crickets had long since completed their dissident concert and lapsed into silence.

Filled with fear and emotion, Comai relived in his dreams the story of Asoná as the wise men had so often told it. . .

Many, many years ago, Asoná was a beautiful Ayoré girl. She was the most beautiful girl, in fact, ever to be born to the tribe. As she grew and blossomed into glorious young womanhood, she had many suitors; but the son of a chief in a far part of the forest won her love and they were married. However, since this warrior's father was a powerful chief and wanted his son with him so that he could pass on to him his power at death, the young couple broke custom and went to live with the groom's mother rather than with the bride's.

There Asoná ran into serious trouble. Her mother-in-law was insanely jealous of the vivacious, beautiful new member of the family. From the very first day, she started a hate campaign which was all too successful; before long, not only the whole camp but even Asoná's own husband turned against her. Her life was made most miserable, and finally she could bear it no longer. She took her own life and departed from this world, but her spirit stayed behind incarnated in the nighthawk. Now Asoná, in the form of the *cuyavo* or the nighthawk, returns to the forest every year to punish her people for the wicked way in which they treated her.

Comai awoke with a start and began to cry. Asoná's power was terrible. She knew everything an Ayoré did. His little body trembled and was damp with perspiration, even in the chill morning air. He reached out a chubby hand and found the comforting bulk of his mother by his side. Through his tears he could see the sun, *Guede,* standing in the sky just where *Edocarate* had been the night before. Usually, he would have thrown off his covering and jumped with little-boy joy to greet the new day. But today the sun did not seem as bright. The events and stories of the night pressed upon him like some great weight. Was there no escape from Asoná and her anger? Must it always be this way? Would she always reign supreme in the country of the Ayorés?

2.

A Mission and a Man

THE GOD WHO HAD MADE the Ayorés and to whom they belonged, did not intend to let Asoná's reign go forever unchallenged. Being omnipotent, He could have found some quick and efficient means of breaking her power over these, her dupes. But God works through a man with a message. It could be no different now.

It was June of 1938, and Bill Pencille* had returned to his home in Rochester, Minnesota, for summer vacation. The grind of a chemical engineering course at Macalester College was half over, and his junior year would start in September. Two more years of study and then a career in chemistry and science! Jean Mitchell would be Mrs. Pencille by then, and the future looked very rosy.

Bill, a stocky red-head, who was full of life, thought that vacations were a waste of time. He had been brought up on a farm where there were no vacations, and he would much rather have been back in the "chem" lab in St. Paul. Or — was it Jean?

His promised job of delivering soft drinks had not materialized as yet because of a chilly spring, so Bill consented to take over a friend's farm for a few days while the owner was called away. Bill's aunt, a devout Christian, lived on the next farm. She recognized this as the opportunity she had been praying for — she wanted this rowdy, worldly nephew of hers to know the Lord. If his boundless energy and zeal could ever be channeled properly, he might some day become a servant of the God she loved so well!

An old-fashioned tent meeting was being held in Rochester, and the aunt asked him to drive her to town

*Pronounced "pencil."

one evening. She wanted to attend the meeting. What teen-ager would turn down the opportunity to drive a new car? Bill hadn't planned on attending the service, but the music attracted him and he slipped in and sat on the last bench with other young fellows.

Bill believed in God; he attended church occasionally; he had been baptized and confirmed. But as the evangelist preached, something deep within him was stirred. What difference had all his religion really made to him? The simple message burned its way straight into his heart. How did that preacher know just what kind of person he was? Bill's dignified Lutheran background marshalled against his "hitting the sawdust trail," but almost before he knew it, he was kneeling at the front of the tent and opening his heart to Jesus Christ.

Before a week had passed, Bill was certain that God wanted him to preach the Gospel. But what about that chemical engineering career? What about Jean? Bill decided to consult his pastor.

"Is it possible to serve the Lord as a scientist?" he asked. It was a loaded question.

"Of course it is!" his pastor replied. He went on to mention various men, Dr. Harry Rimmer and others, who had done so.

This was all the encouragement Bill needed. He determined to finish his course at Macalester, taking his degree in chemistry. The summer was as sunny as his outlook for the future. He made good money delivering soft drinks and grew in his spiritual life by attending the services in the big tent night after night. Summer passed, and the cool Minnesota evenings signaled the approach of fall. It was time to return to Macalester and chemistry.

He quit the job at the bottling plant. Suitcases were packed and loaded into the car. After breakfast, they would begin the eighty-five mile trip to St. Paul. But as he bit into a piece of toast, Bill felt a sharp pain in the right side of his jaw. He tried the left side. That hurt even more. There were mumps in the neighborhood, and within an hour the family doctor was giving his diagnosis.

"Sorry, Bill," he said. "But you've got the mumps. That means at least three weeks in bed!"

Bill forgot his promise to serve God with chemistry. All he wanted now was that junior year in college! Would it be possible to get into the dorm, he wondered? Could he make up back work? Would his old job still be open?

At last the three weeks were up, and the doctor said, "You're all right now. I'll write a note to the dean of the college for you."

The next day, tingling with anticipation, Bill handed the note across the desk at Macalester.

"Your place is still open," he was told. "We are very glad to have you with us again."

There was not a happier young man in St. Paul that afternoon as Bill Pencille bade his mother good-by and unpacked his suitcases. He was tired and nervous, but blamed it on the excitement of the day. He wasn't in the mood for looking up old friends, and decided to retire early.

But sleep would not come. As he rolled and tossed on his bed, the old pains returned, and by morning he was burning with fever. The college physician shook his head gravely. "It's mumps — a relapse. We'll have to send you home. Perhaps you can continue school next semester."

This time it was six weeks in bed, not three. During those long days and nights of suffering, God once again spoke to Bill. This time his reply was unconditional: it didn't have the "with chemistry" tacked on. God was soon to put him to the test.

During the 20° below zero winter that followed there was no soft-drink business, and Bill found work at a soda fountain around the corner from the hotel in Rochester where his best friend, Ben, worked. Ben had spent a year at Northwestern Bible School in Minneapolis, and Bill admired him for his dedication to the Lord.

One bitterly cold day as Bill was leaving his job, he found Ben waiting for him. "How would you like to team up with me and begin preaching in a country school house?" he asked. "The farmers in the place I'm thinking of don't have a church to attend. They might be interested in a Sunday school for their kids, and we could preach afterwards."

"Me?" laughed Bill. "I don't know how to preach! You're the one who has been to Bible School! I'd come out with a bunch of chemical equations."

"You don't have to preach. I'll take care of that. Just come along and help with the children and the songs. And for moral support."

Bill wasn't convinced, but next Saturday found him in Ben's car, canvassing the neighborhood to see what interest there might be in their project. At least, no one was completely disinterested, and the first service was scheduled for the following Sunday.

On Friday, Ben was again waiting for Bill as he left work. "Bill," he said, his face very grave, "something went wrong. I've just been told I must work Sunday!"

"What — what do you mean? How about our service?"

"You'll have to preach, Bill!"

No thunderbolt from above could have stunned Bill so completely. He was nervous enough about leading the singing, let alone preaching! He went to his pastor for advice.

"What in the world can I ever preach about?" he asked in desperation.

The pastor smiled sympathetically and reached for a book on the shelf behind his desk. "Preach on Law and Grace," he said, as he handed the young man Young's ponderous *Concordance of the Bible.*

Bill says, "Those hours from Friday morning until I prayed the final prayer about noon on Sunday, are still hazy in my mind. I lived an eternity in those few hours. Was ever a worse sermon preached? What could those spiritually needy farmers get for their souls out of such a performance? At least, they couldn't see my knees shaking behind the teacher's desk!"

The next time was easier, and that winter gave Bill his first real experience in serving the Lord. Chemistry was forgotten, and he had his sights set on another goal. Jean wasn't interested in either Bill's new religion or his preaching. After two or three letters, she returned his picture and class ring. In September, 1939, Bill enrolled in the Pastor's course at Chicago's Moody Bible Institute.

Bill knew little about foreign missions before attending Moody, but there he learned a great deal. MBI has always been a missions-centered school, and through the years nearly half of the graduates have become missionaries. At first, Bill wasn't interested. It was required that all students attend the Thursday morning missions' hour, and he attended dutifully. But try as he would, it seemed almost impossible to stay awake through the entire period. He often wished, silently, that missionaries would find some more interesting way to talk about their work.

When they showed films however, Bill didn't find it so easy to drowse. Especially, when the man from Brazil told of how two missionaries were killed there in 1930. Bill forgot the names of the two martyrs, but jotted down the name of the Indian tribe who murdered them. The Nhambiquaras. Inexplicably, he sensed a strange inner feeling that someday he would meet these jungle nomads!

Bill wrote: "This feeling did not pass away. Daily, the realization grew that this was God's will for me. I was determined to obey God. The mumps and the struggle between the ministry and chemical engineering were all too fresh in my mind. But what if I were mistaken? What if it were just emotions? How could I really know the will of God? How could I distinguish His will from the desires of my own deceitful heart? These and a hundred other questions raced through my mind. Should I just say 'yes' and then ask God to open the door before me?

"As I read my Bible daily, I was impressed with the frequency of the statement 'the Word of the Lord came unto. . . .' God apparently was anxious to manifest His will to men. Perhaps the only hindrance to my knowing the will of God was my own will! So gradually, I began to ask not for an open door, but for a closed door. I told God that I was giving myself to Him for the Indians of Brazil. I would move in that direction: if it were *not* His will, I asked Him to close the door."

With the decision made, Bill became more active in the Missionary Union and the Latin America Prayer Band of MBI. He learned of the South America Indian Mission, which at that time had some eighty missionaries working with jungle tribes. A letter to the headquarters of the mission brought a most encouraging reply.

During Bill's senior year this activity in missions brought

him into contact with Harriet Carlsen. He was meeting in council with other student leaders when Harriet was suggested as a candidate for office in one of the prayer bands.

"Who's Harriet Carlsen?" Bill inquired. He had always prided himself on knowing all of the thousand Moody students personally.

"Don't you know her?" was the reply. "She transferred last year from evening school. She wanted to go to China at first as a missionary, but now is sure that the Lord wants her to work with the jungle Indians of South America."

At the age of fifteen Harriet had become an orphan. Her father, a wealthy Norwegian jeweler in Chicago, lost all he had in the depression. Her mother died shortly after, and her father, overcome with grief, soon followed her. Harriet was the youngest of seven children. The family was nominally Christian, but Harriet had a haunting desire to know God more intimately. Her conversion came about as a result of reading a Christian novel. After completing high school, Harriet announced to her brothers and sisters that she had decided to attend Moody Bible Institute evening school.

Her announcement met with strong opposition. The family tried hard to get this foolish idea out of her head. But no amount of persuading could change her mind, and that fall she entered the Institute. There the conviction deepened that the Lord would have her serve Him on the foreign field. With this in mind, she transferred to day school.

Working together in Missionary Union, Bill and Harriet soon became close friends. They had many common interests, not the least of which was the Indians of the Amazon River.

Courtship at the Institute in those days was no easy task. Dates (except for church services) were discouraged, but Bill and Harriet enjoyed the Sunday-night-after-church walks down Lake Shore Drive; and before long, the first kiss in the moonlight reflected from Lake Michigan became a promise to share their lives in the Brazilian jungles.

Bill graduated from MBI in August of 1942. The group seated that morning in Torrey-Gray Auditorium, resplendent in scarlet robes and tassled mortar boards, was about equally divided between men and women. It was the last time it would be so until after the war. The men of the Class of '42 had been classified 4-D by the Selective Service, as they had entered theological training a year before the draft went into effect. This was a challenge to Bill for complete dedication to Christ. If his government was willing to free him for God's service at a time when thousands of men in uniform were sacrificing their lives for their country, how much more did he need to dedicate himself wholly to his Lord!

Events now began to move rapidly. Another year at Moody for special missionary courses . . . intensive study for both Bill and Harriet at Wycliffe's Summer Institute of Linguistics. . . marriage in the First Baptist Church of Rochester. . . ordination. . . then, a "honeymoon" trip to West Palm Beach, Florida, headquarters of the South America Indian Mission!

3.

A Simple Way of Life—and Death!

Comai's mother was watchful over her children after the appearance of the red star, *Edocarate.* Now that her boy was no longer a baby, but ran through the forest with the other boys shooting beetles and butterflies with his tiny bow and arrows, there was the ever-present danger that he would awaken Asoná and incur her displeasure. Comai had been badly frightened after hearing of the bird god's terrible wrath and unforgiving memory; but as the season of the closed world advanced, his fears were slowly forgotten. All the *don'ts* made him angry. — Don't kick among the leaves! — Don't turn that log over! — Don't touch the turtle eggs! — Don't do this! — Don't do that! — The bird will surely get you! Did Asoná have no love at all, he wondered? Was she never considerate of little boys who had to play?

Although Comai called his mother *ité,* everyone else called her Natuinate. This was because his older brother's name was Natui. It was really quite a handy arrangement, for once a baby was allowed to live and was given a name, his parents and grandparents were known by the baby's name. Comai had no idea what his mother's or father's first names had been. Now they were always Natuine and Natuinate, father and mother of Natui. All of the Ayoré parents were known by the name of their oldest living child.

Natuinate was expecting another baby. Not that it made much difference to six-year-old Comai. But when he played with the other boys around the women as they spun their endless *doriaquedena* thread, he sometimes heard them talking about the expected event. Even when he heard the old women affirm that the baby would be buried alive if it were not pretty or was in any way imperfect, Comai was not too impressed. How could you feel sorry for someone you had never seen? Or miss someone you had never played with?

When the now-familiar birth pangs began, Natuinate quietly arose from her fireside and walked to the edge of the clearing. It would never do for the baby to be born in the camp. The blood would contaminate everything, and her grass shelter would have to be torn down and destroyed. Here, under the trees, dirt could be thrown on the blood, and evil spirits couldn't molest. The pains were sharper now and more frequent.

Natuinate couldn't remember how many children she had borne. Six or seven, she thought. But Natui, her eight-year-old boy, his sister Naramia, and Comai were the only ones she had kept. The rest had been buried alive.

Natuinate sat down with her back against a huge *curupaú* tree. One by one, the old women gathered around her. They were dirty and unkempt. Toothless gums showed between their thick lips as they discussed the task ahead of them. These were the tribal midwives, and would be the ones to decide whether or not the baby should be allowed to live. The oldest woman, Natuidacode, was in charge. She would be the baby's maternal grandmother — if it lived. In her bony fingers she clutched a clamshell, and on the ground beside her was a half-gourd of not-too-clean water. A handful of wood ashes on a leaf completed the collection of obstetrical instruments.

It was hot in the shade of the *curupaú* tree, but nervousness and pain made the patient feel chilly, and one of the old women carefully blew a few live coals into flame beside the expectant mother.

A few quick, powerful contractions and it was all over. Stomach muscles hardened by years of carrying heavy burdens made the job of giving birth easy. Of course, Natuinate had not cried out — not even once. Had she not gashed herself across the stomach as a teen-aged girl, to show that she could bear such pain?

The baby lay quietly on the ground, still connected to its mother by the life-giving cord. It was a boy. His wizened old judges scrutinized him carefully. No one touched him as yet. Yes, he seemed to be all right. His head was nicely shaped. His little arms and legs were straight and strong. He had ten fingers and ten toes. Really a pretty baby!

There were no signs that the spirits had taken possession of him, so it might be safe to keep him.

But wait! Was he the only one? Was there a twin yet to be born? If so, they must both be buried immediately, for how could you explain two babies born at once? One must surely belong to the evil spirits — but how could you tell which one? The only safe course would be to bury them both alive.

No, there did not seem to be another one. A final contraction and the birth was complete. Natuinate, breathing heavily, relaxed by the fire.

Now it would be safe to touch the baby. Natuidacode cut the cord with the clamshell, while another woman dug a little hole in the sandy soil with the butt end of a spear. They pushed the placenta in with a stick and filled in the hole. They rubbed ashes into the bleeding stump of the cord, and the caustic action of the lye stopped the bleeding and disinfected the stump. The baby's grandmother filled her mouth with water from the gourd and carefully squirted the warmed water over the baby. This she did again and again until he was clean, and then wrapped him in a brand-new piece of the coarse fabric woven from *doriaquedena,* the wild pineapple plant.

Natuinate slowly rose to her feet, picked up the little bundle from the ground, and walked rather unsteadily back to her fireside. Comai had a new baby brother.

Even as a baby, Comai had never been allowed to cry in the jungle. At the first whimpering complaint the comforting breast was thrust into his mouth. Crying babies could too easily give their position away to the white enemies who might be nearby.

Many of his earliest memories were of games of jungle hide-and-seek. All Ayorés were experts at it. It was an important game, the stakes were high, and you played for keeps. A quick burst of fire from a "noise stick" in the hands of a white man would quickly and effectively end the game forever.

Ever since he could walk well, Natuinate insisted that Comai toddle along ahead of her on the trail. It was not easy, as there were so many thorns. And the needle-like ends of the *doriaquedena* leaves always seemed just the height of a little boy's eyes. You simply *couldn't* watch

Life in camp is boring for little boys when the men are away.

A jungle existence is full of hazards for a baby.

Hunting for head lice is one way to while away the time waiting for the men to return to camp.

Honey is the Ayoré staple food. There are 12 species of honey bees in the Bolivian jungle, none of which sting. But they bite, as this honey hunter shows by scratching one out of his hair.

When the honey hunters return to camp they sit in a circle passing a honey-soaked mass of fibers around for sucking and chewing.

out for everything! Sometimes you tripped and fell down over a root. Then all the girls laughed, and you just couldn't keep from crying. Mother would stoop over a little bit and let you take a few swallows from her breast, then she would swing you up over her shoulder by one arm and up onto her pack. It was fun to ride piggy-back, but you had to be careful that one of those branches didn't brush you right off onto the ground.

When Natuinate awakened you in the morning by pulling off your covering, the sun was already up above the trees and the camp was astir. Natuinate would bring a gourd filled with honey and water. It was nice and sweet and it really filled you up. Sometimes, when there was no honey, it might be a roast turtle liver; or maybe just a mashed-up piece of *doria* root — that *never* filled you up!

By the time you finished breakfast, most of the men and older boys had already left camp. They took axes, rope and empty honey gourds in their shoulder bags. You could hear them shouting for a long time. Then the toc — toc — toc of an ax against some hollow tree. There would be honey in the afternoon.

It would be fun to go with the men! Life in camp was boring! All you did was chase lizards and butterflies and shoot at them with your bow and arrows. Comai remembered the day when he shot a parrot. How proud he was when his daddy came home and he presented him with the tail feathers! Natuine smiled at Comai as he tied them among the hundreds of others that he already had on his war bonnet. He said, "Someday you'll be a man and have your own war bonnet!"

Then there was the day when his big brother Natui also had shot a parrot. . . well, to tell the truth, he didn't really shoot it himself. Little Pajei's uncle had just made him a new bow and arrows. No one really took care of Pajei since his parents had died, but occasionally his uncle made things for him. When the boys saw the parrot in the tree, several of them had shot at the same time. The parrot never even squawked as it plummeted to earth. Of course, the boys all raced up to where it fell. Natui was oldest and biggest — and he got there first. He said it was his arrow that was in the parrot. It was really Pajei's. But when Pajei tried to claim it, Natui pushed him down into the dust and walked off with the bird. Then, when Natui presented the tail feathers to the captain that night — how Comai's chest had swelled over the praise heaped on his brother! He was sure to be a mighty hunter some day! Of course, Comai never did tell whose arrow really killed the parrot. He was proud of his brother, even if the other boys called him a bully.

Every day, Comai's people moved camp; today only a mile, tomorrow a little further . . . always moving . . . constantly searching for food. Even at night around the fires they talked about food. Sometimes it was about war and sometimes it was about love, but usually it was about food. War . . . love . . . food . . . You seldom heard anything else discussed. Except maybe water! Not water to swim in or to bathe in, or even to cook with. Just water to drink. Comai tried to remember the places he knew to find water. Water holes, the center of *doria* plants, knot holes or woodpecker holes in the trees, the *cardo*, the *sipoy* root — you grew tired and thirsty digging out the *sipoy*, but it was worth it when you squeezed the water out!

Evening was always the best time of all. The men would have brought back plenty of honey and the women roasted huge piles of *doria* roots in the late afternoon. You filled your stomach and then slept until the sun set. Then the mosquitoes began to buzz around your ears and no one felt like sleeping any longer. The chiefs and witch doctors gathered in their circle by the central fire. Little boys couldn't go too close, but from the shadows they could see and hear everything. You had to be quiet or the chief would scold you and send you away.

What would they do tonight? Would they just smoke and talk about plans for tomorrow? Would they tell the exciting old war stories? Would they discuss a new invasion of the Guidaigosode territory? Maybe the witch doctor would cure someone! You hoped so. That was the most exciting of all. Rather spooky, too. Made you wish you could be a witch doctor when you grew up. Oh, boy! Who's he going to heal? It must be Ajaronate. She has been groaning all day.

Deguide has his feathers on, now. His neck feathers are pointing upward! This must be a hard case! He has blackened his body with charcoal and all kinds of hideous designs are drawn on his face. In the flickering firelight he looks scary. Even the evil spirits must be afraid of Deguide and you almost feel like running to mother! But you want to stay and see what happens. Deguide calls for Ajaronate and she rises, stooped and groaning, from her fireside. She lies down at his feet in the midst of all the men.

The witch doctor sits down next to her and smokes his pipe. But he doesn't blow the smoke out — he eats it. Look at him sweat! Look at his body shake all over! Sidi's power is taking over! He must be talking to Sidi himself. Now he is chanting — he has the answer from Sidi. Some evil spirit must have gotten into Ajaronate's body and caused sickness. Too bad! Deguide's chanting grows louder and he's eating more smoke. Now he has thrown aside his pipe and is kneeling over poor Ajaronate.

His face is right over her body and he's talking to the spirit. Now he is sucking and biting the spot! How hard he has to suck! The spirit is not coming out very easily. Now he has stopped. He's getting to his feet — but he's wobbling around. The spirit must be in *him* now! He looks so sad! He's trying to chant, but he starts to choke and vomit. He's trying to cough up the spirit! Woops — he almost fell on the ground! It's stuck in his throat! Now he's pulling it out of his mouth! What does it look like? It's too dark to see. But he's running with it to the edge of the clearing. Thump — thump — thump — you can't see him, but he must be killing it with his war club. Now he's burying it. Well, at least *that* spirit won't make any more people sick! Where could it have come from? Probably from the white people. They have terrible spirits!

Everyone slept late the next morning. The sun was high before the hunters went off to search for food. The women were slow in packing up for the trail. Ajaronate was much better. Suddenly, the cry of one of the hunters pierced the still morning air. The danger signal came shrill and clear, *"Ayoré quiiiii!"* "Ayorés are coming!" Who could they be? Friends? Enemies? Without wasting a motion, the women grabbed their children and disappeared into the jungle. In a moment the camp was empty and silent.

"Yocurasa suaaaa!" came another cry. "They're our friends!" Indians came running from all sides, and the

A successful day's hunt means roast turtle for dinner.

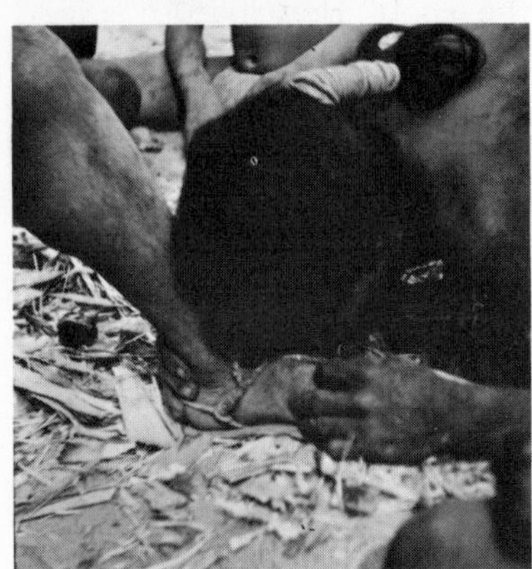

Witch doctors suck the evil spirits out of whatever part of the body is hurting.

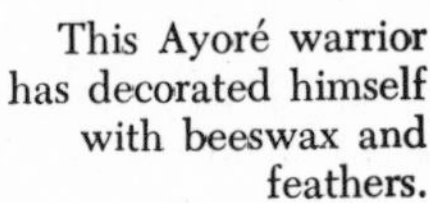

This Ayoré warrior has decorated himself with beeswax and feathers.

women, somewhat embarrassed, returned to their firesides. The visitors stood in the center of the camp. Comai and his friends wiggled their way through the crowd to get a better look. The visitors had prepared for the meeting by blackening their bodies, covering their arms and chests with bees' wax and sticking hundreds of white downy feathers into the wax. Their stomachs and faces were painted a brilliant red, and on their heads were headdresses of jaguar skins with feathers hanging down the back.

The newcomers sat in silence around the fire while the other Indians clustered about them, laughing, chattering and gesticulating. Gifts of honey water and food sat untouched at their feet. Custom forbade their showing how hungry they really were by touching the food too soon. In the interest of courage and prestige the grinding hunger pangs would have to be endured a little longer.

Deguide said the men were from a group that lived many miles to the east. Comai wondered why they had come. They must have brought news! Could it be that Big Chief Idaide was calling the warriors together to fight the Guidaigosode? The story soon came out.

"Idaide has killed five white men.* It was ten nights ago that they walked into our village with their arms held high above their heads. They did not carry noise sticks. Our men were all out planting corn. Most of the women ran away screaming when the white men arrived, but two stayed behind when they saw they were unarmed. The white men removed their shirts and gave them to the women. But when we men arrived, we were sure it was a trap! We were sure they were preparing for an attack on the Ayorés. Idaide pointed to five of us, and ordered us to kill them. The white men couldn't understand our words, and when they saw us coming toward them they just smiled and stood there waiting for us. It did not seem right to murder them — they weren't like other white men we have killed! But Idaide insisted that it was a plot to wipe us all out later. So we killed them and dragged their bodies from camp, buried them, and built fires over their graves."

---

*These were the five men of New Tribes Mission, killed by the Ayorés in 1943. See Preface.

"How about the blood?" Deguide asked.

"We burned the entire village, and the killers did the *tarigai* dance. We will now be well protected from evil spirits."

No one slept much that night. There was too much to talk about. Where had those white men come from? Why didn't they bring noise sticks? Why didn't they try to defend themselves? How could anyone be so willing to die?

Comai lay awake until *qui,* the partridge, began to call just before dawn, and then he dropped off into a troubled sleep. His last thoughts were of Asoná and her judgment for shed blood.

"It's a good thing they took care of that with the dance of *tarigai,*" he thought, drowsily.

4.

Closed Doors—and an Open Door

SINCE BIBLE SCHOOL DAYS, both Bill and Harriet had dreamed of serving the Lord in the jungles of the Amazon Basin among the fierce Nhambiquaras of Brazil. In 1930 these savages had massacred two South American Indian Mission missionaries.* Mrs. Tylee alone lived to tell of the tragic event. When Bill and Harriet heard the story, they longed to take the place of those who had laid down their lives for love of the Indians.

But this dream came to an abrupt end in the Brazilian consulate in Miami. The consul was polite but firm as he said in broken English "I am sorry. In my country we have a new law. Missionaries may no longer enter. Can you not go as a teacher? Or an agriculturist?"

"No," Bill responded. "I'm just a missionary!"

"Then you cannot go!" was the answer.

The young couple returned to the mission headquarters disappointed but not cast down. What should they do now? Brazil was definitely a closed door; but — the door to Peru was still open! And there were many tribes there in need of the Gospel.

They were assigned to work as missionaries with the Campa Indians on the banks of Peru's Ucayali River. As Mission Director Joseph Davis placed his hands on their heads and offered the commissioning prayer, there was no doubt in any of their minds that they would some day be in Peru.

With a sixty-day tourist visa stamped in their passport, they set out for South America.

---

*See Mrs. Arthur F. Tylee's *The Challenge of Amazon's Indians,* (Chicago: Moody Press, 1931).

The year was 1944. D-Day was still three months off, and non-priority travel was difficult if not almost impossible. No ships were available in the Atlantic due to Nazi submarines, and the young couple crossed the continent by train to Los Angeles in hope of finding some means of travel down the west coast. They were finally able to book passage to Lima on an Italian freighter. The submarine net in San Pedro harbor swinging open to allow them to pass seemed to Bill a portent of open doors in Peru. He was soon to learn otherwise!

Meanwhile, Harriet had discovered that she was pregnant. Fearful lest the mission or relatives keep them from sailing because of it, she told no one but Bill. The last mail from the departing ship carried a handful of letters announcing the coming event.

Everyone assumed it would just be a matter of bureaucratic routine to have the sixty-day visa changed to a permanent resident visa once they landed in Peru. But the political situation at the time the Pencilles arrived was in a turmoil and no evangelical missionaries were allowed to enter the country. Now what? The door had been closed to Brazil — could this mean a closed door to Peru as well?

Bill tried everything possible to secure the desired permission, but to no avail. The American Consul was kind but powerless to aid him. "Is there no other place you can go?" he asked. "If not, we'll have to ship you home!"

Bolivia was the last resort. The SAIM had missionaries there working among the Spanish-speaking civilized Indians. This was not for them! They had been called to evangelize the wild Indians, the jungle tribes! But, as far as they knew, there were no jungle Indians in Bolivia. "Someone," Bill said to himself, "has made a mistake!"

But every other door was closed; only the door to Bolivia remained open. So it was that a few days later they boarded a rickety wooden coach of the Peruvian Railroad and began the trip over the Andes mountains to Bolivia.

Exactly three months after leaving Los Angeles, Bill and Harriet arrived in Santiago de Chiquitos, Bolivia. They were met in Roboré by George Haight, veteran missionary of the SAIM. He was smiling under his little square mustache as he pulled the brown Chevrolet truck up in front of the New Tribes mission home where the Pencilles were waiting for him. The hand he stuck out of the truck window in greeting was thick and rough, but his blue eyes sparkled friendship and his lantern jaw jounced a little whenever he performed one of his characteristic swallowed chuckles.

Santiago is only twelve miles from Roboré, but the road up the hill is no freeway. Breaking all speed records as well as a couple of springs, one could conceivably make it in a little over an hour. Two hours is more like average, but if it has been raining and the rivers are swollen, from four to six hours is not unusual. But the road wasn't wet that day and the trip went as smoothly as the road would allow.

As they drove over the last ridge that overlooked the Santiago valley, the sun was just setting. The little town of palm and tile roofed houses nestled in a fertile valley surrounded by rocky hills. The jungle between the hills and the town lay black and foreboding in the evening twilight, while the distant sandstone cliffs were a breathtaking blaze of reds and oranges. The long shadow of the cross on the Catholic church reached almost to the far side of the town plaza.

The new missionaries were speechless. This exotic little village looked like something come to life out of the pages of the *National Geographic*. As the truck circled the plaza and drew up at the mission house, hundreds of questions flooded in on Bill's consciousness, demanding an answer. Santiago was so different from Chicago or Rochester! Would they ever learn to understand this people or their customs? Would it be possible to adjust oneself to life in these simple huts? Would it be fair to their child, yet unborn, to raise him in these surroundings?

The bustling primary school, run by George Haight, was in session at that time of year, and the noise of the children at play, reciting their lessons, or singing gospel choruses constantly filled the air. The little room where the Pencilles unpacked their few belongings was just off the main courtyard. They settled down to study Spanish, the ever-present children around them providing the teachers they needed.

George Haight was continually on the move. He directed the school, maintained an extensive agricultural project to help support it, ran the only regular transportation service

George Haight (without hat), Benigno (far right) and the rest of the group emerge from the jungle after making the first friendly contact with the Ayorés in the spring of 1936. Frank Pickering took the picture.

George Haight

to Roboré, and handled the pastoral responsibilities of the local church. In fact, after they had been there a month or so, they wondered if there would ever be an opportunity for a relaxed conversation with their senior missionary. They chatted once in a while during the afternoon coffee break, but usually George stopped just long enough to swallow a piece of bread and gulp down a cup of scalding hot coffee. Then he was back on the job. Harriet and Bill would sometimes linger behind, talking with his wife, Helen. They were all alumni of Moody Bible Institute, and had a good deal in common.

One afternoon, however, a storm was raging outside. The missionaries had gathered in the dining room. The windows were closed against the storm, and a kerosene lamp furnished both heat and light for the small group sipping coffee around the table. The new missionaries were fascinated by the topic of conversation: the *bárbaros*!

George was in a tale-spinning mood, spurred on by many questions that Bill posed about these Indians. Bill had only recently realized that there were savages in Bolivia!

"The first contact we made with these savages was when I took Frank Pickering along," began George. "You will some day meet Frank. He's tall and soft-spoken and has been in Bolivia almost as long as I have. He and Evangeline are up in San Ignacio now. But when he went on this trip with me he was new on the field and fresh from Wheaton College. We had a curious fellow by the name of Benigno and four other hired men with us — this was the spring of 1936."

Bill made a mental note of the date. In the spring of 1936 he was just two months away from high school graduation.

"This Benigno," went on George, "was our interpreter. He was born a *bárbaro,* but by this time had become perfectly civilized and was working on a cattle ranch. He was captured in a rather unorthodox manner when about ten years old. A small group of Indian boys was gathering palm nuts in a clearing when two cowboys on horseback came out of the woods and surprised them. His companions fled across the field to safety, but Benigno was caught up in the top of one of the palm trees. He jumped down and started to run, but one of the cowboys lassoed him as though he were a calf. He took him home and made him his servant boy, and soon had taught him Spanish.

"Well, just a few days' out of Santiago, we found the *bárbaro* trail. It was a difficult trip, especially for Frank. He showed me a letter later that he wrote home, telling of the backache and blisters, going down that trail sweltering, breathless, and exhausted; fighting insects and clawing the bites, and above all, no water all day.

"After a week of the twisting and thorny paths, we were setting up camp for the night when suddenly Benigno stiffened to attention. 'Did you hear that?' he asked in an excited whisper.

" 'What?' I wanted to know.

" 'The *birulo*! Listen!'

"We were instantly engulfed in a silence you could almost feel. The next moment the sound penetrated the jungle again, and knowing grins spread over the faces of the men. That is, all except Frank.

" 'What are you supposed to hear? What's a *birulo*, anyhow?' Frank asked, guessing that it had something to do with the *bárbaros*.

"I told him it was the *bárbaro* whistle. Just then, we heard it again, but Frank still could not make it out. We felt it was dangerous to go further that evening, and planned to catch up with them the next morning.

"We took the precautions of not lighting a fire. We talked only in whispers. No one got much sleep. We tried to anticipate what would happen when we met the *bárbaros* — no friendly contact had been made with them since the famous massacre of San Ignacio de Zamuco, two centuries ago in the 1700's, when the *bárbaros* killed the priests and fled to the forest.

"The same thing could have happened to us that happened to my friend Hugo Petzault. He was innocently traveling from Santo Corazón to Puerto Suárez with his son and another man when they stopped in a clearing to make lunch. They were careless enough to wander too far away from their rifles, and the savages ambushed them. They split Petzault's head in two with a sharp war club and ripped the other man open with a lance. Miraculously his son escaped.

"Anyhow, the next morning, the *birulo* sounded again,

and this time so clearly and shrilly that even Frank could hear it. We had not seen fresh water for days, so the men cut down some nearby *cardo* plants and strained the stagnant water through handkerchiefs into their canteens."

"What's the *cardo* plant?" Bill wanted to know.

"The *cardo* is a tall plant which traps and holds rainwater in the inner folds of its leaves. Needless to say the water soon becomes filthy, slimy and bitter, but it's the most delicious beverage in the world when it stands between you and possible death from thirst.

"The sky was cloudy and the air sultry. A tropical storm was threatening. As we worked our way quietly through the brush, the sounds of the *bárbaros* became louder. The toc — toc — toc of the chisel against a hollow tree, the *birulo* again, and then the audible sound of human voices. We could see nothing, but soon heard several of the savages coming through the brush toward us. We silently slipped our packs to the ground, and Benigno pulled off his shirt so he would look more like a savage. Thunder rolled ominously in the distance and the sun disappeared behind dark storm clouds. No one would venture a guess as to what the next sixty seconds would bring forth.

"The savages were breaking a new trail to connect with the one we had been following. First came a young fellow blazing the trail. Close behind him was a very large Indian, chanting in a deep, gutteral voice and slashing down the brush with a huge war club. The young man reached the trail and shouted the good news back to his companion; but as he examined the dust on the trail he instantly spied our footprints. His body tensed and he tightened his grip on his spear.

"Benigno stood up in his hiding place and greeted him in the *bárbaro* dialect. The savage glanced briefly at him, and then spotted us. He took a headlong dive back into the brush on the far side of the trail, letting out a shriek of terror.

"Benigno, unarmed, bounded through the jungle in hot pursuit. I yelled after him, 'Benigno, be careful they'll kill you!' and I took off at full speed after him. The rest followed. The *bárbaro* men easily outdistanced us in this mad race through the woods, but some of the women and children couldn't escape. Benigno caught a stout woman who was not much at running, especially with a child clinging to her back like a frightened monkey.

" 'Stop!' he commanded. Surprisingly, she did. Four little children stopped with her, completely out of breath. When we caught up to the woman we convinced her we meant no harm, and she began to chat animatedly. Benigno was so excited at seeing his people again, he could scarcely interpret what she said. She was most intelligent, and gave complete answers to the questions I had Benigno put to her.

"We gave her gifts of ribbons and beads, then arranged with the woman to meet the group again twenty days hence. Then we headed back for Santiago. This was the first friendly contact with the *bárbaros* I know of.

"Just before we made camp that evening, the impending storm broke in all its fury. We finally got a drink of fresh water, but we spent a sleepless night in drenched hammocks."

"Do you mean that was the first contact that has ever been made with the *bárbaros*?" asked Bill when George had finished.

"Well, the first *friendly* one that I know about since the Jesuits."

"The Jesuits?"

"Yes. You know the Jesuits were the first ones who came in and settled this region back in the eighteenth century. They were run out by the King of Spain in 1767. They mostly worked with the docile Chiquitanos, and had ten missions around here — Santiago was one, San José another, San Ignacio, Santo Corazón — there were ten in all. When they left, the Franciscans took over; but they didn't maintain the old missions, and rich landowners took over the Chiquitanos and created a feudal state. Anyhow, the Jesuits succeeded in forming a mission with the *bárbaros* in a place called San Ignacio de Zamuco."

"I remember you mentioned it before," Bill said. "Where is it?"

"That's the thing; nobody knows. It just disappeared. Someone's always looking for it. They say that the golden heads of the twelve apostles are buried there!"

"Are they?"

George just chuckled. "You'll get used to tales like that before long!"

Harriet spoke up. "You told the Indian woman you would return in twenty days. Did you go back?"

"We went back, but it was more like three months than twenty days. Frank Pickering was off on a trip to Santa Cruz. That was when he almost died of sunstroke in Pozo del Tigre; but that's another story!

"I took Bill Hammond with me on the second trip, though I wasn't sure he would be the man for a *bárbaro* expedition. He'd just arrived in Bolivia. It turned out that Hammond had to stay behind with the horses so he didn't get to meet any *bárbaros*.

"Hammond only made one more trip to look for the *bárbaros* with me, in the dry season of '37. That one nearly cost him his life. It wasn't the *bárbaros* — we never did meet any — it was the lack of water. All the water holes had run dry. He's never been on another trip but he says he wants to make a try for the savages up around Concepción where he's stationed."

"Why is it you haven't been able to make a permanent contact with the savages during all these years?" asked Bill.

"More than anything else, because of the school. When this school began with just eight students in 1932, we never dreamed it would develop into what it is now. But I had to make my choice, and felt that the Lord would have me devote myself to this. But Bill, you might be the one the Lord will eventually use to reach these Indians! We have been praying long enough for the right man."

Bill and Harriet looked across the table at each other in silence. The kerosene light was just bright enough to reveal the mist that filled their eyes. The account of the evening had stirred and challenged them to the very depths of their beings. Slowly, they were beginning to understand the plan of God in closing the door to Brazil and Peru only to open wide this door in Bolivia!

The old men may grow beards because they are too old to take part in the bird festival. The oldest man whips the others as they come in from getting honey for the bird god (p. 102).

Jungle life is only for the fit and strong. Before their contact with Christianity, the Ayorés would have buried this old woman alive.

One must know where to find water during the dry season — stagnant rain water caught in the leaves of wild pineapple plant is carefully collected (p. 34).

5.

Just an Indian Boy

COMAI NOW HAD TO USE all of the fingers on both hands as well as the first toe of his right foot to tell how old he was. He liked to think he was nearly a man, and could do many things men do. Natuine had told him that this year when Asoná sang, he could go with the men to hunt honey and turtles as an offering to her. That was a sure sign that he was a man! Always before, he had remained in camp with the old men and boys, making and filling water troughs for the ceremonial bathing, and washing of axes and honey gourds when the men returned from the hunt. Anyone who failed to carefully wash himself as well as everything used on the hunt would be unclean for a whole year, and incur the displeasure of Asoná. But it would be far more exciting to go with the men.

Only one moon had passed since *Edocarate,* the red star, had made its appearance at sundown, and the earth would remain closed for almost three more moons. Even so, Comai could do little but dream of the impending festival in honor of Asoná when he would become a man! He would then leave the camp behind, with the women and girls, and for a whole day and night not even look in their direction. He could eat nothing in all that time — not even lick the honey from his fingers as he removed it from the bee's nest. It would all belong to Asoná. Could he endure going so long without drinking water? On hunting trips with his father, he was already practicing fasting, so that he would not fail when so much would be at stake — maybe, even his life! Sometimes, he became impatient and a little angry at Asoná. But he never dared tell anybody how he felt . . . or even think it very long. If Asoná was so powerful and had such a good memory, would she not also know one's very thoughts?

As always, Comai's people were traveling. Sometimes, when the rains came, the old men would order that huts be built and squash, melons and beans planted. Then they might not move for a whole moon. But now that the world was closed and everything was dry and burned, the camp moved a little each day to find food. Often, there was no water to drink, but the *chicore* root grew everywhere. One could always dig it up and squeeze enough water from it to quench one's thirst. When Asoná would sing to open up the world for a new year, they would have to move near a water hole, for then all the men and boys must bathe carefully. But that was still at least three moons away.

For some time now, the tribe had been moving southward. The old men said that the big, new, white man's road* was only two or three days' hard travel away. Comai had never seen this road. In fact, he had never seen a white man! He knew about the road, however. Some of the young warriors had gone down to the Salt Lake in the territory of the hated Guidaigosode, and crossed this new road both going and coming. What would those white men do next? As the young men told it, they pushed whole trees down, riding on the back of great, roaring yellow monsters! They had no idea of what kind of animal that might be, and called it the white man's *gachidi,* or pet. It looked as if twenty arrows couldn't possibly pierce it! Then, in the big beast's trail other white men laid down some short pieces of tree trunks side by side, all in a row. On top of them they fastened two long pieces of iron side by side, just a little ways apart — about as far as you could step.

Those two pieces of iron went far in the distance and came together there! Well, it seemed as if they came together, anyway. But when you went down to where they came together, they were still apart! Then a tremendous monster — even larger than the yellow ones — ran right up those pieces of iron! It had one eye in front and its mouth was in back where it ate firewood. Fire was in its stomach and smoke poured out its side and top. The white men didn't seem to be afraid of it although it looked as though

---

*Railroad cutting through eastern Bolivia from the Brazilian border.

it could eat up ten Ayorés at once! There were white men right up by its mouth, and it pulled houses along after it, filled with white people.

Comai longed for the day when he could see this marvel with his own eyes! It sounded almost too fantastic to believe! But it was true — the braves had said so.

One day there was new excitement in camp. The hunters had returned, breathlessly, much earlier than usual, saying they had found white men's footprints near the village. The footprints showed that they had gone away, but no one knew whether or not they might return. A guard was set around the camp that night. Comai found it hard to sleep. He tingled with anticipation. Or was it fear? He wished he could see a white man!

Next day, it was decided to follow the white man's trail into the forest to see how far they had gone. Of course, it was out of the question that Comai and the boys go; only the men went. The whole camp awaited their return with great anticipation. They weren't gone long, and when they returned, each of them carried a brand-new machete or wore a colorful shirt.

Everyone crowded around the braves as they marched to the center of camp. Comai, with the other boys, forced their way to the front of the group. Everyone wanted to hold the knives and touch the wonderful shirts! All were talking at once. When chief Deguide was able to restore a measure of order, the warriors told their story.

"We did not meet the white men, but we saw where they had rested. Their smell was everywhere. What a strong odor they have!" One of the braves spat at just the thought of it.

"They went as far as the old village around the bend of the trail," another explained. "But they had left all of these things tied to the branches of the bushes with pieces of vine!"

That evening's session of the council of elders was stormy. Why had these hated white men left the knives and clothing on the trail? Did they really want to be friends? Or was it a trick to throw the Ayorés off their guard? Some of the chiefs said this would be a good time to make a friendly contact with the whites. But most of the older men felt that they should immediately flee further into the vastness of the jungle. The argument continued far into the night. The stars of the constellation *Guiguinai Piragoi* (Orion) were high overhead before Comai curled up in the sand by the fire and drifted off into a fitful slumber. He hoped they would decide to meet the white men! How exciting that would be!

The peacemakers finally carried their point, and the whole tribe began a cautious move southward in the direction of the new iron road. They followed the trail of the white men. Perhaps there they would find those who had left the gifts! Although there were more Indians than Comai could count, they traveled fast. Comai overheard the chief saying that ten Ayorés would not have enough fingers and toes to count everyone in the group. They felt safer since there were so many of them. In case of trouble, they could defend themselves well!

When they reached the iron road it was many days before they could decide just how they should approach the whites. Every man seemed to have a different idea as to how it should be done. Finally, they all agreed to follow chief Deguide's plan.

They had already noticed that the huge, fire-eating animal that pulled little houses behind it passed by only once daily. But several times a day a little house* with round feet would go rushing past. Usually, only one or two white men were in it. It would be safer to stop one of the little houses and see if the white men were friendly. The big, black fire-eating ones went too fast, and there were too many white men in them. It would be dangerous to try to stop them.

When they heard the clattering of the next little house in the distance, they were ready for action. They had noticed that it slowed up whenever it went around the nearby curve, so half of the group stood on the iron road around the curve where they couldn't be seen. In their hands they held only feathers and rattles. The spears and war clubs were hidden nearby in the brush, in case of trouble.

As the little house came into view, around the curve, the Indians saw the white men inside suddenly sit up tall in

---

*Small, gasoline-powered inspection cars.

their seats. The little house with round feet stopped with a screech. The white men looked afraid and nervous. Then the house started to move backwards, but by this time the other half of the tribe had stepped out in the road behind them. The little house couldn't go either way, and the white men shut the doors tight and stayed inside. The bravest of the Indians from either side walked slowly forward, shouting and waving gifts of feathers. Comai and his friends could hardly hide their excitement as they watched from the bushes by the side of the road. What would happen next?

When they saw they were helplessly trapped, the white men finally opened the doors of the little house and stepped out. They had taken off their shirts and held them up in a sign of friendship. Then all fear seemed to vanish and the white men were surrounded by a laughing, shouting mob of Indian men. The white men handed over their shirts and accepted the feathers the Indians proffered them.

A long time later, more white men appeared. Natuinate and the other mothers hid their children behind their skirts, ready to flee; but nothing happened. These new white men brought gifts for everyone! Knives, axes, shirts, pants, beads — Comai had never seen so many wonderful things before!

The sun moved so quickly across the sky that day that no one noticed until it reached the tops of the trees in the west, casting long shadows across the road. With one glance skyward, Deguide gave the signal and in minutes not an Indian remained in sight. Though not one intelligible word had passed between them and the white men, the Ayorés felt that at long last here was the beginning of a real friendship!

From that time on, Deguide's people were never far from either the railroad or one of the white men's villages. Although they still slept in the jungle and hunted for their food along its tangled trails, almost every day some of them would visit the whites in their houses. The white people were still afraid, but no one shot with "noise sticks."

One day a woman with yellow hair came. She knew some words that the Ayorés could understand, but she didn't say the words quite right! Natuinate took Natui and Comai to the house where she lived. The woman with yellow hair gave Comai some food. Comai smelled it and felt like vomiting! He threw it on the ground. How could anyone eat food that smelled so terrible!

The woman with the yellow hair who gave Comai the food was Jean Dye, widow of one of the five missionaries murdered by the Ayorés in 1943. Jean and others gathered the Indians together and moved them northward away from the railroad, near the village of San Juan. The Indians were attracting too much attention and the missionaries saw at once that it would be better to remove them to some more isolated spot. At San Juan, however, disaster struck. A measles epidemic was in full force when they arrived. The men of San Juan told them of a spot along a stream near some red sandstone cliffs, about fifteen miles away. Along both banks of the stream the jungle was so dense that the white men had named it Tobité, or darkness.

Hardly had they arrived at their destination when the Ayorés began to come down with the measles. They were very ill, and each time anyone died, the Ayorés, fearful of the spirits, insisted that the camp be moved a mile or so upstream.

So many people died that they could not be counted on the fingers and toes of one Indian! The fingers and toes of another Ayoré would have to be used before coming to the end of the death list. Comai's baby brother died. Then one day, Natuine and Natuinate awoke with their bodies hot. Little red spots covered their faces and spread over their bodies. Jean and her friends were most kind and loving. It was plain to see by the way they looked and what they did, that they really did care. Each time they would come to the clearing to give medicine to the sick, they brought along something for the children to eat. Comai along with the others, did not like this food at first, and spat it out. But when his mother and father could no longer rise from the ground to cook for him, hunger drove him to eat it, until he found himself actually enjoying this white man's food. The yellow-haired lady called it *pan* (bread).

As soon as the missionaries returned to their houses, the witch doctor came and smoked and chanted over Natuine, blowing smoke on his fevered body, and sucking the evil spirits out of it. These were apparently spirits of white men, for they resisted all efforts of the witch doctor to bring them out. As soon as the witch doctor was finished, Natuine dragged his weakened body to the little river nearby and sat down in the cool water. How good it felt on his hot chest and legs! But he coughed more when he crawled back to his fireside. Every day he was weaker. When Natuinate died in the night, the white men dug the grave and buried her. Since she had died suddenly, though, her spirit had escaped and was abroad. She should have been buried alive the night before to avoid this. The witch doctor said the only hope for the well-being of the group was to move the entire camp, sick ones and all.

It was a sad, bedraggled procession that struggled down the path along the river. Many were so ill they had to be carried. Before they left, they burned the little leaf shelters that had served them as houses, and cut down a few trees to generally change the aspect of the camp. In this way, they could confuse the spirit of Natuinate, so that it could not find them again. Finally, only Natuine and a few others were left. Since he had learned of his wife's death, he had not spoken. Now, when friends offered to carry him to the new camp, he refused to go.

"I am too ill," he said. "And I miss *Caratabidate* (the mother of my children). I have no desire to live. Dig my grave for me!"

Sadly, his relatives dug a shallow round hole. Natuine dragged himself painfully to it and let himself down into it in a sitting position. They spread a rough blanket over his head, and pushed the dirt back into the hole, burying him alive. His honey gourd was broken on top of the dry, loose earth, and his spear and bow stuck upright over the grave. Comai stood watching, dry-eyed, until the earth over the grave stopped its violent shaking. An Indian was not supposed to cry, even though his heart was breaking. He turned and walked slowly after the others down the trail. He was alone and an orphan.

He knew the rest could not be far ahead. It wasn't necessary to move a great distance to confuse the spirits of the dead. As he threaded his way among the thorns and fallen branches, following the faint footpath of his people, he wondered what *naropie* was like. Every Indian went to *naropie* after death and there was no return. His father and mother were both there, now! It was a place of darkness and deep mud, with no honey nor turtles. All of the very worst of this life was concentrated there for one to suffer every day. At least, that was what the old men of the tribe said, and they knew everything.

Comai remembered when Deguide had told them about *naropie,* and why Ayorés must go there after death . . .

Deguide, the witch doctor, had stood watching the children at play in the little clearing between the houses. His body, blackened from head to foot with charcoal, glistened in the afternoon sun. War feathers dangled from his neck and down his back. His jaguar-skin war bonnet with its mass of parrot tail feathers sat squarely on his head. Catching the attention of the children, he called them to him. Stopping their noisy play they surrounded the witch doctor expectantly. Deguide was in a story-telling mood. "My little children," he began, "it is time you know who you are, and what life means."

Comai and the others seated themselves in a half-circle in front of Deguide, eager faces turned up toward his. The witch doctor's face was inexpressibly sad. He leaned heavily on his spear.

"We are Ayorés," he said slowly. "We are the first people to come to earth. We came from the moon, *Guedoside.* He was our father. But one day, long ago, *Dajusui,* the tapir, tried to win us away from *Guedoside.* He proposed a race between them.

" 'If I win the race, all the Ayorés must go to *naropie,* the place of darkness and mud, in the center of the earth, where there are no turtles, and no honey. All will go there, and none will ever be released,' boasted *Dajusui.*

" 'I agree to race with you,' answered *Guedoside.* 'But if I win I shall take all of the Ayorés up with me to live in my lovely home in the sky.' "

Deguide paused, his voice choked with emotion. "Who won?" asked the children, breathlessly.

"They raced, and *Dajusui* won."

When Asoná sang that year, most of the Ayorés were still too weak to do much in the way of offerings of honey and turtles. But gradually their strength returned. They did not go back to live permanently in the jungle, but stayed near the railroad, learning to travel in the trains between the little villages of the whites that were springing up along the right-of-way. One of the largest of these villages was the old Jesuit mission of San José de Chiquitos.

They enjoyed going to the towns to sell, trade or beg. From one of these trips Comai did not return. He had dropped behind the group as they walked up one of the grassy streets, and a white woman had beckoned to him from the doorway of her house. In her hand was a piece of bread. By now, Comai was very fond of bread. Fearlessly he approached the woman to take it from her outstretched hand. But at the doorway she grasped his wrist and pulled him quickly inside, shutting the door firmly behind him! For six months Comai's people searched for him in vain, and finally gave him up for lost.

Although Comai was a slave in her house, his mistress did not mistreat him. Only when the Indians were in town was he denied access to the streets. The Ayorés spoke no Spanish, so could make no intelligible inquiries for the lost boy. And for fear of his captors' sharp tongues, no neighbor would reveal his whereabouts to the Indians. Often, when the Ayorés were not in the village, Comai would be sent out to sell little plates of sweetened rice. And always, when he returned, the money would be carefully counted against the amount of rice sold. Comai longed to run away, but he was not too sure in which direction his people had gone.

Months passed; and Comai began to enjoy the civilized life more than the endless wanderings of his tribe. There were few bugs here; water ran out of a faucet and there was an abundance of it. When it rained, he could lie under a roof of tile and listen to it without getting wet. This was better than the drip-drip-drip of the rain through the leaf shelters that had always been home in the forest! True, he missed the honey and turtles, but he was learning to like rice and *empanizado* (brown sugar). He spent many hours listening to the white people talk, and soon found he could understand much of what they said. He was slowly able to talk with other boys he met, and they understood him. He would have learned even more rapidly had he been allowed time to play with them in the streets.

One day, the inevitable happened — or was it God?

While out selling his little plates of rice, a train arrived with many of his people on it. They were overjoyed at seeing Comai, and surrounded him, fingering the ragged shirt and pants he wore as they excitedly conversed together. Tattered and torn though they were, Comai's clothes were more than any of the others had! Suddenly, the call of the wild flooded in upon the lad, and setting down his tray of rice on the ground, he hitched up his trousers, climbed up on the flatcar beside his people, and returned with them to their camp. He was immediately a hero and a leader among the young people. Not only was he the proud possessor of pants and a shirt, but he could even speak the strange language of the white people!

6.

Missionaries Are Made—Not Born!

It wasn't long after the Pencilles arrived in Santiago that George Haight predicted: "Bill Pencille is the man we have been praying for to contact the *bárbaros*." His prediction proved true. But first, Bill was to go through a long process of refining. Jungle missionaries are made, not born.

Football players lining up for the kick-off of the big game, marines storming a strategic beach, astronauts ready to go into orbit — all have had months and years of rigorous training before they are called upon to use their skill. Before Bill Pencille saw his first *bárbaro* out in the jungle he, too, needed training; although at the time he failed to understand why God had called him to Bolivia and then allowed him to "waste so much time"!

Later, he was to realize that he had experienced with his own life just what God had done to many others. Moses herded sheep for forty years; Joseph was sold as a slave and then jailed like a criminal; John Mark abandoned Paul's missionary band. Our Lord Himself spent many years planing and sawing lumber in Joseph's carpenter shop.

This was all part of what the Apostle Peter meant when he wrote that a Christian's faith is much more valuable than gold, which, "though it be tried with fire might be found unto praise and honor at the appearing of Jesus Christ."

Bill Pencille, like so many other new missionaries, arrived in Santiago with a shiny diploma and suitcases filled with the latest books on theology, eager to accomplish the task set before him. He had many lessons to learn, and needed a five-year postgraduate course on jungle living.

Without it, he could never have been successful with the *bárbaros.*

The first few months in Bolivia were not too trying; studying Spanish was a necessary and not unpleasant prelude to future work. Bill and Harriet made good progress in the language, and being in isolated Santiago and in such close daily contact with the Spanish-speaking population helped a great deal.

Three months after their arrival, their first child was born. It was a boy, and they named him Richard. When Harriet returned from the hospital in Santa Cruz she noticed that Dick wasn't gaining much weight. Then dysentery struck. How he contracted it in spite of the meticulous care Harriet took with whatever touched her baby's lips, no one knows. In a country where sanitation is almost unknown, it could happen — and it did.

They took him immediately to the army doctor in Roboré, but medicine didn't help. They changed the baby's formula, thinking that this might help him, but it proved too strong for his weakened system. As the illness continued week after week, he wasted away to a mere skeleton, and all he could hold on his stomach was a bit of rice water. He lay in a semi-coma, his little heart beating weakly under the loose skin on his chest. He reminded Bill of the pictures taken in India during a famine!

The young couple were desperate. Bill, especially, had been growing increasingly bitter as the baby's condition worsened. How could a loving God allow this to happen! He had brought them to Bolivia — why did He not answer their prayers for Dick? Would they not have been better off in Rochester? This would never have happened there! A thousand questions, all unanswered, plagued him.

The Haights were most loving and thoughtful, and did all in their power to help the stricken parents. One morning, George entered the house as Harriet was attempting to feed the baby. He was too weak to drink from a bottle, and she was carefully feeding him with a medicine dropper. He was barely breathing.

"I'm going to call that army doctor again!" said George abruptly. "We can't move the child — he'll have to make the trip up here!" He stood a moment longer, silently looking at the baby. George had served in the Canadian artillery during the first World War, and was not given to a show of emotion, but his eyes were moist as he turned to leave.

He put in the telephone call, then went over to a friend's house and purchased two boards. The coffin wouldn't have to be very large, he thought, but it would be best to have it ready.

Harriet was at the limit of her endurance, both physical and mental. As she carefully placed the baby in his little crib, the tears could be restrained no longer. Bill felt as though his own heart would break, but he kept his arm around her till she regained her composure. "To think that the house we left in Rochester," Harriet whispered brokenly, "was only a few blocks from the Mayo Clinic!"

The God who had brought them to Bolivia had not abandoned them. He had no intention of leaving the crucible in the fire beyond the best refining point. As Bill stood over the pitiful bundle of life, steadying his sobbing wife, a sudden tenderness flooded in upon him, dispelling the rebellion in his heart.

"Dear," he said to his wife, "I have been wrong in my bitterness toward God. And I fear I haven't been too much help to you in this trial, feeling as I have!"

Harriet smiled up at him through her tears.

Bill went on, "It was wrong to ask God 'why?' I should have known I could always trust Him to do all things well, and not have asked why He does things as He does! Will you kneel with me? I think we ought to give our baby to Him anew, and ask God to restore him to health or take him home to heaven, as He alone sees best."

They slipped silently to their knees beside the tiny crib. Words were no longer necessary. Their prayer was more an attitude of surrender and trust, than an outpouring of words. As they rose to their feet, there was a light knock at the door. Beth Earle, fellow missionary and nurse, had come to stay with the baby while Bill and Harriet got some much-needed rest.

Though their hearts were again at peace, they could not sleep. A half-moon was in the sky, and Santiago was silent, shrouded in peaceful sleep. Bill and Harriet, hand in hand, walked slowly through the deserted streets. They spoke little. Each knew the other's thoughts. *God does all things well; if He chooses to take our baby home, we will accept it joyfully as the will of a loving Father!*

The hour was late when they returned to the little bedroom, and they rejoiced to see that Dick was still breathing.

"The dysentery seems to be stopping somewhat," whispered Beth encouragingly to Harriet.

By morning, it was obvious to all that the crisis had passed, and there was great rejoicing in the mission compound. Bill was in the street when the army doctor came hurrying toward the house. "How's the baby?" he asked.

"Better," replied Bill with a broad grin.

"Better! What did you give him? What did you do?"

"We prayed, and God healed him!"

The doctor laughed incredulously. These *evangelistas!*

As Dick slowly regained his health, the testing seemed to die down. But it flared up and became even more intense after George Haight sent Bill on his first assignment to Aguasucia.

Aguasucia was where George Haight had had fleeting contact with the Ayorés fifteen years earlier. Now, waiting and hoping for another contact with the Indians, George maintained an outpost and kept cattle there. It was a lush pastureland in the flat jungles twenty-five miles south of the Santiago hills, and could easily support five hundred head of cattle.

Haight had great expectations that Bill Pencille would be the man for the Indian work he envisioned. He had a burning desire to reach the *bárbaros,* coupled with a feeling of frustration caused by his administrative duties in the school and mission station of Santiago. He knew it would be a long term job to find the Indians, and he hoped that Pencille would have the patience and perseverance needed to do it.

As the months in Aguasucia lengthened interminably into a year. Bill Pencille felt himself slipping. Separated from his family he had given up reading the Bible. Once in a while he tried to concentrate on singing a hymn to himself but he rarely got through the first stanza without other thoughts coming into his mind.

These other thoughts were invariably bitter ones. Why in the world had George Haight sent him out to this desert? Even the water hole in Aguasucia had dried up, so they had had to drive the whole herd to another ranch where there was still some water.

Indian work, my eye! We haven't seen an Indian since we've come. I doubt if there's one within 500 *miles. If Haight works at this rate of speed no wonder nothing's been done with the* bárbaros. *I came to Bolivia to be a missionary, not a cattle-herder. He doesn't mind it up there in Santiago, eating all those canned goods, and sleeping in a nice soft bed with clean sheets.*

What a gang he sends with me! Illiterate, stupid peons. Why, they're just as happy here as if they were at home with their families — that's what gets me.

That rice — I don't think I'll be able to eat another plate of it.

I didn't know this Mission was a dictatorship. Didn't we missionaries out-vote Haight and decide to close down the school? Over his dead body, he said. Maybe that's the kind of democracy they have in Canada. If Mr. Haight were an American things would be different. Moody didn't do him any good. He must have slept through his classes.

I'm not going to put up with this much longer. There are plenty of churches in the States that need pastors and you can get things done for the Lord there.

Harriet will — Harriet! I can't take being away from her for six, eight weeks at a time. It isn't natural. When Haight comes I'll give him a piece of my mind!

When George did come Bill never had the courage to express his thoughts. But Haight was observant enough to realize he had a malcontent on his hands. The inevitable blow-up came when George, on one of his visits, ordered Bill to take the cattle back to Aguasucia.

"But how do you know there's water?" objected Bill.

"This is December. There's always water there in December. Besides it's rained plenty here and that means it's rained there, too."

"But why don't we go down and see first? It's an awful job to round up these half-wild cattle and drive them that far."

From these peons in Aguasucia (above), Bill Pencille received a post graduate education in jungle living, including how to make hammocks and how to hunt the tapir, the largest land animal in South America (below).

"Mr. Pencille, I'm in charge here! The cattle are going back to Aguasucia." George Haight laid the reins on the side of his horse's neck, whirled around and cantered off towards Santiago.

Bill was boiling inside during those long days of riding in the dust of a cattle drive. And then when they got to Aguasucia there was no water! It was just as dry as it had been in June!

Bill decided to write Haight a letter. It was typical of what a young, impatient, disillusioned missionary might write:

Dear Mr. Haight,

We arrived in Qurupaocito (sp?) last evening(Thurs.) and left the cattle pointed this way while we came on in to see about the water. We picked up the 2 *paridas* and the bull in San Joaquín. The bay cow is in San Francisco now, at least so says Moreno in Santiagoma. The men got back this AM and reported the cattle all in Aguamana.

The catch to the whole thing is that it hasn't rained since we were last here. There is no water here except the hole. . . . The Cola, Toro Muerto — even the Salitral are dry as can be. Taromá has water, however.

Although a Junior Missionary isn't supposed to know anything, you will remember that I suggested another trip in to look around before we brought the cattle out. Even the water here would not last with 72 head of cattle. Yes, I know it can all change in 2 hours, but the simple truth is that it hasn't and this is January 10. Last year at this time everything was full and the rains were letting up. I should think we might as well face the possibility of this being a dry year.

Well, I'm not in too good a humor so I'd better be careful not to speak all of my mind. What I'll do is this: we are taking the cattle to Toromá this PM and closing the gate behind us. In 2 days what little water is here would be undrinkable. Then beyond Casa Bárbara I'm making another gate and Pedro and I are going to make camp in the *potrero* — the one off to the right of the road before entering the *monte alto*. I have no desire for the bugs of Taromá. The pasture along the road and in the *potrero of Taromá* will give for awhile. Also the road is now dry and hard enough for a cart if you should desire.

This will have to be temporary; as for my part I will not continue as a cowboy out here. You know that I have no objection to cattle here and that I'm more than willing to cooperate with you. However, I fail to see where cattle at present, under these conditions, are an asset, and when we put them and the *chacos* first and *bárbaros* later if and when there is time and money, then I think we're "off the beam."

The men think to leave Saturday morning. They can confirm what I've said and fill in the details. If the letter seems strong, I trust you and Mrs. Haight will not take personal offence. I've felt more and more that we were giving secondary things first place, and the events of the last days only confirm it to me.

I trust you are all well, and will be awaiting your decision.

In His Name,
Wm. R. Pencille

The day after George read the letter he headed for the cattle ranch. The atmosphere was icy as he dismounted in front of the hammock where Bill was relaxing. Bill looked him straight in the eye. George could hardly control the emotion in his voice. "Mr. Pencille," he said, "you're through in Aguasucia! I had hopes that you would be a good man for the Indian work — from this moment on you're through! You failed your test!"

Bill had expected the reaction. He flushed with anger. Nevertheless he said nothing but "All right," saddled his horse, rolled up his hammock and rode back to Santiago with his senior missionary. Few words were spoken on the ten-hour trip. It was dark and raining when they arrived.

Back in Santiago George Haight turned the church over to Bill. The congregation, composed mostly of students from the grammar school, presented little challenge. And Bill's relationship to George, although always correct and polite, was not the kind of warm fellowship that all missionaries are thought to enjoy.

Bill began to scout around for some place else to serve. He went up to visit Bill Hammond in Concepción, and the two made an exploratory trip to the Guarayos, far to the north. "This is the place for me," thought Bill. But when he talked it over with Hammond he soon detected that Hammond was most cool toward the idea and would not back him in a committee meeting. Unable to see that this was all part of a greater plan of God, the young missionary returned to Santiago, still troubled in spirit. In the next field meeting, he told George Haight he wanted to work in nearby Santo Corazón.

This decision broke the ice and put the relationship between the two men back where it always should have been. Haight had been apprehensive that Bill would go up to the "northern section" of the field to get from under his direct jurisdiction. But when he decided to stick it out under Haight's leadership, George reformed his opinion of the man. "He'll make the grade," George said to Helen as Bill walked beside the pack oxen up the road toward Santo Corazón.

The Pencilles weren't in Santo Corazón too long, not long enough for their ministry to have a permanent effect. In fact the only things some people in the area remember about Bill Pencille in Santo Corazón is that he is the only missionary they knew of who got drunk!

Bill had to visit a home about three miles out of town one morning. He couldn't take a horse because there was no trail cut through the woods, so he went on foot. The last kilometer or so was through deep sand and under the blazing noonday sun. Bill says,

"When I arrived I was extremely thirsty. They were very poor people. In fact all they had to offer me was a bowl of *chicha* that they made out of the *totaí* palm plant. You can see how poor they were because they didn't even have *yuca* or corn, so they were making *chicha* and living off this *totaí* palm. They offered me this gourd of *chicha* and I took it. Of course the stuff was steaming hot, and it wasn't cooled at all. When I took the first drink of it I knew it was strong — as we say *picante.* But I rather prefer the *chicha* not too fresh anyway. It is much better once the corn or *yuca* taste is gone, as well as the musty tang which comes from the jug.

"I was thirsty enough, so I just gulped it down in two or three swallows and handed the gourd back. I suppose we talked for fifteen minutes and I didn't notice anything. Everything was all right as long as I sat down, but then I stood up to say goodbye to them, and — couldn't find the door! I staggered, took a few missteps, and finally grabbed hold of the doorpost to hold myself up. I got outside and went wobbling down the road. I could hear them laughing back in the house, and of course, knew what they were laughing at."

In mid-1948 the Pencilles were sent to Concepción to relieve the Hammonds who were due for furlough. Here finally a measure of real and permanent victory became evident in Bill's life. Now he says in retrospect:

"I needed maturing, and I now realize just how valuable that 'boot camp' really was. It had made a man of me. How could I have better perfected my Spanish than by living under a grove of trees, in hammocks, with a dozen Indian peons who spoke no English? How could I have learned to exist in the jungle except by being forced to do so with men who knew it as intimately as I knew the streets of Rochester? They taught me to ride a horse. From them I learned the secrets of the hunt. They were experts at stalking deer, tapir and peccary. I found that the South American honey bee does not sting, and that there were a dozen different species that made delicious honey. I could now pass a comfortable night in the most torrential downpour with only a hammock, a mosquito net and a poncho. I could build a house out of just what the jungle provides. They taught me to clear and plant the land with nothing more than an ax and a hoe. Eighteen years on a Minnesota farm could not prepare me for all of this!"

Even with this new realization and victory in his life, Bill could little imagine how necessary this jungle "post-graduate course" was to be in the years still to come!

7.

Peace With the White Man—Almost!

WHILE THE MEASLES EPIDEMIC raged along the railroad line, another chief, Nuine, and his people were camped at the base of a big rock over two hundred miles north of Tobité. They knew nothing of the contact their friends had made with the white men.

The forest was parched, and the clay in the bottom of the dry water holes caked and cracked; but *cucaratedo* on top of the rock was full of sweet, clear water. Some pre-historic cataclysm had carved a huge, deep fissure in the rock, and this filled with rain water each year. When all moisture on the forest floor had long since disappeared, *cucaratedo* still retained its water. Each year, Nuine brought his people to this rock during the months Asoná had the earth closed. It was a good place to be when she opened the world again in the August full moon. There was sure to be sufficient water for the ceremonial bathing and washing of axes and gourds, when they washed away *puyai*. *Puyai* was the uncleanness of a whole year of offense to Asoná, and only careful bathing could remove it.

Nuine's group was not large. They could be counted on the fingers and toes of three Indians. This year, there was not only an abundance of water, but the honey and turtles were unusually plentiful. The wise men of the group, after a long night's session over the pipe, decided that they should remain in the vicinity of the rock and plant their gardens there at the new year.

This decision was greeted with a great spurt of activity early next morning. Every man and boy in camp attacked the brush and trees with their axes and knives. But the flurry of activity did not last beyond mid-morning. As the burning sun rose higher in the brazen skies, the budding farmers retired, one by one, to *cucaratedo* to drink from its cool waters. Refreshed, they stretched out to rest on top of the rock in the shade of the few scrub trees struggling for existence there. By the time the sun reached its zenith, all sound of ax and knife had long since ceased in the new clearing, and the men either slumbered or sat silently in little groups. Weapons were scattered carelessly on all sides, but within reach of their owners. No Ayoré was ever caught far from his bow and arrows and his war club.

Suddenly, as if on signal, the group was alert. The low hum of an airplane could be heard off to the east. Even as they strained to listen, the hum swelled into a mighty roar. The great silver bird was heading straight for their rock, and was just skimming the treetops! As it passed overhead, the Indians instinctively ducked, and the huge rock seemed to tremble beneath them. Before they could collect their wits and reach for their weapons, the great bird was gone!

But now — it was turning so sharply it seemed to stand on one wing! Then it came straight back toward them. It must have seen them there on the rock! The more timid plunged into the foliage along the steep sides of the rock. The braver warriors stood their ground, arrows fitted to taut bowstrings, bows pulled nearly double, ready to see if the great silver bird might be brought to earth by the sharp points of their arrows. As it roared overhead a flood of arrows rose skyward, but not one succeeded in reaching the bird. It flew so fast that even their swiftest arrows fell far short. Now it turned again and came thundering back, even lower! The rock trembled and the very leaves of the trees shook at its passing, as though caught up in some mighty gale.

Then it was gone. Watching it fly toward the horizon, it seemed to fall into the trees and disappear. So they named it *cuchabasui*, a thing that falls. No one had any idea of just what this gigantic bird might be. But of course, there was no question about its being alive. No dead thing could make that much noise or fly so swiftly!

Work on their gardens didn't progress very rapidly. But then, there was no hurry. There never was in the jungle. Even if they never planted their gardens, there were always plenty of honey and turtles in the forest, Sporadically, between hunts, they did work. It was on one of those days that a most exciting thing happened. Everyone was out at the clearing, even the women. There was really more noise than work, but a few trees were falling to the blows of the narrow chisel-like axes. Jara went for water to *cucaratedo.* She had been gone for about the time it takes to cut down one tree, when suddenly her scream pierced the jungle air, sending shivers of apprehension down the spines of even the most courageous!

"Coñocho quiiiii!"

"White men!" Axes and knives were tossed aside, and weapons grasped in brown, sinewy hands. Terrified women gathered up their children and fled. The young people disappeared into the jungle surrounding the clearing at the first syllable of the dread cry. Then Jara burst upon the scene. "Run for your lives!" she shouted. "Three white men are on the trail to the waterhole!" In less time than it takes to tell it, the group had melted into the forest, their naked bodies blending perfectly with the boles of the trees.

The Indians fled according to pre-arranged plan, fleeing separately in every direction and leaving behind as few signs as possible. They expected momentarily to hear the white man's noise stick boom out behind them! But not once did they hear it, as they had on so many other occasions, echoing and reverberating endlessly through the trees.

Several miles away, they regrouped in an old abandoned campsite. Nuine counted them carefully. No one was missing. The white men had been outwitted and outdistanced this time! They breathed easier now.

Then Jara told her story. At the waterhole, three men had suddenly stepped from the brush into the trail. The leader was tall, and his head was round and shiny. (No doubt, he had pulled out all of his hair in respect to his god!) His clothing was strange — like a skirt that went all the way down to the ground. The second man was dressed like the first, but the third one looked just like any other white men they had glimpsed from time to time. Yes, they all carried the fearful noise sticks. They were tying axes and knives to the bushes with pieces of jungle vine when she saw them. But she really could not tell exactly, for she was frightened and had not taken time to notice too closely.

It was deemed wise not to return to *cucaratedo* immediately. A wide circle would be described in their wanderings, and then after a whole moon, they would cautiously swing back toward the rock. When they finally did approach *cucaratedo* once again, scouts were sent ahead. They announced that all was clear. The footprints of the white men were still visible in the dust of the trails; but there seemed to be two sets of prints, one fresher than the first! Just as Jara had said, there were pieces of vine hanging from the branches — but no axes or knives were to be seen. Each piece of vine had been severed, and now hung empty, swaying gently in the breeze!

What did it all mean? Why had the white men not followed them and tried to kill them, as they had always done before? Why had they not plundered the Indians' village? Had they really tied axes and knives to the bushes? If so, where were they now? What did the second set of footprints mean? These were questions that even Sidi and tobacco could not answer! Life in camp was livelier than it had been for many moons as these intriguing questions were posed again and again.

Finally, the young warriors proposed a solution. Why not follow the white men's footprints to his house, and approach it at midday, unarmed! In that way, they could tell if the white men were really trying to be friendly!

Most of the younger men were heartily in favor of this plan. The women and sweethearts openly opposed it, seeing only disaster and death as the outcome. The old men smoked endless pipes of tobacco, invoking Sidi's help and wisdom. Finally, it was decided that a few of the warriors should carry it out. It would be wonderful if a way could be found to make peace with the white men! Perhaps they would then be prevailed upon to use their big noise sticks to help the Ayorés fight the hated Guidaigosode, the enemies to the south!

The sun was directly overhead as the small group of men stepped out in plain view of the white man's house. They had hidden their spears and arrows in the brush. Now they slowly advanced, shouting, toward the house, holding their hands high above their heads. They were frightened; their bodies trembled and their voices wavered. What would the white men do? Would they receive them in peace?

They did not have long to wait. At the first shout, the white men had run into the house, hurriedly closing the door behind them. Then a window opened cautiously, just a trifle, and a rifle cracked twice. Simultaneously, there were two high-pitched whistles over the Indians' heads! The white men's noise sticks! The warriors turned and plunged headlong back into the protection of the forest. Whatever had been the object of the whites in their visit to *cucaratedo,* they obviously were not looking for peace . . .

8.

Probings

Bill and Harriet had no sooner moved into the big mission house in Concepción where the Hammonds had lived, than they had a visitor. Bill was working on the fence in the back patio when he heard the clap-clap-clap of hands at the half-open Dutch door. Clapping, rather than knocking, was the customary way of announcing a visit.

A huge stranger, not unlike the hero of some western movie, stood at the door. Although his features were hardly Latin, his perfect Spanish proved conclusively that he was a Bolivian. He introduced himself as Constantino Flores, and said he owned the house across the plaza. After a few of the customary Spanish courtesies, he got down to the point of his visit.

"Don Guillermo," he said, "I would like to know if you are interested in reaching the *bárbaros*?" He looked at Bill keenly, trying to anticipate his answer.

"Of course!" was the ready response. "But I understood there weren't any *bárbaros* around here! That most of them were along the railroad line and near San Ignacio."

"Very true," Flores replied. "But there are plenty of them around my ranch as well, and I wish you would do something about them!"

Bill's interest quickened. This man apparently knew what he was talking about, and he tried to draw him out. "Have you seen any on your ranch?"

"Not personally. But my peon Nicolás has seen them and he tells me there are plenty of signs nearby. If you wish to go after them, I'll tell him to help you all he can!"

"How do I get to your ranch?" Bill tried, not too successfully, to conceal his enthusiasm.

"It is about seventy-five miles east of here. You can get there easily on horseback!"

Bill assured his new friend of his interest, and promised to visit his ranch as soon as possible. At the same time he was wondering why Flores, a Catholic, would encourage a missionary to go after the wild Indians on his ranch! Why didn't he offer this opportunity to the priests?

As don Constantino rose to leave, Bill asked, "What is the name of your ranch?"

"El Encanto," was the reply.

Two months passed before Bill was free to plan a trip to El Encanto. He didn't own a horse or saddle at that time, and was so new in the village that he hardly knew where to borrow one. Bill finally brought up the subject with a casual acquaintance, don Germán. Don Germán immediately offered him one of his horses! He wouldn't charge him a thing!

Bill was amazed that a virtual stranger would be so generous. He was not as yet familiar with the Latin way of doing a favor with the expectation of a favor in return! He was soon to learn.

He planned to leave that afternoon. But as he was getting his gear together a boy came to the half-door and said, "Padre Luis sent me to tell you he is leaving for El Encanto this afternoon!"

Padre Luis! Bill had seen this Padre Luis, a large, robust German priest, many times, but had never spoken to him. Why was he going to El Encanto — and why had he made it a point to tell Bill about it? Was he also interested in the Indians? How did he know of Bill's projected trip?

Bill's thoughts were abruptly interrupted by the appearance of don Germán at the door. His wife, he claimed, was very ill out at his ranch and needed to fly to Santa Cruz the next day for medical treatment. Would Bill be so kind as to postpone his trip to El Encanto for just one day and bring his sick wife to town in the jeep so that she could catch tomorrow's plane?

This was all part of the initiation of a first-term missionary into Bolivian life. As Bill drove out to the ranch he began to understand something of don Germán's motives in loaning the horse, and suspected that he was working hand in glove with the priest! How else had Padre Luis learned of his projected trip? Bill wasn't too surprised to find don Germán's wife in perfect health, busily preparing for the journey. "Oh, yes," she smiled. "I'm much better! But since you're here I'll just ride to town with you. . ." By the time they reached Concepción, it was too late to start for El Encanto.

That evening Bill paid a visit to his friend, Luis Buceta, the Panagra agent in Concepción. Buceta was short and very round. He dressed immaculately and his white shirt and khaki trousers were always well-pressed even in the humid tropical heat.

Luis was one of those people whose business it was to know everyone else's business, and not much happened in Concepción that Luis didn't know about. He was proud to be a self-appointed authority on everything. Perhaps, Bill thought, Luis could clear up the mystery of the past few hours!

"Of course I know why Padre Luis is going!" don Luis said as soon as they were comfortably seated on the verandah. "You know about his trip with Padre Salvador last July . . ."

"What trip?"

"Why, the one he took with the priest from San Miguel! Surely, you've heard about that?" Luis raised his eyebrows questioningly.

"If I have, I must have forgotten," replied Bill. "Tell me about it."

Just then doña Nellie, Luis' wife, entered with *cafecitos*. Bill wished he might refuse, but knew it would be impossible. He wasn't too fond of the little cups of strong black coffee, thick and sweet as syrup. As they sipped from the tiny cups, Luis began his story.

"Last June, the Panagra DC-3 was coming here from San Ignacio, on its regular run, when pilot Norman Smith spotted the savages on a big rock east of here. You know Norm, don't you?"

"Sure, I know him," Bill said. Down in that lonesome corner of the world, every American knew every other one. "What did he do when he saw the *bárbaros*?"

"Well, if you know Norm, you won't be surprised. He banked sharply, dove down as if he were flying an army trainer plane, and went into a tight circle just over the rock. The passengers thought sure they were going to crash and were all screaming and praying back in the cabin. As a matter of fact, one of them registered a complaint with me when he arrived, but I just laughed!"

"I would have liked to have been in that plane!" Bill exclaimed. "Could they see the Indians?"

"See them!" don Luis laughed. "The radio operator was taking pictures of them as fast as he could roll the film through his camera! In one picture, you can actually see the arrows flying through the air under the plane. The *bárbaros* kept shooting at them as they circled. I've got a copy of the picture somewhere around here. I'll show it to you!"

"Too bad nothing was done to reach them."

"Now, just a minute! I did *my* part! The pilots left the compass reading and the exact location with me. You know who the first one I told was? I didn't tell a soul until I saw Bill Hammond! But he said he couldn't do a thing about it. What could I do then? I had to give the information to *someone* who could use it. So I told Padre Luis Ofner!"

"Luis Ofner! He's the one who left for El Encanto this afternoon, isn't he? Was that big rock near El Encanto?"

"Exactly! As soon as Padre Luis heard about it, he got in touch with Padre Salvador from San Miguel and they headed for the rock. They found the *bárbaro* village but no one was around; so they hung the gifts they had brought on the bushes around the waterhole. Just then, a woman came for water and gave the alarm. The *bárbaros* fled into the woods, and the priests felt it best to leave, too. They wanted to let the impact of the gifts sink into the *bárbaros'* mentality — if they have any!"

Don Luis' last words were typical of the whites' attitude toward the wild Indians. They considered them animals to be hunted down and killed off. Bill ignored the remark, and Luis continued.

"When the priests arrived back in El Encanto, don Constantino was there branding his cattle. He's the man that lives across the plaza from you — you know him?"

Bill nodded.

"Anyway, the priests told them what they had done and told them not to shoot at the *bárbaros* if they should come out at the ranch house. The priests said they would be back in El Encanto in a month, and rode off.

"Constantino grew worried. Priests or no, he didn't want savages coming out at *his* ranch! What if they thought he was the one who had left the gifts and wanted to be friendly? As soon as the Franciscans were safely out of sight, Constantino sent his peons out into the woods for the gifts the priests had left!"

"Constantino stole the gifts!" Bill exclaimed.

"Not only that. That's only the beginning of the story! Some time later, the *bárbaros* did come out at El Encanto in broad daylight. Maybe Nicolás would have been OK if he had been there alone, but a Brazilian was in the house with him at the time. He panicked. He took two shots at them with a rifle! He was too nervous to have hit a tapir at five meters, but it scared the *bárbaros* away!"

"What then?" Bill asked, sitting on the edge of his chair.

"Oh, the priests were furious when they heard about it. They stormed over to don Constantino's house and did everything but excommunicate him! The shooting wasn't poor Constantino's fault — he wasn't there! But don't think Constantino takes abuse like that without striking back!" Luis was really enjoying himself.

"Just about everybody's mad at everybody else," he concluded. "Constantino's mad at the priests. They're mad at Constantino. And the *bárbaros* must be mad at white men in general — first they steal their gifts and then they shoot at them!"

Bill had arranged to leave at daybreak for El Encanto, and it was nearly midnight now. He thanked Buceta for an informative evening, and walked home through the silent streets. Now all was clear. Constantino was out for spite. The priests wanted to keep their "inside track." By the time he finished recounting to Harriet all he had learned the first roosters were beginning to crow. It was time to saddle the horse and leave.

Bill was not familiar with the road to El Encanto, but found it fairly easy to follow the trail. He was accustomed to horseback riding, but the borrowed animal was lazy and slow. With the energy he wasted in urging him on, Bill wondered if it wouldn't have been easier to have shouldered his pack and walked!

He had not yet finished one term of missionary service. As he rode along the trail, he wasn't anticipating an encounter with a veteran priest who had spent half a lifetime in Bolivia. His one consolation was that Ofner was considered by all to be a "good priest." He was popular wherever he went, and if he sinned he didn't do it as publicly as some of his colleagues. Like Bill, he had worked in Santiago before going to Concepción, and had once challenged George Haight to a public debate. Since then, he and George had always been the best of friends.

It was a three-day trip to El Encanto. By mid-morning of the second day, the road came out of the thick jungle into open grasslands. There were signs of cattle everywhere. Far to the east of the trail Bill could distinguish in the distance a huge rock of solid granite towering above the surrounding forest — a silent eternal sentinel guarding the endless expanse of grass and trees. Bill continued down the trail toward a small stream with a cluster of palm-thatched houses beside it.

The only person in view was a Chiquitano woman dressed in a shapeless, faded blue dress. Bill rode up to her, but did not dismount. She sat on the ground busily sorting dried beans, and did not look up as he approached.

"What ranch is this?" he asked.

"Zapocó," was the answer.

"Who is the owner?"

"Don Gervacio Nogales."

It was apparent that the woman was in no mood to waste words on useless conversation, and Bill urged his mount down the road.

For the next eighteen miles the road followed the river upstream. The summer rains had not yet begun. The water that remained had collected in large holes in the riverbed, and the numerous fords were dry. What would it be like in flood season? The highwater marks were fifteen feet up the tree trunks.

Bill thought he had never seen a more beautiful place in all of Bolivia! The wall of forest fell back on each side of the river, giving way to lovely carpets of lush green grass. *Motacú* palms gracefully draped their fronds over the river. Egrets, snowy-white, rose gracefully from the water, startled by the sudden intrusion of horse and rider. Deer frolicked on the outer fringes of the grass, scampering, when startled, into the jungle. Fish darted to safety in the crystal pools as the shadows of horse and rider fell upon the waters.

"What a place to live!" thought Bill. He had no way of knowing that in less than two years the land for ten miles on both sides of this gorgeous valley would belong to the South America Indian Mission, and that he and Harriet would be living on the banks of this river with the first of over four hundred Ayoré Indians!

It was evening of the third day when Bill arrived at El Encanto. No one appeared to be at home, and he dismounted and tied his horse to a post in the yard. He walked around the corner of the house and came face to face with the German priest. Padre Luis' eyes expressed surprise as he said, "What? You out here?"

"Yes," said Bill. "I see you are here also!" They shook hands coolly.

The sole inhabitants of El Encanto were don Nicolás, his wife María, and a teen-ager named Esteban. The ranch was not at all what Constantino had led Bill to expect. It consisted of a tiny two-room thatched hut, a dilapidated corral, and fifty head of scrawny cattle, surrounded by endless miles of swampy sawgrass and jungle. "Why does Nicolás remain in a forlorn place like this?" Bill wondered while relaxing in his hammock. "The wages must be mighty attractive!"

One night after Padre Luis had gone to sleep, Nicolás Chuvé told Bill his story. "I once worked for a good *patrón*," he began. "He was a merchant and we traveled these roads with ox carts, selling to the ranchers. Once we were traveling at night. The day had been hot. Oxen don't travel well in the heat — you know that."

Bill assured him that he knew indeed, and Nicolás continued. "About midnight my *patrón* grew sleepy and told me he was going to ride on ahead to the river and make camp. There was a full moon. Well, I stayed with the ox cart. It would take me two hours to reach the river. As they plodded along, the oxen suddenly panicked. I thought they must have sensed a jaguar! Nothing else would make them act like that! I grabbed my shotgun. Then I saw a dark object just off the side of the road, took a good aim and fired. Not a sound — whatever it was toppled right over!

On the rock *Cucaratedo* (above), the priests left gifts for the Ayorés. The gifts are hanging on the stick in the foreground. A peon with a gun keeps a sharp eye out for Ayorés. *Below*, Padre Luis Ofner stands beside the abandoned Ayoré huts at the base of *Cucaratedo*.

Nicholás and María Chuvé (right) stand in front of their house with Esteban and his wife, in El Encanto.

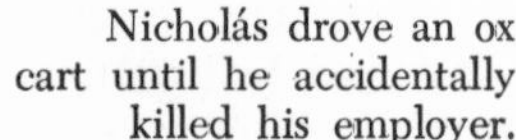

Nicholás drove an ox cart until he accidentally killed his employer.

Nicholás Chuvé and another peon stand in front of an Ayoré hut in the jungle.

"I didn't go right up to it. What if the jaguar was only wounded — that's what I thought! But nothing moved and so I slowly crept over to it. It wasn't a jaguar at all! It was my *patrón!* I struck a match and saw blood trickling out of the corner of his mouth. How could I know he was going to be there? He must have become too sleepy to go on and sat down by the road to rest. I thought he would be at the river! His horse was tied up just around the next bend in the road. I didn't do it on purpose! You do believe me, don't you, don Guillermo?"

"Certainly I do, Nicolás. It's one of those things only God can explain. What happened after you saw your *patrón* dead?"

"The police put me in jail. Then after a long time don Constantino told me he had paid my fine and that I would have to work for him out here at his ranch. He never gives me any food, not even salt! I don't know how much I owe him — I don't even know how much he pays me! But I can't leave! The police would put me back in jail!"

When Bill returned home, he discussed the trip with Harriet. Padre Luis had shown him where he had left gifts at the foot of a huge rock. There was sweet fresh water in a fissure on top of the rock. At the base were abandoned Indian shelters and gardens. It seemed as if the Catholics were in on the ground floor, and would allow no competition. Time and again Bill and Harriet found themselves on their knees praying for God's leading in this situation. The call to work with jungle Indians that they had both received many years before at Moody Bible Institute was real enough! Were they drawing closer to the fulfillment of their dream? They could only pray.

Two weeks later, Padre Luis himself appeared at the Pencille's door. Bill invited him in, but he preferred to stand in the doorway, obviously nervous and ill at ease. It wouldn't do to have his parishoners see him enter the house of the *protestantes*.

"Don Guillermo," he began, "I have come to say good-by!"

"Good-by?" Bill echoed. "Where are you going?" The thought flashed across his mind that he must be going back to El Encanto.

"I'm taking the afternoon plane to Cochabamba. The bishop has transferred me to the city."

"You won't return to Concepción?" Bill was not too sure he had heard aright.

"No, I will not be back. *Hasta luego!*"

They shook hands and the priest was gone. His huge shoulders seemed stooped as he made his way up the bricked corridor toward the Catholic church. Why had he come? Bill could only surmise. Perhaps Padre Luis was really saying, "This ends my chances of making a contact with the savage Indians. Now it's up to you!"

9.

The Long Search

It was 1949, and only a year remained before Bill and Harriet's furlough was due. Could anything be done about contacting the Ayorés in that brief time? Would it not be better to let the matter rest until after furlough? But another year might be too late to reach them! It must be done now or never! Bill set himself heart and soul to do the job.

He had a full-time occupation already, caring for the little church in Concepción. When he spoke to the congregation of the burden upon his heart, they were indifferent. A few were openly hostile. The *bárbaros* were animals, without souls, and worthy only to be wiped from the face of the earth, they said! Bill and Harriet gave themselves to prayer; and as a result it was not too long before the believers began to share Bill's love for the savages, and prayed with the missionaries for their salvation.

But if Bill were to dedicate all of his time to reaching the Indians, to whom could he entrust the teaching of the new converts, and the preaching in the little church? Harriet was capable, but a woman would not be accepted as a teacher of men. God was blessing, and the chapel was filled for every meeting. A number were baptized. Preaching points were established in several outlying ranches. It was at one of these meetings on the ranches that Bill first noticed don Victor's talent. Victor had been a Christian for several years, but only recently had begun to grow in the things of God. At first, he would do no more than give a short testimony or lead in prayer; but this gave him confidence, and he soon developed into a good preacher.

In February, Bill learned that Julio Flores, don Constantino's son, planned to visit El Encanto. Bill decided to go along. He sought out don Victor and said, "I want to go to El Encanto again to see what I can do about the Indians. Will you take charge of the meetings while I am gone?"

Victor hesitated only briefly, then said with a bright happy smile, "I'll do it, don Guillermo! God will help me!"

The rainy season was in full force. The rivers were at flood stage. Ten of the crossings beyond the ranch of Zapocó had to be made by *"pelota."* The word in Spanish literally means "ball." Bill was to learn that crossing these rivers at flood stage was hardly a ball! He describes the experience in this way:

"When you get to the edge of a swollen stream you dismount and unsaddle the horse. Then you lay out your rubberized poncho on the ground and place the saddle, hammock, food and other equipment in the middle. You add your clothes to the heap. Finally you carefully tie up the corners of the poncho, making a big ball or *pelota.*

"Once the *pelota* is securely tied, you ease it slowly into the water until it is floating, free but precariously, like some cumbersome, top-heavy ark. Then comes the big move! You chase your horse into the water and the instant he begins to swim you must grab his tail with one hand and the *pelota* with the other and start the trip across the river. The horse does the swimming. All you have to do is to hang on and keep out of the way of his churning hoofs. If you did a good job of tying the *pelota* your things arrive nice and dry. If not . . ."

Nicolás greeted Bill as a long-lost friend. Now that the priest was not present he showed a keen interest in the Bible and its message of salvation. Julio, however, tied his hammock between two posts on the porch and scarcely stirred for the next three days. Nicolás and María were forced to wait on him continually.

Bill got Julio's consent to let Nicolás go with him into the jungle to examine the trails of the Indians. After several days of fruitless search they came upon a well-worn trail. The condition of the trail told Bill that it must be one of the principal "highways" of the Ayorés.

Nicolás was nervous. "What do you plan to do?"

It did not take Bill long to decide. "We'll leave gifts, and come back later."

Forcing a contact at this time would be premature and perhaps dangerous. The Indians would be angry at the white men who left gifts for them and then changed their minds and collected the gifts again and even shot at them when they tried to make friends! Bill felt he must allow the Indians time to make the first gesture of friendship. They tied their shirts and one of the machetes to branches over the trail and turned back.

Swinging leisurely in their hammocks back in El Encanto, Bill and Nicolás chatted intimately. Having worked most of his life for Bolivian nationals, Nicolás spoke acceptable Spanish, although he used his native Chiquitano when speaking to his wife. He was a member of an oppressed race, a man with no social rights in his country, a baptized Catholic with no idea of what Christianity was really all about, a convicted murderer, a slave.

In spite of his deep poverty Nicolás was remarkably well adjusted to life. He hadn't given himself over to self-pity or bitterness against the society that had treated him so harshly. He showed no hostility toward either his tyrannical boss or the demanding son. He was at peace with the world.

Bill was reluctant to leave El Encanto. He wanted to prepare Nicolás for that day when the Indians would again appear at the edge of the jungle clearing. He was certain they would come again. It would just be a matter of time. He repeated his instructions over and over again.

"Don't shoot at them! Gather your wife and child into the house, then you block the doorway. Offer them gifts of food, but don't let them in your house! Whatever you do, don't ever turn your back on them. If they become unmanageable show them your gun, but don't threaten them or shoot at them! That is, unless it is the only way you can save your lives. Send word to me just as soon as you can. I will repay you for anything you have given them!"

Home again in Concepción, Bill was pleased at the way things had gone in his absence. Victor had done well, and other men had become interested in helping out. When Bill gave them details of his trip and told of the fresh Indian trails, they were enthusiastic, and several men offered to accompany him on his next trip to the forest.

The only break in the monotony of life in the sleepy village was the weekly arrival of the Panagra plane. Almost the entire town would go to the airport to glean what news they could from the passengers. For many this was the only link with the outside world.

In March, when the plane landed from San Ignacio on the flight to Santa Cruz, Frank Pickering was on board. During the fifteen-minute stopover Bill briefed Frank on the latest trip to El Encanto. Frank was deeply interested, and asked a number of questions. Just as the bell announced the departure of the plane he said with a great deal of enthusiasm, "Say, Bill, why don't you come over to San Ignacio next month! El Encanto is closer from there than it is from Concepción! I think we can make it in my Power Wagon and it will save you three days of hard horseback riding. We can go together and check on those gifts."

Frank was already half-way down the ramp running toward the plane when he finished talking. Bill shouted after him, "I'll be there in the middle of April!"

It rained nearly every day for the next month, and when Bill arrived in San Ignacio the roads were flooded and a sea of mud. Frank was confident that the Power Wagon could get through. "As a last resort," Bill said wryly, "we can always walk! It won't be the first time!"

Preparations were under way for the trip when the red Stinson 150 belonging to the New Tribes Mission circled the Pickerings' home. Frank and Bill raced down the street and out to the airstrip in time to see pilot Mel Wyma and Joe Moreno step from the plane. They had flown in from Tobité on the railroad line where they had been working with the Ayorés of that area.

Joe Moreno was the field representative for the New Tribes Mission. A Mexican-American with one-quarter Cherokee blood, Joe was one missionary who looked like a Bolivian — dark and handsome with a tight crop of curly hair. He was not very tall but could pick up a 55-gallon drum of gasoline and toss it on a truck all by himself. He could walk a jungle trail for hours and hours after everyone else had given up, and he wouldn't even sweat under a noonday sun. Perhaps this inability to perspire was what made him able to exist comfortably on practically no water.

Mel Wyma had brought the Stinson 150 with him when he came to Bolivia with NTM. Mel is a typical "swell guy." Tall and good looking, he has a winning smile under a

ain, mud and a tree stump effectively kept Joe Moreno (in cab), rank Pickering (on bumper), Mel Wyma and Bill Pencille from reaching El Encanto with the Power Wagon.

Frank and Evelyn Pickering

Crossing a river at flood stage with an ox cart is relatively simple: the cart floats, the oxen swim. If you don't have an ox cart, however, you cross by *pelota* (p. 86).

buttonish nose. From the first minute you know him you can't help liking him. He has that ability of making you feel important.

When the Power Wagon started off the next morning, Joe and Mel went along. Three months had elapsed since Bill had left the gifts on the Indian trail, and he was anxious to see if they were still there.

In spite of mud and water, Frank was confident they would get through to the ranch. He probably would have been right had it not been for the mahogany stump hidden in the high grass in the center of the road! No one saw the stump, and the truck hit it with enough force to bend the tie rod nearly double. With the wheels toed in and no way to straighten them, they abandoned the truck and walked the last twelve miles to El Encanto.

It was midday, and the tropical sun beat down mercilessly. Most of the road led through open country, and no one remembered Frank's sunstroke years before in Pozo del Tigre. By the time the little thatched roof came into view, Frank was exhausted. But still no one had any premonition that it was anything that could not be cured by a good night's sleep!

Nicolás welcomed the men to his home with his usual courtesy and enthusiasm. Knowing the poverty of the Chuvés, Bill and Frank had brought their own supplies. This they tried in vain to share with Nicolás and his family. Nicolás insisted that it wasn't proper to accept food from his guests.

"What's the news about the *bárbaros,* Nicolás?" Bill asked as they sat around the fire that evening.

"Nothing at all. I have been expecting them every day. And I haven't forgotten what you told me, either! But there are no signs of them."

"Have you been out to check on the gifts?"

"No. I intended to go. But I have been just too busy here! I couldn't get away!"

The missionaries chuckled silently at this whopper. Nicolás would never admit that he had been afraid to go alone into the jungle!

"All right," Bill continued. "We'll go tomorrow and have a look. Are you game, Frank?"

Frank was already stretched out in his hammock on the

porch. He had eaten no supper and his face was flushed. "I've been thinking," he replied in a tired voice. "It might be best for you fellows to go alone. I've got an idea as to how to fix the tie rod. I'll go back to the truck tomorrow and have it ready to roll when you all get back!"

Frank slept fitfully and was still in his hammock the next morning when the others left for the jungle. They were gone three days. The Ayorés had not returned to the area, and the gifts were still intact. They arrived back at the ranch long after dark on the third day, the path illuminated by the light of a brilliant full moon. Coming up to the porch, they were surprised to find Nicolás and María sleeping outside! When she heard the men arrive, María was instantly on her feet.

"Frank is dying!" she exclaimed.

"Where is he?" Bill asked quickly.

"In there — in the house! He got sick right after you left!"

"Do you mean that he has been sick for three days now?" demanded Mel.

"Yes, yes! Very sick! He's dying!"

The men hoped that María might be painting too gloomy a picture. But Frank's close brush with death that time in Pozo del Tigre suddenly loomed before them. They immediately surmised that this was a recurrence of the sunstroke!

Mel was the first to open the door into the little mud-walled one-room hut. He coughed and stepped back into the cool night air. The room had been closed tight for three days, and Frank had been completely without nursing care! The stench was overpowering. Poor María was beside herself with grief. She had had no idea of how to treat a sick *gringo,* and so she had left him a little water, closed the door tight and left Frank to his own resources in the dark, smoky room! He had drunk a little water, but had eaten no food.

Bill and his companions were deeply concerned as they did all they could to make Frank comfortable. Their first thought was to repair the truck and take him home in it. But they had neither tools nor spare parts! Furthermore, they doubted whether Frank would be able to bear the hot, bumpy ride to San Ignacio. They had no medicine that would help him in his condition, but realized that something must be done, and done soon! Frank's condition was serious.

It was Mel who spoke first. "Let's bring the plane in!"

"Fine! But where in the world could you land?" Joe asked, sceptically.

"Let's take a look at that open space over there," Mel answered as he began walking out past the corral.

They explored the place by moonlight, as best they could. It would certainly take some backbreaking work to get it ready for the Stinson to land!

"If you fellows can knock down those ant hills and fill in some of the biggest holes, I think I can make it," Mel said finally. "You will have to cut down the biggest trees on the end for an approach. What do you think?"

"We'll have to try it!" Bill agreed grimly. "It's Frank's only chance. Who should go to San Ignacio with you?"

"I'll go alone. You'll need every strong arm you have here to get the place ready in two days! I should be back here Monday night."

"O.K. But let's get some sleep first. I'm bushed!"

At daybreak Mel Wyma left for San Ignacio, walking. Bill, Joe, and Nicolás began work on the airstrip. For the next two days they pushed themselves to the gray edge of exhaustion. But by the time they heard the distant hum of the approaching plane they had only cleared about 300 yards, and the lower half of the strip was still covered with high thick swamp grass! This would act as a brake. But how about take-off? You don't want brakes then!

The strip was barely distinguishable from the air. While Mel circled in the plane the men hung handkerchiefs, shirts, underwear — anything they could lay their hands on — on the bushes along the sides of the cleared area to give Mel something to aim at. Satisfied at last that he knew where the strip lay, Mel brought the plane in beautifully over the tree tops and set it down to a perfect landing. Helped by the grass, the plane rolled to a stop in less than half the length of the strip.

Frank was now half delirious with fever, and unable to walk. They carried him on board the plane and strapped him in his seat just as the sun dropped behind the trees beyond the clearing. The wind died with the sun, and without added lift, three hundred yards was a mighty short distance! "Are you sure you should try it, Mel?"

"I think we'll make it," he replied, with a calmness bred from years of jungle flying. "But just to make certain, let's try something. When I rev up the motor, the three of you take hold of the tail and pull back! When I stick my hand out the window, push for all you're worth. Then pray!"

Mel opened the throttle full. The plane jumped and bucked. Then he released the brakes and stuck his hand out the window. They all gave a mighty push. The Stinson catapaulted forward — but would it clear the grass? If not, it was doomed to crash into the stumps and brush at the far end of the runway.

Frank was sitting limply, strapped to the seat. He clenched his teeth, praying silently. The plane grew lighter and he felt the tail lift off the ground. He glanced at Mel, whose face was calm but serious. Then they were in the grass, midway down the strip. The plane slowed; the tail dropped. The set of Mel's jaw tightened, and drops of perspiration broke out on his forehead. He tried the throttle, but it was already at full. Frank took a last look at the stumps rushing at them. Then they were at the end of the strip. Mel pulled back on the wheel and miraculously the plane lifted! He looked down at his shaken passenger and grinned. "Thank God!" he said.

During all of 1949 Bill continued his search for the Indians. To the east — to the west — to the south — every rumor of their whereabouts was carefully tracked down and checked. Bill came to know and understand the jungle as well as his Chiquitano guides who had lived there all their lives! There was no lack of signs of the Indians. The forest in every direction was honeycombed with their trails! Abandoned villages and empty bees' nests gave mute testimony to their presence. He left gifts for them along their trails. But knowing nothing of their language, he did not push for a definite encounter with them. To the Indians, he would be but another white man — and white men had always shot at them on sight! No, the Indians themselves must make the first advance of friendship. They must not be pushed into a situation where they would attack. If shots were ever fired, even in self-defense, it would be difficult if not impossible to convince them later of genuine friendship.

10.

Still Searching

NOVEMBER CAME. Furlough was but a few months away now. Perhaps there would be just time to attend the annual church conference in Santiago and then make one last trip into the jungle to check the gifts! This might be the trip that would produce the contact Bill had prayed and worked for so long!

During the conference at Santiago, Bill met Angel Bravo. When the Santiago school had first begun in 1932, Angel was one of the students. Between sessions of the conference, Angel and Bill became close friends. Angel had spent some time with the Ayorés in the first contact along the railroad line, and had a deep love for them. Bill spent long hours talking of his hopes and plans for the Ayorés of the north. In Angel he found an interested and sympathetic friend. Near the end of the conference, Bill turned to Angel as they were eating dinner. "Is there any reason," he began, "why you can't come along with me to Concepción? I'd like to have you go along on this last trip!"

Without a moment's hesitation Angel replied. "I'm ready to go!"

Both men felt it would be wise to look for an interpreter from among the Ayoré Indians along the railroad line — one who was no longer completely wild, and who perhaps had picked up a little Spanish.

Bill consulted some of the New Tribes missionaries at the conference, and they agreed heartily to help find an interpreter. But who should it be? Perhaps Degui would be the best man to take. In his mid-twenties, he had shown himself friendly toward the missionaries. He knew no Spanish, but being an Ayoré, was at home in the woods and would, of course, be able to help in a contact with his own people.

Plans were quickly made. Bill would fly directly to Concepción and arrange for horses and supplies. Angel would proceed to Tobité and find Degui; from there they would go to San José by train and then fly to Concepción. As they parted in the Roboré airport, Bill gave Angel the typical friendly embrace as he said, "I'll see you in a couple of weeks!"

The two weeks stretched into five, and still there was no word from Angel! Bill had almost given up hope when Angel finally stepped off the plane, followed by an eleven-year-old boy!

Angel was quick to explain. "I'm terribly sorry, don Guillermo," he began. "But I couldn't make Degui come with me. He got as far as San José but when three Panagra flights were rained out he grew tired of waiting and went back home!"

"I understand," Bill said, "but who is this boy?"

"Well, I didn't want to come without an Ayoré," Angel continued. "So while I debated what to do a group of Indians arrived in San José on the train. This boy, Comai, was with them. The missionaries told me that he was a fresh kid and hard to handle. But he does know a little Spanish. It seems that a woman in San José had held him as her slave for a few months."

Comai was a sight — dressed in filthy rags, his hair long and unkempt. Bill tried a few words in Spanish on him, but got no response. His only reaction was raised eyebrows for "yes" and puckered lips and wrinkled nose for "no." Bill found it difficult to hide his disappointment! He had counted on the mature Degui to help them make a contact! But this boy —

Everything was in readiness for the trip. By this time the Hammonds had returned from furlough. Bill Hammond was thrilled when he heard of the attempts to contact the Ayorés and wanted to go along on the coming expedition.

The start of a trip was always the most difficult. Four riding horses and one pack horse had to be saddled. Endless repairs and adjustments had to be made on the gear at the last minute. Saddlebags, bedding, ponchos, machetes, guns, canteens — a place had to be found for everything, and still leave room for the rider! Bill had hoped they might leave at dawn but it was ten o'clock

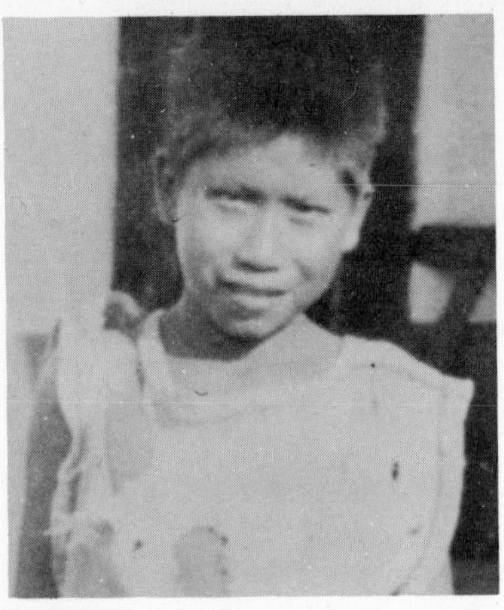

In 1949 no one foresaw the important part Comai would play in reaching his own people.

Degui got discouraged when three planes were rained out and went home (p. 95). Comai came instead.

Bill and Harriet with sons Dick and Bruce stretch out a snake skin while Comai looks on – before he got his new clothes.

Comai in his new pants and shirt rides a donkey at El Encanto.

before they were finally ready to mount their horses and head south toward Lomeríos.

At that moment a little boy came running up the street waving a paper in his hand. "This is a note from don Hugo," he said, breathlessly, handing the paper to Bill.

"Don Hugo! Which one?" Bill knew several men by that name.

"Don Hugo from Alta Vista," was the answer.

Bill hurriedly read the note, and could hardly believe what he read. His friend had written to tell him that the Indians he was looking for had come out at his ranch just the day before! They had killed the watchdog and stolen the ducks and tools. Then they had headed back into the jungle in the direction of El Encanto. The note concluded, "Come immediately! You are only two days behind them!"

Instead of heading south toward Lomeríos, Bill, Angel and Bill Hammond turned their horses east toward Alta Vista. Surely, this was the hand of God leading them in right paths!

Comai had never ridden a horse before, but he seemed unafraid. Soon he was completely at home in the saddle, bouncing about from side to side as he rode along.

By mid-afternoon they were at the tiny outpost of the ranch where the Indians had staged the raid, but neither Angel nor Comai could pick up the trail of the fleeing savages. It was not until the next morning that Angel suddenly shouted, "They went this way!"

As the rest clustered around him, he pointed out a tiny twig, broken as some Indian had stepped on it in passing. It was near the river, and bent in that direction. Bill found a tree that had fallen across the water, and over this precarious bridge they were able to cross with their packs and equipment. The horses had been left at the ranch in the care of the cowboys.

Once on the far side of the river they continued their search in ever widening circles. Finally they picked up the trail again, and toward evening located the spot where the Ayorés had regrouped and headed east down a dry creek bed toward El Encanto. There was no difficulty now in following the trail, and by dark they found where the Indians had slept both before and after the raid. Here they called a halt, planning to continue in the morning.

Bill had never before been this close to the Indians! The trail was less than forty-eight hours old! The weather had been clear and the Indians had built no shelters for sleeping on the two nights they had spent in this camp. There had been some twenty men in the party, and each had cleared a little circle of ground for a bed. With a fire on each side for warmth and protection, they had slept out in the open. Here, too, they had made the spears used on the raid. They were nothing more than hardwood sticks of two inches in diameter and sharpened to a point. Their regular weapons would have been left behind, Comai explained, lest they be contaminated by the blood of their enemies!

In the middle of the little camp was a post about a yard high. One side had been flattened with an ax, and on the clean, white wood were an assortment of circles, dots and crosses, drawn in charcoal and red dust from some soft stone.

"What does this writing mean, Comai?" Bill wanted to know.

"It doesn't mean anything," Comai replied laconically.

"Oh, come now!" Bill urged. "Don't be that way! Surely it must say something!"

Comai scrutinized the symbols closely and then said gravely, "It says, 'I killed the dog because they killed my wife.' "

Ignorant of the ways and customs of the Indians, the missionaries believed Comai. Years later Bill was surprised to learn that Comai had made up this interpretation just to appease him! There are seven clans in the Ayoré tribe. The signs simply indicated the names of the clans which had been represented on the raid! Ayorés have no other markings or writings.

As Bill and his companions drifted off to sleep in their hammocks they had high hopes of catching up with the Indians the next day. There had been lightning in the north earlier in the evening, however, and by midnight it began to rain. Gently at first, but steadily harder came the rain, until it was a torrential downpour. The men, huddled in their hammocks, tried in vain to keep dry under the ponchos spread tent-like over them. With the first light of dawn the the stream bed beneath their hammocks, dry the evening before, now flowed with a foot of swift-running water!

The Indian trail, which had followed the bed of the stream, was washed away forever!

No one wanted to turn back. El Encanto must be somewhere ahead. No one knew exactly in which direction. Finally they decided on a compass reading of 150 degrees and set off through the forest, hoping that they might come out somewhere near El Encanto. Or perhaps they would cross the Ayoré's trail again on ahead.

Now Comai's upbringing in the jungle began to show to advantage. Both Bill and Angel were experienced jungle men, but their knowledge of the woods could not begin to compare with that of the eleven-year-old boy. He was able to follow the seemingly invisible turtle trails, and by some uncanny sixth sense catch the turtles every time. He could track the bees in flight and lead the group unfailingly to honey. Bill tells of one experience they had on the trip, in his diary:

> *Friday, 9th.* Before leaving camp I mentioned to the men the necessity of discipline in the matter of water, and not to drink more than necessary. About nine we came upon an *arroyo* (stream) but it was dry. On examination we found the ground damp, and by digging got sufficient water for drinking and cooking our meal. We pushed on breaking the trail while the food was cooking. The sweat-bees were so bad that we had to eat walking around. They were everywhere — in our eyes, our noses, our mouths, our ears. If you stood still your plate was instantly black with them!
>
> We got under way immediately after eating. At noon, Angel took his turn at cutting the trail; but with the sun overhead he got turned around and I neglected to check with the compass. As a result we came out again on our own path where we had passed about an hour before . . . We had made a complete circle and wasted valuable time and strength! After this, I was careful to check the compass!
>
> In the afternoon we were plenty thirsty and there was no prospect of water for the night. Suddenly, Comai, up front with me, pointed to an old rotten, spongy tree trunk and said, "Don Guillermo, *aqui hay aqua!* [there's water here!]" I cut out a piece of the tree trunk, soft and rotten, with my machete, and found it full of good, sweet water. Like a sponge, this old fallen tree trunk had soaked up

> water from the rains, and we drank our fill and replenished the canteens. We had coffee to drink with our dry corn flour that night, thanks to Comai!

On the sixteenth day, weary and footsore, the men broke out of the forest into an open clearing. At first they thought it was the open grassland surrounding El Encanto, but soon discovered it was just a small island of grass in the midst of a tangled sea of jungle. Not anxious to plunge immediately into the jungle wall on the far side of the clearing, they relaxed a few moments, enjoying the clear view of the sky, the cooling breeze and freedom of movement. Then while the two Bills sat quietly by a little crystal-clear stream, Angel and Comai went to scout around. It wasn't long before they both came running back with the same report: there were fresh Indian trails leading off in all directions!

The newest of the trails was only a few days old. Now what? Food was long since gone, and the men were exhausted. Bill Hammond was sick and needed a rest. No one knew where they were at the moment. After prayer, it was agreed that to attempt to contact the Indians under the circumstances would be too risky. They would be at too great a disadvantage if things went wrong. So again, gifts were placed on the trail. Finally, after three more days of cutting their way through the dense jungle they came out at last at El Encanto, almost completely exhausted, their clothes torn to shreds. Nicolás was speechless at the sight of his friends walking out of the jungle instead of riding up the road from the opposite direction.

Bill was disappointed and discouraged. More than a year on the jungle trails, and not a single contact with the Ayorés! Furlough had already been postponed, and there was no putting it off any longer. He and Harriet would spend Christmas in Concepción and then leave for the United States. Angel Bravo decided to stay on in case of some new development with the Indians.

Bill bought Comai a new pair of pants and a bright green shirt and put him on the plane for San José and the railroad line. Then on New Year's Day, 1950, he and Harriet and their three children flew out of Concepción for home and furlough.

11.

Asoná's Due

NUINE AND HIS GROUP were frightened by the shots fired at the young men when they tried to make friends with the white people. They decided to remain at the village of *Cucaratedo,* but were always careful never to hunt or walk in the direction of the white man's house, lest their presence so near be discovered. The witch doctor was sure that the visit by the men in the long skirts was directly connected with the flight of the big silver bird over the camp, and forbade anyone to stand on the rock at any time when the big bird was heard.

By now, four moons had passed since *Edocarate* had first appeared in the east, and *Guedoside,* the moon, was nearly full-grown again. It was almost time for Asoná to sing and begin a new year. All was in readiness for the big festival and offering in her honor. The old men lay awake each night now, listening for the first notes of her song. Nuine the chief heard her first. It was nearly daylight, and the big full moon hung heavily just over the treetops, ready to plunge to its rest. Then Nuine heard the notes of her song! Clear and beautiful it sounded in the quiet of dawn. Asoná had opened the world for another year. Nuine awoke the sleeping camp with a shout, and immediately the men made preparations to leave for the hunt. They decked themselves in their finest feathers. As the sun rose, they picked up their axes, whistles, bags, and fire, and moved their camp away from that of the women.

The first part of their ritual involved the lighting of new fires. Then, all facing south, they shouted and whistled with all their might. The forest rang with hideous noises, but all for a purpose. They were calling out to Asoná to protect them during the coming year from their enemies down south, the hated Guidaigosode.

Then each man made a little pile of leaves and sticks. This was his altar to Asoná, his prayer for an abundant harvest. One pile for peanuts, one for corn, one for squash, one for beans. If they neglected this recognition of Asoná's power, they might go hungry next year.

A warrior quenched the fires with water from a gourd, and they blackened their naked bodies with the remaining charcoal. Then they started on the honey hunt, each man alone, and required by Asoná to bring back his offering for her. No one carried his regular honey gourd — it would be unclean and taboo at the end of the day. A hollowed-out piece of *toborochi* tree would be used to carry the honey, and it would be discarded later.

While the men were hunting, the old men and boys were busy making troughs for the ceremonial bathing. Some of them made crude crosses of sticks and placed them around the edge of the camp to ward off evil spirits. The women wove belts of red thread made from the *doriaquedena* plant. These they would present to their husbands or boy friends after the ceremonial bath. Of course, the men couldn't go over to get the belts themselves. They couldn't even look in the direction of the women's camp! The little boys would be the go-betweens who took food and belts to the men. The belt was the only covering the men wore, and they would tie the new one right over the old one. A new year — a new belt.

The oldest man in camp — the old men no longer went on the hunt — had fashioned a whip from a green sapling. He stood at the edge of the men's camp as one by one they returned from the hunt. Each hunter put down his bag and leaned his sweaty body on his spear. The old man beat him twice over the back with the rod. Thwack! Thwack! The evil spirits were driven out for another year!

When all had returned, they placed their offerings of honey in a hole and buried it. In this way they showed their appreciation to Asoná, asking her for a good supply for the coming year. Before going to sleep that night, the men painted themselves red and chanted a special "hymn" that was strictly reserved for this occasion. Next morning they abandoned camp and returned to their women. Another year had begun. The world was open now. The Ayorés were content and at peace, they hoped, with the bird god.

Soon the rains came and the forest was green and alive again. The smaller birds and animals now were everywhere. New gardens were cleaned, and the green shoots of *dutuhe* (squash) and *guenai* (corn) were poking up through the rich, black earth. Between trips back to their village to hoe their gardens, Nuine's people traveled together making a wide circuit through the forest hunting for food, and then back again to care for the crops. It was on one of these hunting trips, many days' walk on the opposite side of the camp from the white man's house they knew so well, that they came unexpectedly upon fresh trails of white men! The footprints came from the sunsetting, straight out of the woods, where no white men lived for many days' walk! They came from where the young men had stolen the ducks! Could they be following their trail to seek revenge?

The Indians often passed through this part of the jungle, and now the white men had found their trails and had even rested in one of the old campsites! They could see where they had scraped the ground clear of thorns and sticks to sit down. But it had been quite a while ago, for the white man's smell had disappeared. When the Indians followed their trail a bit further, they came suddenly upon knives and axes tied to the bushes! Whoever those white men were, they had evidently left these for the Ayorés! Wherever they might have come from, they seemed to be heading for the house of the white man beyond the Indian village.

What did all this mean? Why did the white men leave gifts, and then shoot at them? And now they left gifts again, in another distant part of the jungle! Could these be the same white men? If they were others, why were they going to the house of those who shot at them? Were they friends? The ways of these strange whites seemed beyond comprehension! Long after arriving back at the village, the discussion each night was over these questions.

Finally, it was one of the young girls who had the answer. "Let *us* go to the white men!" she said. "Perhaps they won't shoot at us since we are girls!"

It was decided that Dijere and Jara should make the trip to the white man's house. Perhaps they would succeed where the warriors had failed!

12.

Contact!

Bill and Harriet Pencille were glad to be getting back to the States again. The first furlough is always the most exciting, and they were looking forward to seeing friends and relatives, hearing English spoken, and buying that first ice-cream soda in a corner drug store.

But as they flew north through the tropical night they knew they weren't really happy. What had they accomplished this first term, anyhow? Called to preach the Gospel to jungle Indians, they had not seen even one *bárbaro* during a year of incessant labors. So many times they were within a few hours of the Indians, but no contact was ever made. Their hearts were heavy with a sense of failure and frustration.

When the Pencilles arrived in California and went to a friend's house a letter was waiting for them. It carried a Bolivian postmark and the return address was "Hammond." Bill ripped open the envelope and almost shouted when he read the first lines:

> Dear Bill,
>
> Greetings from Bolivia. I'm sure you'll be happy to know that we have finally made a friendly contact with the Ayorés. Just a week or so after you left they came out in El Encanto and . . .

He didn't read any more. "Harriet," he said hoarsely, "I just can't believe it. Look — they made the contact!" He handed her the letter.

Bill sank down into a chair as Harriet stood reading. A baseball game he once saw flashed across his mind. The relief pitcher had come in in the top of the ninth, pitched one ball, the batter hit into a double play, and the side was retired. His team went ahead to win in the bottom of the ninth — and the pitcher was listed as the winner after having pitched only one ball!

It was difficult for Bill to analyze his feelings. The contact was made — wonderful! Prayer had been answered. But why was it that God would deny Bill the joy of such a moment after so many months of sweat and sacrifice in the jungle? It didn't make sense. He felt a twinge of envy toward those still in Bolivia. The contact had actually been made while he was still in Cochabamba on the way home. But then he recalled what the Apostle Paul had said, "I have planted, Apollos watered, but God gave the increase."

Nicolás Chuvé was making a new girth for his saddle. The day before, the old one had broken and he was almost thrown from his horse while chasing a calf. A Bolivian-style girth consists of eight or ten thin, yard-long strips of leather, braided between two large rings, and tied to the saddle on both ends. Nicolás had tanned the leather himself with the bark of the *curupaú* tree.

María was pounding corn in the *tacú,* the wooden mortar and pestle affair that the Chiquitanos consider their most essential kitchen utensil. She was grinding it to flour for *chicha,* the corn beverage that Nicolás liked so well.

The knife he was using dulled, and as he took a few steps over toward his sharpening stone, he glanced down to the far end of the El Encanto clearing, and froze in his tracks. In a low voice he said, "María, you and Esteban get in the house! Hurry!"

Two Ayoré Indian girls had come out of the jungle and were standing about fifty yards away, watching Nicolás and his family. They were alone.

Nicolás tried to remain calm. When María and Esteban were safely inside the house, Nicolás walked to the doorway and stood there. "Load the gun and put it next to me inside the door," he whispered back to his wife. "Then hand me some corn!" Although the girls were alone, Nicolás imagined that back in the shadows of the forest lurked a score of braves with arrows fitted to their bowstrings!

For a few moments there was complete silence in El Encanto. Then the girls took a few hesitant steps toward the house. Nicolás remained in the doorway within easy reach of his gun. As the girls drew nearer, he held out a gourd full of dried corn and said, "Welcome!" in Spanish. The girls were shy and fearful, but accepted the corn. Someone must have sent them on this scouting mission, Nicolás thought. Once they had the corn in their possession, the girls turned and fled for the woods as though pursued by all the spirits of the white men!

The Chuvés slept with the doors and windows well barred that night. Nicolás and María were restless and uneasy, and expected momentarily to hear savage war cries. The night passed uneventfully, however, and the new day dawned. Ominous clouds hung forebodingly in the north when Nicolás went to the door to see if the Indians had returned.

At mid-morning they were back. This time there were thirty of them, men and women together. They were friendly and things went well at first. But as the day wore on, they began to help themselves to everything within reach. One of them picked up a shovel, looked it over and started to carry it back to the woods. Nicolás left the teenager, Esteban, in the doorway of the house and followed him.

"Leave that here!" he said. The brave didn't understand the words, but he got the idea. He threw down the shovel and picked up his lance. He walked toward Nicolás and stopped about ten feet away. He stuck out his left foot and stamped twice on the ground with a loud shout each time. Then he made menacing motions with his spear toward Nicolás. Frightened, Nicolás backed slowly toward the door of the house.

"Esteban," he said in an undertone, "my horse is around the corner of the house. Don't bother saddling him. Ride bareback to La Esperanza and tell them the *bárbaros* are here!"

The savages settled down as though they intended to stay. They built campfires and cooked the corn that Nicolás had given them. By mid-afternoon, the Indians seemed to have always been a part of the El Encanto scenery.

Toward evening, Nicolás was surprised to see a rider come galloping up the road. Could it be Esteban already? He soon made out the figure of Angel Bravo — the only Bolivian within hundreds of miles who had been with the

Ayorés and knew some of their language! And now he appeared right at the time he was needed most!

When the Indians saw the horse and rider galloping into their midst, they scattered precipitately into the forest.

Bill Hammond had been praying with the believers in Concepción for an opportunity to continue the search for the Ayorés in Bill Pencille's absence. He had an overwhelming urge to form an all-out expedition to reach them. While talking over the possibilities with Angel Bravo, they decided to go to El Encanto and use it as their base. There was much work to be done in Concepción, but Hammond could not disobey what he felt was a clear command of the Lord to search for the Ayorés.

While Bill purchased the supplies, Angel hired two Bolivian companions. La Esperanza was on the direct road between Concepción and San Ignacio, and El Encanto lay to one side, twelve miles to the north. Angel and his helpers were to take Hammond's horse and supplies to La Esperanza and await him there. He would take Sunday's Panagra flight to San Ignacio to pick up Frank Pickering and proceed to La Esperanza with him. From there, they would all continue their journey to El Encanto, for the big push. No one could predict how long it would take.

Everything started on schedule. Frank was at the airport when Bill landed. They discussed the coming expedition through the long afternoon hours, and that evening Frank invited Hammond to preach in the little church.

As he was nearing the conclusion of his sermon, Bill noticed the two men he had sent from Concepción with Angel hovering in the chapel door! They seemed nervous and excited. Hammond's curiosity was aroused — what were they doing here? What had gone wrong? He cut his sermon short and while the congregation was singing the last hymn he went outside to the men. He found them across the shadowy street, seated on the grass next to their sweat-streaked horses.

The men started on the long routine of Latin greetings, but the missionary cut them short. "What happened? Where is Angel?" he asked impatiently.

"Angel went to El Encanto," replied the one named Luis.

"To El Encanto! Why on earth — he was supposed to wait for us in La Esperanza! And you two weren't supposed to come here!"

"We know it, señor." Luis said. "Please pardon us. But the *bárbaros* came out!"

"Where? Did they attack you?"

"No, they came out in El Encanto."

"How did you find that out?"

"As we were riding up to the house in La Esperanza another rider came down the road from El Encanto. It was the boy Esteban, riding his horse into a sweat. He shouted that the *bárbaros* had come out and threatened Nicolás with a spear!"

"Then what?"

"Don Angel never even dismounted. He told us to get you. He headed toward El Encanto at a full gallop."

"How many *bárbaros* came out?"

"I don't know, señor," Luis replied. He glanced over at his companion, who shook his head.

"We'll leave at daybreak!" Bill said, a tremor of excitement in his voice.

Luis handed him an envelope. "Don Rivero sent this letter to don Carlos Mayser."

"Who's Rivero?" Bill wanted to know as he examined the envelope.

"He's the schoolteacher in La Esperanza. *Muy católico.* (A strong Catholic.) He insisted that we wait until he wrote this letter to bring with us."

"I'll give it to don Carlos," Hammond said, putting it in his pocket. Carlos Mayser was a German storekeeper and his friend. "He may want to send an answer with us in the morning."

Carlos ordered *cafecitos* brought to the front corridor of his house where he chatted with Hammond a few minutes later. Bill had given him the letter, but Mayser stuck it in his shirt pocket without opening it. They conversed about the savages and speculated as to how things were going in El Encanto. Hammond finally said, "You'd better read your letter, don Carlos. There may be some word to send along with me tomorrow. We're leaving at dawn."

Carlos' face was thoughtful as he read the letter. Then, without a word, he handed it to Hammond. His scornful glance told the missionary that something was not to his liking. When Hammond finished reading it, he said, "Well, what are you going to do?" The letter instructed don Carlos to inform the priests about the Indian contact and send them to La Esperanza in their truck that very night!

"Nothing," the German replied. He shook a stubby finger half-angrily at Hammond. "You are the ones who have done all the work! Don't think I don't know what Bill Pencille has been doing to try to reach those savages! The priests have no right to step in now!"

Sleep did not come easily to Hammond that night. As he swung gently in his hammock, the stars in the black tropical sky shone like diamonds. He gave thanks to God — Angel Bravo was on the scene at precisely the moment he was needed for the contact! Hammond himself had arrived just in time to head off a possible take-over by the priests. Surely God was leading them on toward a friendly contact with the Ayorés!

It was late afternoon next day when the four riders, two *gringos* and two Bolivians, reached La Esperanza. The school teacher don Rivero walked up to Luis and angrily demanded if he had delivered the letter. He had expected that the priests' truck would have arrived ahead of the *protestantes.*

Before dawn they were again on the trail. They expected to see Indians when they arrived in El Encanto, but were disappointed. Angel Bravo was there, however, and greeted them joyfully.

Even before they dismounted Bill Hammond asked, "Where are the *bárbaros*?"

Angel stretched out his right hand and wiggled it back and forth in the Bolivian way of indicating that they were not there.

"Let's sit in the shade and hear what's happened," suggested Frank. Since his near-death in El Encanto a year before, the sun had become his worst enemy.

They settled down on stools made out of tree stumps and Angel began, "I met Esteban in La Esperanza. He told me that the savages had come out, so I rode directly here. As I came over the little hill there they were all over the place, completely surrounding the house. Nicolás can tell you."

Nicolás nodded his head in agreement.

"When the savages saw me they ran for the woods. They left their belongings in the ranch clearing, so I knew they wouldn't go far. Nicolás told me that they had been cooking the corn he had given them. There were a dozen little fires around. I figured they had run because they didn't know me and were afraid; so I called out in Ayoré, 'Come back! I'm your friend!' It took a while, but soon one by one they returned and I could talk with them with the few words I learned in Tobité. They were very friendly, and surprised that I could speak a bit of their language. They had not heard of Tobité, but when I mentioned some of the names of the *bárbaros* there, they recognized them. I made them understand that I was a friend of the *bárbaro* chiefs in Tobité."

Hammond and Frank were full of questions. Most of all, they wanted to know if there were any chance of the Indians returning to El Encanto.

"They said they would be back in two or three months," Angel replied. "First they said a month, then they said two or three."

"And you let them go, just like that!" exclaimed Hammond.

Angel shrugged his shoulders. "There really wasn't much else I could do!"

"Let's see if we can find them!" suggested Frank.

They took what they might need for the afternoon, and started to follow the Indian trail. They had not planned on going very far this first day. The trail was easy to follow, but soon rain began to fall and in minutes they were drenched to the skin. They returned to El Encanto to wait for the storm to pass.

It was three days before the skies cleared. By then the entire area was flooded. The men were in water up to their knees most of the time when they again followed the Ayoré trail. Most of the signs had been erased by the storm, but the men headed in the general direction, splashing and sloshing, until they found a recently-abandoned Indian camp. Soon they came upon a small lake and on the other side of it saw the smoke of the savages' fire. There were several Indians in the camp, and for the first time the missionaries actually saw what they had been searching for — wild Ayorés!

Angel Bravo stepped out into the clearing and shouted to them. They were startled at first, but soon calmed down. Angel made his way to them, wading through the grass in the shallow part of the lake. He was in their camp for some time making friends, and then motioned for his companions to join him.

The Indians showed no signs of hostility, and it was evident that they wanted to be friends. The missionaries recognized the hand of God opening the way for them. After giving the Indians pieces of cloth and iron they were able to persuade them to return with them to El Encanto. Never again was contact completely lost with this group.

Back in El Encanto the missionaries had their first taste of what life was really like among the savages! If it hadn't been for Angel, things would have gone badly. After two or three days Angel said to Frank, "We need an interpreter. If we don't get one, we're liable to lose this contact! I can't understand enough of what they say to control them!"

The missionaries could see only too plainly that he was right. Angel continued, "I wish we could get hold of Comai! He did well the last time he was with us, and he does know Spanish. I wish he were with us right now!"

Frank said, "But how in the world could we find him? Who knows where he might be!"

"I think he's in Tobité," Angel said.

Frank looked at Bill Hammond. "I guess one of us should go for him," said Bill, slowly.

Frank answered, "You go if you want to. I'll stick it out until you get back. But how long will it take?"

"I could get a plane to Roboré tomorrow. By the time I reach Tobité on the train and find Comai, I'll be lucky to be back on next week's plane. A week would be the shortest time — possibly two. This is the rainy season, and travel is difficult."

"Two weeks!" mused Angel aloud. "I doubt if we'll hold them here for two weeks. I wish Comai were here now!"

"If I'm going, I'd better not waste any time!" Hammond untied his hammock and began to fix up his blanket roll.

When he arrived in the Roboré airport he saw Mel Wyma's red Stinson parked over to one side of the apron. He spoke a word of greeting to the station manager, and headed down the hill to the town. It was Sunday, and nearly noon. In order to complete its weekly run the Panagra airplane would go on to the border town of Puerto Suárez, then return to Santa Cruz in the afternoon retracing its route of the morning: Roboré, San José, San Ignacio, Concepción.

Angel went directly to the mission house but found no one home. He had forgotten for the moment that this was Sunday, and they would all be in Sunday school.

He retraced his steps to the chapel. Without going in, he beckoned Mel Wyma who was standing near the door, to come outside into the street.

"What in the world are you doing here, old fella?" demanded Mel as he gave Hammond a Bolivian-style *abrazo*.

"Mel, we've made a contact with the Indians!" he said.

"No kidding! Boy, that's great! Praise the Lord! Can we be of any help?"

"What we need most is an interpreter. There are about thirty Indians with Angel and Frank at El Encanto, and they're beginning to get nasty. They already threatened Angel's life — he wouldn't let them steal María's cooking pots!"

"Brother, I know how that is!" Mel said. "We went through plenty of that in Tobité, and it is just the power of the Lord that will see you through!"

"Well, do you think you could help us out with an interpreter?"

"I don't see why not. Who do you want?"

"Where's Comai?"

"Out in Tobité, I guess. That kid's hard to keep track of."

"I'd like to get him as soon as possible. I don't know how long Frank and Angel are going to last out there. I'd like to take next Sunday's plane back — unless your Stinson is running."

"Sorry, Bill — no gas. Some is supposed to be coming from Santa Cruz, but you know how that is! I've been grounded for three weeks!"

"Do you know if there are any trains to El Portón today?"

"We've never been able to have any luck on Sundays. There's always something on Monday mornings, though. Stick around until tomorrow, why don't you? Come to Sunday school and tell us about the contact."

The two missionaries started in the door of the chapel

when suddenly Mel halted. Leading Bill back outside he said, "Say, I just had a thought — some Ayorés came into town last evening. They might know where Comai is! Why don't you go down and talk to them. Look, buddy, I don't want to keep you from Sunday school, but if there's a chance . . ."

"O.K." Hammond replied, "I'll take a run around town and see if I can locate them. If not, I'll be back."

The missionary had no trouble in finding the Indians. They were by the river, and were still enough of a novelty to draw a crowd whenever they came to town. As he approached, Bill thought he saw a green shirt — not a bright green one — a very dirty green one, but could it be — it was! Comai! The green shirt had not been washed since the day Bill Pencille put it on the boy. His trousers were long since discarded.

"Comai," Hammond said, "how would you like to go to El Encanto with me?"

The boy dropped his head for a moment and didn't seem to answer.

Hammond was perturbed. Could it be that he would turn down an airplane ride? He was sure that Comai understood enough Spanish to know what he was saying. He tried again — then it suddenly dawned on him! Angel had once told him that the Indian way of saying "yes" was just a slight raising of the eyebrows. Bill hadn't been watching Comai's eyebrows.

"Would you like to go, Comai?"

Up went the eyebrows!

"Come on, then!" and without further ado, Hammond turned and began to walk to the airport. Comai didn't have to worry about getting ready — he was wearing all his worldly possessions. He just put both hands on top of his head in a gesture that was very characteristic of him in those days, and followed the missionary up the sandy road to the airport.

It was Monday noon, and Frank was seated in the shade of the porch in El Encanto. Suddenly, an Indian boldly picked up Frank's saddle and walked swiftly towards the woods with it. Angel was watching, and ran after him.

The brave was very indignant, and started jabbering unintelligibly, with his face held close to Angel's.

Angel laid hold of the saddle and half-wrestled it from the Indian's hands. The warrior grunted fiercely and gave Angel a blow on the chest that almost knocked him down. Angel's right hand automatically reached for his gun, but he checked himself in time. With a scornful look at the warrior, he turned his back deliberately on him and walked away.

Frank had been watching the whole affair with interest. Suddenly he jumped to his feet and yelled, "Look out, Angel!"

Angel whirled around, dropping the saddle. The Indian was rushing at him with a war club raised threateningly over his head. It would have been an easy matter to bring it crashing down on Angel's skull! The Bolivian stood motionless, feet widespread, gazing steadily into the eyes of the maddened brave. Confronted by such raw courage the savage began to lose his nerve. He stopped short, lowered his weapon and smiled uncertainly.

Without a word Angel picked up the saddle and returned it to its place near the house. "I'm afraid this is the end of our friendly contact," he said to Frank in a low tone. "Before long, things are going to blow up. We'd better get back to San Ignacio and try again some other time!"

"You may be right," Frank agreed slowly. "We'll simply never be able to hold out until Hammond and Comai come next week."

They were interrupted in the middle of their disheartening conversation by María's call for lunch. As they were eating, Angel's fork suddenly dropped with a clatter to his tin plate. "Look!" he said.

Up the trail came horses carrying a missionary in a sun helmet and a brown boy in a faded, dirty green shirt. Bill Hammond had been gone only three days!

13.

Zapocó

CONSTANTINO FLORES, the owner of El Encanto, showed his true colors shortly after he heard the news that thirty *bárbaros* were on his ranch. Bill Pencille had been right when he suspected that Constantino's only motive for encouraging the missionaries was to get revenge on the priests. Now that the contact had been made he plotted to use it for his own gain, and planned to use the *bárbaros* as his slaves.

Three months had passed since the first contact, and with the help of Comai and Angel, all was going well. Ray Frazier, a missionary who had been working in the Santiago school along with his wife Alma, was assigned to help Frank with the Indian contact. Bill Hammond returned to Concepción to handle the supplies.

A base was needed from which to reach out after other Indians still in the forest. Don Constantino had hinted that he might sell the ranch, but he proved to be an impossible man to bargain with. Also, he refused to allow them to remain in El Encanto with the *bárbaros*. But where could they go with thirty savages?

Gervacio Nogales, a slightly-built, large-mustached Bolivian, was one of those fortunate individuals who had fought through the Chaco War between Bolivia and Paraguay and lived to tell the tale. (The Chaco is the vast dry, sandy area of eastern Bolivia and northern Paraguay which is covered by low, scraggly, thorny brush and trees, with occasional patches of palm forests and salt flats. The war was fought over oil discovered in the area in the late thirties and was won by Paraguay.) But his most significant war story did not have so much to do with the shooting in the trenches as with an inward battle in his own life. It was during the war that he first heard the Gospel.

Although he was deeply convicted of sin and his need for Christ, he did not make his decision at that time. He promised instead to get right with God after the war.

When the hostilities ended, religion no longer seemed so important. He married a dark-eyed girl from Santa Cruz and was content with subsistence living for some years. Then came World War II, and the United States' Rubber Development Corporation entered tropical Bolivia. Gervacio spotted the opportunity to get rich quick, and the RDC gave him the supplies and credit necessary to set himself up in the rubber business. With the unusual combination of U.S. credit and a flood of German agents in Santa Cruz who offered premium prices for black market rubber, the shrewd contractors made themselves fortunes — although playing two world powers against each other turned life in the area into an exciting game of cat and mouse.

Gervacio Nogales was wise enough not to squander his money as many of his friends did. After the war he bought 2,000 acres of land near Concepción, and two hundred head of cattle. He named the ranch after a river flowing through it — Zapocó.

He also built a nice home in Concepción and opened a small store there. When Bill Hammond moved in to take over the work, it wasn't long before he learned of Gervacio's Chaco War promise and led him on to fulfill it. Some years later circumstances worked out so that Gervacio decided to sell Zapocó and move to Santa Cruz — just at the right time!

Frank Pickering, Ray Frazier and Angel were with the Indians in El Encanto, discussing what could be done to keep don Constantino from taking the Ayorés from them and making them his slaves.

"Say, why don't we move them to Zapocó?" Frank suggested.

"But suppose don Gervacio pulls the same stunt that Constantino is doing!" Ray replied.

"At least Gervacio is a Christian!" said Angel.

It was decided that this was the only move possible, and they were soon packed and on their way. Zapocó lay some thirty miles southwest of El Encanto. This would be the first time any of the men had traveled through the jungle with Indians, and they hardly knew what to expect.

It proved to be quite an experience. The thirty miles took six days to traverse, and by the time they arrived at their destination all but ten of the Indians had abandoned the group and returned to the forest. They had left, saying that they were only going to find their friends and relatives and bring them back. Angel, especially, doubted that they would ever return.

On the third afternoon they had crossed a trail made by a herd of wild pigs. The Indians immediately became uncontrollably excited. They said that there had been more pigs than could be counted on the fingers and toes of three Ayorés. Throwing off their packs, they were off on the run, following the trail of the wild pigs. There was nothing the missionaries could do except wait until they returned. They were gone over an hour and when they returned, Comai proudly announced that they had killed two pigs. From his description of the hunt, it was evident that they had not used much strategy or they would have undoubtedly killed many more. When they were close enough so that they could smell the acrid odor of the pigs and hear the ominous clacking of their razor-sharp tusks, the men had simply rushed ahead pellmell into their midst. Shooting arrows in every direction, hurling their spears at anything that moved, they had succeeded in killing two pigs. Miraculously, they did not kill one another in the process!

By the time the men arrived carrying the dead pigs, the women had a huge fire burning. As the missionaries looked on in wonderment, the animals were thrown, whole, on the fire. The stench of burning hair stung their nostrils. Angel turned in disgust to Comai. "Don't they clean the pigs, or take out the entrails?" he demanded.

"Oh, of course," the boy answered.

"But they just threw the whole thing on the fire!"

"Yes, you have to cook the blood first. Asoná doesn't like bright red blood, and the Ayorés are afraid of it!" Comai explained.

Only ten Indians arrived in Zapocó, and within a few days they were all sick with grippe. Angel had loaned them tools to clear the land for their farms and to build their houses. After only a few weeks, however, they returned the tools to Angel and announced that they were leaving to hunt turtles and honey. They promised to return in fifteen days.

The camp was unbearably quiet without them. This was just a foretaste of what was to come, a token of the constant setbacks and heartaches the missionaries were to suffer in the attempt to make jungle Indians accept a sedentary way of life. Many times during the next fifteen days, and countless times in years to come, they asked themselves if it were really worth the trouble and waiting.

They knew, down deep, that it was. Sooner or later the tribe would meet up with twentieth-century civilization. The question was when and under what circumstances. The missionaries had an unshakable conviction that, in spite of its drawbacks, the Indians should come in contact with the Gospel of Christ simultaneously with civilization. To them it was simple obedience to the Great Commission to "preach the Gospel to all creatures."

It soon became clear that the Indians always kept their word when they promised to return. If they said fifteen days they would appear on the fifteenth day. If they said one moon, they would appear at the end of the month. It was August when the ten returned to Zapocó, and they were not alone. They had met thirty-two of their friends in the forest and convinced them to come with them to live with the white men. The Indian population of Zapocó now stood at forty-two!

When don Gervacio was approached about the purchase of the ranch, he had already decided to sell. As a Christian, interested in the welfare of the Indians, he was most cooperative and in a short time Zapocó was deeded to the South America Indian Mission, for the ridiculously low price of a few cents an acre!

14.

Communications Problem

THE PENCILLES returned to Bolivia in the fall of 1950, shortening their furlough because of the contact with the Ayorés. They planned to move to Zapocó just as soon as they could build a place to live. While Bill worked on the house, Harriet and the children lived in Concepción.

The road between Zapocó and Concepción was a nightmare — even for an ox-cart road. It took a good deal of maneuvering and plain hard work to take the jeep over the ruts, stones and mud holes. (The jeep was a gift from several of Bill's friends in the States.) Every few weeks Bill would drive to Concepción on the day before the Panagra DC-3 was due to arrive, in order to get mail into the post office. The following day he would head back to Zapocó after the plane had left. On the return trip he always had a full load of food, equipment and building supplies.

His major problem was to escape from Zapocó before the jeep truck filled completely with Indians. They wanted to ride to town and see the "falling thing" — the bird that flew without flapping its wings, and seemed to disappear in the distance by falling into the treetops. Bill told them that it came to rest on the ground in the white man's village, but no Indian had ever seen it from close by, on the ground. Their greatest desire was to go to town and see the great silver bird. Bill could never move the jeep without its filling up with Indians. The springs simply could not carry so much weight over the rough roads, especially when Bill would have an additional load of food and supplies on the return trip.

After several frayed tempers as a result of telling them they had to stay home, Bill hit upon a plan that promised a quick, safe getaway. The night before the planned trip he would unobtrusively park the jeep on the top of the hill on the road leading to Concepción. After dark he loaded what he needed in the front seat: ax, machete, gun, canteen. Then at four in the morning he arose and dressed in the dark. Quietly slipping out of his house he dashed for the jeep, ignition key in his hand. The dogs in the Indian camp started to bark furiously at the sound of the jeep door opening; but the motor caught on the first try, and he was off, roaring down the hill in a cloud of dust. He had made it!

Next time, however, the Indians were ready. The moment the dogs began to bark, they sprinted for the jeep. By the time the motor started there were fifteen or twenty men in the back of the truck. Bill knew he needed a new plan!

At daylight, he called a council of the leaders of the tribe. With Comai helping to interpret Bill spoke to Chief Tarane. "I have to go to town," he explained, "but I simply cannot take so many Indians along. They'll break 'our' truck." (The Indians never spoke of the truck as Bill's, but as "ours".)

"The Ayorés only want to go along to see the big bird!" expostulated Tarane.

"All right. I'll take all of the Ayorés to see the big bird!" But only two at a time. I'll take two this time. You pick out the ones who should go. Next time, I'll take two more!" Bill said. He could use the extra help to chop the fallen trees from the road and push the jeep through the mud.

The first time the savages drove into town it caused quite a sensation. Bill was wise enough not to allow them to appear clad only in a few feathers, as was their custom. The clothing problem was solved by taking along a couple of pairs of trousers and two T-shirts. At the last waterhole before driving into the town Bill stopped, made the Indians bathe and helped them put on the clothes.

It wasn't too difficult to convince his helpers they should dress up for the gala occasion of their first visit to town! Putting on the T-shirt and pants, however, was quite another matter. Grown men though they were, they were as adept at putting on a T-shirt as a two-year-old. Invariably they got their head in an armhole and their arms where their heads were supposed to be. Eventually, though, the job completed, they drove down the main street of town. This occasion turned out to be a real "ticker-tape parade" with the whole town lining the streets to stare at the long-haired savages standing erect and proud in the back of the jeep truck as it bounced down the grassy main street.

The high point of the visit of course, came next day when the great silver bird was to land. When Bill took his friends to the airport a crowd of curious children surrounded them. Station Manager Luis Buceta was hard pressed to keep them from crowding into the airport building. Bill took the two Ayorés around to the front of the building and found a vantage place under the eaves, looking out on the apron. He later tried to describe the actions and emotions of the Indians as the Panagra DC-3 roared in from Santa Cruz and taxied up to the loading platform. "I'm sure I've never really learned to think like an Indian!" Bill said, "and I had no idea what thoughts were coursing through their minds as they saw the huge bird come roaring up. They stood there, trembling, half ready to flee, torn between two emotions — curiosity and fear."

But with Bill by their side they stood fast. When the belly of the "bird" suddenly opened, however, and twenty-four people stepped out alive, their eyes fairly bulged with amazement. To the amusement of the Bolivians the Indians began to count the passengers who emerged from the bird. They counted in a loud voice, using their fingers and toes. When they had finished all of the fingers and toes of one Indian they began on the right hand of another. The spectators roared with laughter, but the Indians seemed unaffected. They signaled to Bill that they wanted to go closer to the bird and touch it.

Buceta nodded his permission, and Bill walked out on the runway with them. First, they stepped gingerly up to the plane and touched it. Then they began to caress it gently, as though it were alive and they were anxious to be on good terms with it. After they had thus "made friends" with it, they unwound the ropes that bound their long, black hair.

"What are you going to do with those ropes?" Bill asked, worriedly. He wondered if they might not plan to tie the thing up and take it captive!

"Oh," they replied, "we want to measure it."

"What for?"

"If we don't measure it, our wives and children will never believe us when we tell them how big it is!"

From wing tip to wing tip and from nose to tail they carefully took the plane's measurements. Then they meticulously wrapped the ropes back in place around their hair.

Sure enough, when they returned to Zapocó they marched out to the middle of the plaza and again unwound their ropes. With great care they drew the measurements of the plane on the ground. "For those two," Bill said, "it was their supreme moment of glory!"

When Chief Tarane heard the report he decided that he himself must go next time to see this great marvel. As Bill prepared for the trip, Tarane served notice that it would not be necessary to take pants and shirt for him. He had his own. Bill glanced up, and there Tarane stood, resplendent from head to foot in a pair of Frank's cast-off "long Johns." His face was blackened with charcoal. His inky-black hair was tied back into a long pony tail. His war feathers stuck up proudly. His dirty hands clasped a vicious-looking war-club. *"Yico!"* he said. "Let's go!"

Bill decided to take the pants and shirt along anyhow and try to convince him to change at the waterhole. But Tarane staunchly refused to exchange his shiny, white suit for such mundane covering as pants and T-shirt. Only after prolonged argument was Bill able to persuade the chief that he simply couldn't go to greet the big bird in such an outfit. Still unconvinced, Tarane submitted to the indignity of surrendering his most prized possession and struggled into the khaki trousers Bill handed him.

It was noon when they arrived at the Hammond house. Dinner was ready, and Dorothy had prepared a big pot of rice for the Indian men. Bill took charge of them and filled their plates, seating them on the woodpile back of the kitchen. Harriet was still in Concepción awaiting the completion of the house in Zapocó, and the two couples enjoyed a pleasant meal together. Bill and Harriet were seated with their backs to the door of the little dining room, and Dorothy sat facing them. Midway through the meal she suddenly blanched, dropped her fork on her plate and gasped, "Oh, help!" Covering her face with her hands she rushed out of the side door and into her room, shutting her door.

Bill Pencille whirled around to see what had happened. In the doorway stood Chief Tarane, once again resplendent in his long, white underwear! A big grin split his face from ear to ear.

The sign language the missionaries had been forced to use to communicate with the Indians when Comai wasn't around was clearly inadequate. If the Indians were ever to understand the Gospel, they would have to hear it in their own language, according to their own thought pattern. Nothing pointed up the absolute need of learning the Ayoré language more than the visit of the traveling preacher to Zapocó. He was from New York, and had learned a little Spanish in Argentina. He announced that God had sent him to Zapocó to preach to the Indians!

Bill consented reluctantly, and explained that he would have to use Comai as his interpreter. It turned out to be Comai who suffered by the experience. The sermon bristled with such terms as "justification by faith." "sanctification," "redemption." Poor twelve-year-old Comai had never even heard the words in Spanish, let alone try to express their meaning in his own tongue! When he was unable to translate them, the preacher lost patience with him and the whole attempt was a failure.

After a few days the preacher announced that he was ready to preach again. Bill took him aside and told him, "Look, brother, if you want to preach again, I'll bring Comai over this afternoon to your room. We will carefully go over your message first, and then —"

"Go over my sermon! How do I know what I'm going to preach on? I never study for a sermon! The Spirit gives me my sermons as I preach them!"

Bill admits that perhaps his reply was not too kind. "I'm glad you get your sermons from the Spirit," he said. "But as of now, the Spirit has given you your last message for the Ayorés!"

When Bill first began to study the Indian language he started by asking Comai the names of the parts of the body. It was the most convenient thing around, since both had one, and both had names for its parts. This was the begin-

Chief Tarane of Zapocó wears
a necklace of human hair.

The Ayoré camp in Zapocó.

ing of the dictionary. As Comai repeated the word in Ayoré Bill would attempt to reproduce it, and then decide how to write it down.

Comai was but a boy, and an Indian boy at that. He had never been to school and had not learned to think and concentrate for long periods of time. It was hard to keep his attention through the long, tedious hours of endless questions about words, words, words. Bill finally found a way to hold the boy's interest. Comai had always been fascinated by the ringing of an alarm clock. Bill brought one to the class, and Comai agreed to work hard for fifteen minutes and then have fifteen minutes off for play. The ding-a-ling of the bell on the clock would signal the end of the study time.

This worked fine until one bright morning when an Ayoré woman walked in with her little baby in a shoulder-sling. At that moment the alarm sounded — diiiiiing! The baby screamed and nearly lurched out of the sling. When the mother finally succeeded in quieting her baby, she turned furiously on Bill. "Now look what you've done! You split his gall bladder!"

From that clue Bill learned that for an Ayoré the seat of fear is the gall bladder. If you are an Ayoré you don't get scared to death, your gall bladder splits! Also, in Ayoréland, you don't love with "all your heart," but with "all your stomach"! A starry-eyed Ayoré lover would ask his girl, "How is your stomach toward me?"

The language was not as simple as Bill had hoped. As he worked with Comai, he soon realized the tremendous complexity of his task.

The Pencilles practically adopted Comai. He lived right in their house, although he never would consent to sleeping in a bed of his own. He preferred to roll up in his blanket on the bricks of the kitchen floor.

One day, Comai entered the house in the middle of the morning and said in broken English, "Good morning, how are you?" Bill and Harriet realized that they had been making the mistake of talking too much English in their home, and from then on made an effort to speak only Spanish when Comai was present. Working in two languages would be difficult enough without complicating the process with a third!

Every day, either Bill or Harriet would spend several hours teaching Comai to read the Spanish Bible and to write. They used the Laubach method of teaching illiterates at first, and with good success. Comai became completely bilingual — just as much at home in Spanish as in Ayoré.

They also encouraged him to spend as much time as possible in the Ayoré camp so that he would continue to develop his mother tongue. Comai soon got the knack of picking up new information. Whenever Bill asked him something that he couldn't answer, he'd just tuck it into a corner of his mind and make his own investigation later. Usually, within a day or two he'd have the answer Bill was looking for.

As a little boy, Comai would become nervous and fearful whenever he had to interpret Bill's preaching. It wasn't that he couldn't do it, especially after going over the sermon several times with Bill beforehand. It was just that little Ayoré boys weren't supposed to stand up in front of those hard-eyed chiefs and wizened witch doctors and say *anything,* much less tell them that they all were sinners! Comai would take a deep breath and stand trembling by Bill's side as he preached. Soon Bill noticed that an unfamiliar word kept cropping up. Comai seemed to preface everything he said with *chi.*

Bill said, "All are sinners and no one pleases God."

Comai interpreted, "*Chi,* all are sinners and no one pleases God!"

Chi turned out to mean, "He said it, I didn't say it!" Comai didn't want to get into trouble with his elders, so he always put the blame on Bill!

The Ayorés had no word for heaven. As Bill and Comai talked it over between rings of the alarm clock, the only thing they could come up with was *gueodeuechai,* "Beyond the clouds." The Ayorés believed that all the dead go to *naropie* in the center of the earth. But they had no concept of heaven. *Gueodeuechai* was sort of the great blue yonder, with no real idea of how far away it actually was. Bill hoped to use this word and imbue it with some of the Bible's teaching about heaven. Until now, all the dead simply "*chicai numi,*" "went into the earth."

Soon after translating this word and attempting to explain its meaning to the Ayorés, Bill and Harriet with their children left Zapocó for a week and went to Santa Cruz in the airplane.

When they returned, the entire tribe of Indians approached them with quite a formal air and sat solemnly down around the front door. A committee interviewed Bill and Harriet in front of the others — the Ayoré version of a press conference. The missionaries hardly knew why all the special fuss, but began to understand with the first question: "What did God have to say?"

Bill rejoiced over this religious interest, but didn't understand the intent of the question. So he countered, "Do you want me to read you what God has to say in His Book?"

"No," they chorused. "We want to know what you talked to Him about when you went on the airplane to *gueodeuechai*!"

Bill spent a difficult hour trying to convince them that he had not paid God a visit in heaven! Since the plane often flew above the clouds, they were positive it must meet God up there somewhere!

The Ayorés had two ways of making new words to describe the things they saw and learned about after coming to live with the white men. Either they made descriptive compound words by using their already existing vocabulary, or they adapted a Spanish word. Nowadays, they call an airplane the Spanish *avión*. But while they were still in the woods they called it a *cuchabasui*, or "falling thing."

On the other hand, they knew nothing of rice until the missionaries showed it to them, calling it by the Spanish name *arroz*. But Indians' tongues couldn't twist around the Spanish pronunciation so they said *aose'*, ending with the characteristic glottal click. Thus even while Bill was working on the rudiments of what would later be the Ayoré dictionary and grammar, the language itself was growing and expanding.

Bill was not long in discovering how brutally frank the Indians could be. There is no such thing as a bald Ayoré, and Bill's bald head caused them no end of merriment. When they became angry with Bill, who was farm boss, police chief, storekeeper, banker and many other things to them, they would scowl and spit out the name "Squash!" in Ayore. Here comes "Squash!" they would say — "*Purua ee di.*" To them, Bill's bald head looked exactly like the shiny, white squash they grew in their gardens. When they shouted this word after him, Bill knew they were angry about something.

Bill was the most curious person the Ayorés had ever seen. He was always pointing to something and saying "*Irique*" — "what's that?" Then out of his shirt pocket would come a notebook and pencil and he'd write down the word phonetically. This, of course, didn't make any sense to a people who could write nothing more than the signs of their seven clans with a piece of charcoal. It gave rise to another, this time not so derogatory, nickname. At the same time it must be one of the strangest coincidences in the history of linguistics.

The Ayorés had no idea that Bill's last name was Pencille, much less what "pencil" means in English. But their nickname for Bill was *Gueguerai* the Ayoré word for charcoal or pencil because he always had one in his hand.

As Bill learned more and more of the Ayoré language, and as Comai grew more proficient in Spanish, fellowship between them became more satisfying with each passing day. A real father-son relationship was springing up in spite of the enormous cultural and language barrier which separated them.

There were several Christian Bolivian families now living at Zapocó, and Bill encouraged Comai to spend much time with them. Spanish was their native tongue, and Bill could never hope to speak it as well as they did. He was anxious that Comai, with his bright mind and quick tongue, learn good Spanish with all possible speed. This mixing with the Bolivian brethren soon had a second and more far-reaching effect. Comai grew rapidly in his Christian life as he watched these simple people at their prayers and devotions. He learned much from them, listening to their testimonies of what Jesus meant to them.

Anxious as Bill was to preach to the Indians, he still had no adequate term to use for God. Time and again, he had questioned Comai about it without much success. Comai insisted that the only god of the Ayorés was Asoná, and he broke out in new spasms of trembling when Bill questioned him as to just who this god was and what she did. Even though he was now a Christian, Comai was still not completely convinced that Asoná did not hold some mysterious power over him. The Ayorés all insisted that he would probably not live the year out unless he set his new God aside, temporarily at least, and took part in the festival to Asoná which would be celebrated in just a few months. Bill felt that it wouldn't do to use Asoná for God — she was a god of vengeance, and how could you possibly say "God is love" when everyone knew that love was one quality conspicuously missing from Asoná's character? For want of a better term, Bill had settled for the Spanish name for God, *Dios,* but was not satisfied with it. Understanding of the Gospel was slow in coming to the Ayoré's hearts and minds, for the word *Dios* meant nothing to them.

One day, Comai suggested the name *pai* for God.

"Who is *pai*?" Bill wanted to know.

"A missionary."

"What do you mean, a missionary!" How would the Ayorés ever have a word for missionary in their language!

"Well, it is a white man who teaches about God and teaches about heaven!"

Bill dismissed Comai before the alarm clock rang, and began to turn this piece of information over in his mind. *Pai* could easily be the Ayoré pronunciation of the Spanish *padre,* priest. Bill recalled Comai's telling him the legend of Jerai, the great hero of the Ayoré tribe. No one could remember when Jerai lived — perhaps he was the first Ayoré, Comai had explained. At any rate, he was the one who saved the Ayoré tribe from the white man!

At one time, the Ayorés lived with the white men, according to the legend. But the whites didn't dress like Bill and the other missionaries. They dressed more like Harriet, with long skirts. They forced the Ayorés to build a great tower that reached to the sky, but if they didn't work well the white men beat and mistreated them. Finally, Jerai took charge and the Ayorés followed him. They killed all the white men and went back into the jungles to live.

Bill felt that this was perhaps the Ayoré version of the fate of the mysterious Jesuit mission of San Ignacio de Zamuco! Two hundred years is a long, long time for a people with an unwritten history, and now it seemed to them that Jerai must have lived at about the beginning of time.

Perhaps, Bill reasoned, *pai* came into the language at the time of the Jesuit rule. At any rate, *pai* wasn't the word that he was looking for! He struggled with the problem for months. How can you preach to a people unless you can at least tell them who God is?

Then one day, the honey hunters returned and Bill joined the group that gathered about them as they busied themselves dividing the food among their families. Their bags fairly burst with gourds of honey and fat turtles.

The hunters began to talk of Dupade.

Bill was curious. "Who is Dupade?" he wanted to know.

"Oh," they said, "We don't know who he is."

"Come on, now! You must know who he is! Why, you were just talking about him!"

"No, we don't know anything about him."

"Well, why were you talking about him, then?" Bill asked, suddenly aware that he just might be on the verge of an important discovery.

They said, "When we don't find honey or turtles, we pray to Dupade." This "praying," they explained, was done standing by a tree and shouting in a loud voice, "Dupade! Give us turtles and honey! We are hungry!"

"Does he do it?" Bill wanted to know.

"Sometimes he does. This time, he gave us honey!"

"Where does Dupade live?"

"We don't know. Maybe he is the sun, and lives in the sky."

"Do you think he is the sun?"

"We don't know."

"Is he bad?"

"Nobody knows!"

"Is he good?"

"Nobody knows that, either!"

After more questioning, Bill was certain that he had at long last found what he was searching for. Recalling the Apostle Paul's tactics when he preached on the unknown god at Athens, he said, "This Dupade whom you don't know — I know him! He's my God! He's the One who sent me here to you."

They were immediately interested.

"Do you know that Dupade wrote a Book?" Bill went on.

"No! We didn't know that!"

Bill held up his New Testament and explained that it wasn't only for white people, but for Ayorés as well. "Someday, this book will be written in the Ayoré language for you to read and obey!

"Did you know Dupade has a Son?" Bill queried, further.

"No. How could we know such a thing!"

"Well, He does. And His Name is *Jesucristo!*" Bill used the Spanish name for Jesus, since they were learning Spanish names, anyway.

Bill and Harriet rejoiced at this major victory. Sounds and symbols were becoming words and concepts. They had a long way to go, but they knew that they were beginning to break through the language barrier and communicate with the Ayorés.

15.

Counterattack

DURING THE SECOND YEAR the Indian population of Zapocó grew from forty-two to four hundred. The Indians themselves were responsible for bringing most of these, their friends and relatives, to live at the Mission. On their extended hunting and fishing trips into the jungle they came upon scattered groups of their own people and brought them back to live with the *coñone* (white men).

Asoná had been severely threatened, but she was not to be so easily defeated. She was not about to surrender without a struggle those who had been so long under her control.

Invariably, the new Indians would be frightened and shy the first few days after their arrival. And they always engaged in elaborate ceremonies to keep the white man's sickness from attacking them.

When Diraidaquide brought his people to Zapocó, he gathered all of the women and children into a tight circle, and as they huddled together like a flock of frightened sheep, Diraidaquide, dressed in all his witch doctor's regalia, drew crosses with his lance in the dust. He made a complete circle of the trembling little group, entirely hemming them in with the crosses. "This will keep away the spirits of the white man's sicknesses," he explained.

But of course the crosses didn't work. Nothing did. The usual diseases so common in civilization, had never penetrated the vastness of the Ayoré's jungle habitat, and they had no resistance to them whatsoever. What to the missionary was nothing worse than a common cold, turned into double pneumonia in the Indians. Measles, sore eyes, flu — epidemic after epidemic of the "white man's sickness" rolled over the camp at Zapocó. It seemed to the Pencilles and Fraziers that they were doing little but work, day and night, just to keep the Indians alive! They injected penicillin and applied sulfa drugs; they treated eyes with antibiotics and rubbed ointment on fevered chests; then more penicillin! Bill felt that the job of reaching these Indians would have been almost impossible before the discovery of modern antibiotics. And even so, the mortality rate was heartbreaking. After the spiritual, by far the most serious problem was the health of the Indians.

Bridging the gap medically between the Stone Age and the Space Age was no easy task. The apparently simple matter of swallowing an aspirin tablet became a major challenge with the Indians. Although they seemed to be able to eat vast quantities of corn with little or no chewing, to swallow an aspirin was nearly impossible. Bill would break the tablet in four, and even then it took gourdfuls of water before the pill disappeared! They would gag and choke and make a big fuss until eventually it simply dissolved and they swallowed it unawares.

Bill recalls one old-timer who came complaining of a stomach-ache. For want of anything better, Bill gave him an aspirin — at least, it probably wouldn't do him any harm. The Indian took the aspirin and put it in his little mill which he used to grind hot peppers, and ground it to powder. But he then poured a few drops of water on the powder, mixing it into a paste. Before Bill could intervene, he extended his stomach and rubbed the white paste over it! After all, it was his *stomach* that hurt, not his mouth!

It was almost impossible to convince the Indians that the way to relieve a fevered body was *not* a plunge into the cool river; or that sitting naked in the chilly evening breeze was not the best way to cool off after sweating under a heavy load of firewood. Harriet, worn and half-sick herself from long hours of nursing the Indians, would often try to tell them what caused their illness. Seated on the dirt floor of a dark, smoky hut, she was rubbing one of the women with alcohol to ease her aching back. "Taranate," she said, softly, "do you know why you are sick?"

Taranate was silent.

Harriet continued, "You're sick because some germs got into your body."

The woman looked at Harriet blankly. There was no word for germ in the Ayoré language, and Harriet had used the Spanish *microbio.* "Germs?" she asked. "I don't know what a germ is!"

Harriet did her best to explain, but with little success. Then Taranate turned to her and said, "Have you ever seen a germ?"

Of course, Harriet had to admit that she never had seen one. Before she could tell why, Taranate interrupted, "If you can't show me one of these germs, then don't tell me what makes us sick! We know very well. It's the evil spirits!"

Taranate turned angrily to the wall. The implication was all too clear. The spirits were white spirits. After all, they had lived with fellow Indians all their lives and had not been bothered by illness until coming to live with white men. Tears ran down Harriet's cheeks as she silently continued to make the woman more comfortable. Was it right to even try to contact the Ayorés knowing, as they did, that the very contact would condemn many of them to a premature death?

Harriet was not the first missionary to weep when faced with this problem. But the twentieth century cannot be stopped in its relentless march. Civilization was pressing in upon the Indian from every side. Soldiers, ranchers, explorers, oil men, adventurers — all would give the same diseases to the Indians. And instead of the Gospel they would also bring murder, rape and slavery.

Still more important, were the souls of these people. Thousands would be doomed to an eternity without Christ if no one took the message of salvation to them. And only men and women could carry that message, even though they also carried deadly germs! The risk had to be taken. What harms the body is insignificant when compared to the suffering of a soul in hell.

Constantly caring for the Indians in their tiny grass-roofed huts, always exposed to their sickness, Bill himself finally came down with fever. It was not too serious, and after a few days in bed he was back at work again. While he was ill, Harriet noticed the Indians were most solicitous and continually asked about his health. On the day she announced he would be getting up from his sickbed, every woman in camp appeared at the door with a gift. Some brought honey, others had corn, or roast turtle or palm heart. Bill felt flattered for a moment, but soon realized that the gifts were not really for him, but for the spirit of his sickness! Since Bill was getting well, quite obviously the spirit which caused his illness was about to leave him. The idea behind the gifts was to buy off this spirit lest he leave Bill and pass directly to the Indians!

Dealing with the witch doctors wasn't easy. In their visions they claimed to see the spirits which caused illness. Often, Bill would walk to the Indian houses at daybreak and find a post painted with weird symbols — circles, crosses, lines — planted in the middle of the path, blocking the way to their houses. "Aside ordered us to put it up last night," they would explain. "Don't touch it! It is a magic post and will keep your spirit from harming us!"

"But what makes you think my spirit is going to hurt you?" Bill asked.

"Oh, Aside had a dream last night. He saw quite clearly your spirit coming up this way to make us sick!"

Bill couldn't help feeling that this was not exactly the best way to begin a new day!

Gradually, Bill and Harriet lost count of the times when some Indian, after the death of a relative during the night, would appear at their door at daylight threatening to kill them. It was a case of revenge for what you had done through your spirit the night before. All of the witch doctors were able to kill, long distance, by putting a curse on their enemies. Were not the missionaries with their syringes, bottles, pills and salves nothing but witch doctors?

On the initial trips into the forest seeking contact with the Indians, Bill was always well armed. Now, however, after explaining to them who he was, he never kept a loaded gun in the house. Bill explained his position this way: "Yes, I went armed into the forest for the first contacts. You see, to the Indians I was just another white man — another rancher or gold miner or soldier. And the white man had always shot at the Indian on sight. With a gun, I was able to hold them at bay until I talked with them and told them who I was. But once they were in Zapocó I told them I was a child of God and that God had sent me to them. I explained that God always took care of His own children, and I never went armed among them, or kept a loaded gun in my house."

Bill went on to tell of those dangerous days. "When they would come to kill me over the death of some loved one, I would always try to back into a corner so they couldn't spear me from behind. They are not especially courageous, and I felt if I could look right into their eyes they might not have the courage to throw that first spear. I won't say I have never been afraid. On the contrary, I have been so frightened it took all of my strength just to keep the wild beating of my heart from showing up in my voice. I would try to keep my voice level, for they are great admirers of courage.

"Of course, it is a good idea to get in a testimony about now. It might be the last one, you know! I would tell them that they could go ahead and kill me if they so chose, but that I was different from them and wasn't afraid to die. This was because I had trusted in Jesus who had cleansed my sins and opened the way to God's house for me. Furthermore, I was the best friend they had ever had among the white men. I had never lied to them or deceived them. But, if they still wanted to kill me, they might as well get it over with!"

Bill soon learned that it was best to beat them to the draw at such a time. When an Indian had died, Bill would go immediately to the house of the bereaved. Finding them sullen and scowling, he would express his sorrow over the death of their loved one, and then give them a gift to assuage their grief. Then he would come directly to the point and ask if they intended to kill him because of the death. Caught thus off guard, they would invariably stammer and become embarrassed, and finally say, "Why, of course not! You're our friend! Our brother! We would not think of killing you!"

On at least two occasions Bill was saved by animals. Once the Indians, for no good reason, killed the riding ox belonging to an army sergeant while he was visiting Bill! This created quite a problem with the sergeant, and required a good deal of diplomacy on Bill's part. But more important was the fact that the sergeant had the grippe. Eventually, the Indians also sickened, and twelve died. Bill asked the Indians, "Are you going to try to kill me for the death of these people?"

"No, no," they answered immediately. "It was not you.

It is the spirit of the ox! He is getting even with us!"

The same thing happened right after they killed a horse on another occasion. This time twenty-six of them died, but the witch doctor saw the horse's spirit in his dream and Bill once again escaped.

But eventually they did see Bill's spirit in the visions, and that almost ended his missionary career. A grippe epidemic hit Zapocó and witch doctor Sirine abandoned camp with some 40 other Indians. Bill wasn't willing that the contact be broken, so he started out after them, not knowing that Sirine had seen his spirit in a vision and was plotting to kill him in revenge.

He realized that something was drastically wrong, however, when he caught up to them in their camp. They were sullen and angry. The atmosphere was electric. One false move and there would have been one less missionary in Eastern Bolivia within thirty seconds. Bill kept a stony look on his face and slowly backed up against a tree and sat down. He wanted to make sure that no one attacked from behind. His body felt as if it were being stuck by a thousand tiny pins.

"Why have you followed us?" Sirine finally asked.

"I've come to take you back to Zapocó," Bill said.

"You will not take us back. You are a murderer! The spirit of Guillermo killed six Ayorés. We would fix you if you didn't have a gun." Bill was wearing a .44 revolver strapped to his waist.

Bill stood up. Three or four Ayorés who had been sitting perfectly still went into action and grabbed their spears. Was this going to be the end? The possibility of a fight to the death with such a band of maddened Indians had often occurred to Bill.

He held up his hand. "Wait a minute," he said. He felt the hair on the back of his neck stand up. Beads of perspiration came out on his forehead and trickled down his temples. "You think I trust in this gun? I do not! I've told you many times that I trust in something much more powerful than this gun — I trust in God."

As the Indians looked on open-mouthed, Bill reached down, drew his revolver and with the same motion flung it 30 feet away in the bush. "Come on now," he said, "We're going back to Zapocó." And he turned his back to them and walked down the trail without so much as another glance in their direction.

They might have been primitive, stone-age savages, but one thing they understood was raw, masculine courage. They picked up their bags and meekly followed Bill Pencille into Zapocó.

In trying to explain further why he felt that the Indians had never carried out their threats of death, Bill feels that the 34th Psalm has the answer: "The angel of the Lord encampeth round about them that fear him and delivereth them!"

On one occasion Chief Enune and his wife were both ill. At first, it didn't seem too serious. They had a tiny three-month-old girl, but the mother seemed well able to care for her. Then the wind changed suddenly to the south and the temperature dropped to near the freezing mark in a few hours. Seated in the open beside a tiny fire, Enune and his family took a turn for the worse. As they dispensed medicines that evening, Bill and Ray Frazier both noted the change. They had seen this happen too many times to be unconcerned now! They injected them with penicillin, and hauled firewood to them so that they could keep warm through the night.

On the midnight rounds of the Indians most seriously ill they did what they could, but felt it to be pitifully inadequate. Enune and his wife, with the baby asleep in her arms, could not be persuaded to go inside their hut. They said the cold wind felt good on their fevered bodies.

At daybreak, Bill and Ray were again in the camp. At once they noticed the absence of Enune and his wife and baby. Their fire had died down to a cold heap of ashes. The Indians were sullen and angry, and were muttering dire threats. The missionaries wondered where the sick ones could have gone! They were too ill to have walked far. Could their friends have possibly buried them alive!

Then Bill espied two large bags, sewed shut, at the far wall of the hut. Both Enune and his wife had died during the night and their bodies were in the bags, ready for burial!

"Where's the baby?" asked Bill.

There was no response. Only defiant glares at the white men whose spirits were killing them, one by one!

Uneasy over the threatening attitude of the savages, the

Above and right: Little Julia clowns for the camera. She was rescued from her parents' burial bag on the 4th of July which accounts for her name. Beside her stands Tagaca, the first Ayoré after Comai to be baptized (p. 151). After her baptism a number of young people were baptized. Some of the young men are shown below. Comai has on a dark shirt.

missionaries were about to turn away. Then they heard it — the faint cry of a baby! It came from the smaller of the two burial-bags. Bill and Ray looked at each other incredulously. "They're planning to bury the poor thing alive!" whispered Ray.

"We're in a tight spot!" Bill murmured in response. "How will we ever save the baby? We'll be lucky to get out of here alive ourselves!"

Ray clenched his fists and closed his eyes tightly. Both their hearts were crying out to God for wisdom.

Then Bill had a sudden inspiration. He turned toward the scowling group by the campfire and said, "You're all so sick and weak — I feel so sorry for you. We will dig the graves and bury your dead so you won't have to do it!"

A few grunts of assent assured them that the Indians, in spite of their anger, were willing to get out of that unpleasant task. Instantly, Bill and Ray each shouldered one of the bags and headed for the cemetery. As they passed the Pencille's house they placed the smaller bag on the porch, made a quick slit in it and took out the whimpering baby. Bill quickly handed her to Harriet and went on to fulfill their part of the bargain.

Bill wrote later: "What a pitiful piece of humanity she was! During the last hours of life the mother had been too weak to take care of her, and she had rolled into the fire. Her thigh and hip were badly burned. Seven complete baths were necessary to soak all the dirt off! It was the Fourth of July. We were undecided whether to call her Independence or Julia, which is Spanish for July. Julia it finally was."

Although by this time Bill and Comai were able to explain quite clearly who Dupade (God) was, and what He wanted to do for the Ayorés, old customs and beliefs do not easily lose their grip on hearts and minds. Always it was the same — if not the spirit of some animal which caused death, it was Bill's spirit. If not Bill's spirit, then it was Asoná, angry and vengeful over some half-forgotten offense!

At first, Bill tended to ridicule the bird god in his teaching. When the Indians affirmed that some strong, robust man had been killed by her, Bill would ask in mockery, "Do you mean to tell me a tiny bird can kill a big man like that?"

They would become furious and one of them would step directly in front of Bill and shake his finger in his face as he shouted, "Listen! You might know the birds where you come from. But you don't know the Ayoré's bird! You don't know Asoná! You stick to what you do know! We *know* the power of the bird!"

It did not take Bill long to realize that his approach had been wrong. It was too negative. He became more sympathetic and loving, as well as more positive. "I know that Asoná has power," he would tell them. "I feel so sorry for you who must spend your whole lives serving her! She is so vengeful!"

Nods of assent told him that they agreed.

"I have come to you in the name of Dupade," Bill would continue. "He is stronger than Asoná! In fact, He made her. He made everything. If you will just trust and obey Dupade, he will deliver you from Asoná and protect you against her vengeance!"

Comai was one of the first Ayorés to lose his fear of Asoná and learn that her spell could be broken. One morning, he told Bill of a discussion he had had with one of the old Ayoré women the day before. He had suggested that she leave her fear of Asoná and receive God's Son as her Saviour. She became angry and took hold of Comai's shirt as she said, "Comai, you be careful! Something terrible is going to happen to you! You have left the customs of our people, and Asoná will punish you!"

"Do you believe that, Comai?" Bill asked the boy.

"Of course not! But say, may I borrow the shotgun? I'd like to see if I can kill a deer."

Bill watched him as he sauntered carelessly down the trail toward the river, shotgun slung over his shoulder. He prayed silently for this lad, the first to have the courage to break with age-old customs and fears. Surely, Satan, the god of Asoná, could not be pleased with him, Bill thought to himself.

Only a few minutes had passed before Comai was again at the door. He was white and shaking.

"What in the world is wrong with you?" Bill exclaimed,

quickly pulling the boy down beside him on the couch. "You look as though you'd seen a ghost!"

Comai's voice trembled with emotion. "You know that log across the path down by the river?"

"Sure I know it. I step over it every day. Why?"

"So do I. But this morning, I stepped over it and just as I set my foot on the ground on the far side, I heard a rustling and rattling. I looked down, startled, and there right by my foot was a rattlesnake as thick as my arm! It was coiled and ready to strike! I jumped back, and the snake just stayed coiled where it was. I don't know why it didn't strike me!"

"I do!" Bill said, gently, putting his arm about the frightened boy's shoulders. "Asoná is angry because of your testimony to the old woman! But God just proved that He is stronger than Asoná!"

Comai breathed a sigh of relief. "It's good to belong to God!" he said.

16.

Orphans—
Advance on a New Front

The average life of a tribe of Amazon jungle Indians after contact with the whites, is five years!"

These are the words of General Rondon, founder of the Indian Protective Service in Brazil. He was speaking of those tribes in Brazil who come in contact with ranchers, rubber gatherers, or gold miners, and then in five years are never more to be found, having died from the diseases the white man brought into his domain. General Rondon was not speaking of the missionaries who were willing to spend time and money nursing the Indians back to health, and helping them until they have built up enough resistance to be able to recover from an attack of grippe or measles.

Although many Ayorés were to die in Zapocó, the tribe was not destined to disappear, and since 1960 it has been increasing rapidly. The early days, however, were heartbreaking for many of the aged and the very young did not survive. One of the immediate results was the large number of orphan children due to the death of either parent and the remarriage of the other. True, these children never lacked food. Tribal law demanded that they be fed. But the Indians would spend months at a time away from the mission station, hunting and fishing in the jungle. This was a great trial to the missionaries, since all language study and spiritual ministry to the Indians would come to a complete halt during the long months of their absence. During this time the silence of the station in Zapocó, cut off from the world by miles of virgin forest, was hard to endure. More than once during those times of loneliness they wondered how long it would take to civilize the Ayorés and bring them to a saving knowledge of Christ! They seemed to be as fearful of Asoná and of the spirits of the dead as they had been on the day of their arrival.

On one occasion, Harriet noticed that the orphans seemed most unwilling to be dragged off on one of the hunts. She had a sudden inspiration.

"Why do you make the children go to the jungle?" she asked one of the older women who was passing the house leading one of the orphans by the hand. "You know they don't want to go! They say the woods are bad, and that there are too many mosquitoes there!"

"What can we do?" replied Ebiadate. "They cry all the time in the woods now. They like it much better here in Zapocó! But there is no one to feed them if they remain!"

Without waiting to consult Bill, Harriet quickly answered, "You leave that little girl with me, and I'll give her food until you come back. And tell the other orphans that they can stay at my home, too. We will see they aren't hungry!"

The results were better than anyone could have anticipated. During the next hunting trip, Harriet found herself with fourteen orphans. The youngest was six, the oldest perhaps fifteen. The Pencille house was overrun with lovable little savages, and they practically took it over. When the Indians returned, the children refused to go back to camp. In addition to seeing that their stomachs were full, the Pencilles had given them the same loving care they bestowed upon their own children, with the result that the Indian children had no desire to be separated from their new father and mother.

Thus began the orphanage. With three children of her own in addition to the fourteen orphans, Harriet tried to keep things as simple as possible. The children were responsible for the cleaning of their own rooms, were taught to cook their own food, and learned simple hygiene. By now the missionaries had learned that the Indians frowned on physical punishment, so other means of discipline had to be found. Anyone who refused to do his task found his plate empty at the next meal. It was an excellent means of punishment, for they loved to eat; there was seldom any trouble with the children.

Of course, with so many children in a small house, order was important. Everything had its place and everything had to be kept in its place. It was Sunday. Harriet was busy with dinner when Jecuresi came for his tin cup to take a drink of water. But instead of returning it to its place on the shelf, he simply threw it on the floor and turned to walk out. Harriet asked him to please pick it up, but he sullenly refused and stood stubbornly staring at her.

Bill was reading in the inner room, and Harriet called to him. When he understood the situation he, too, asked Jecuresi to pick up the cup and put it back in its place. Instead of complying, there was an outburst of vile words in the Indian tongue as Jecuresi snatched a small hunting knife from his belt and lunged toward Bill.

Quicker than the time it takes to tell it, Bill pulled off his belt with one sweeping motion and struck the boy across the hand, knocking the knife to the floor. Harriet picked it up, hiding it behind her. It took two more strokes of the belt before the boy stooped, picked up the cup and returned it to its place. This was the only time Bill ever whipped an Ayoré or resorted to any physical violence.

While this was transpiring Paoi, one of the younger braves, silently looked on from the corner of the kitchen. As Bill threaded his belt back through the belt-loops of his trousers, Paoi snarled, "If I had my spear with me I'd have killed you!" Then, turning to Jecuresi he continued, "Come back to camp with me! Why do you stay with a man like this? Don't you know that evil spirits have been driven in where the belt hit you?"

"I'm not going to camp!" Jecuresi replied. "It hurt plenty, but I deserved it. And I don't believe all of this about the evil spirits any more!"

Now, for the first time Bill and Harriet had a permanent audience to teach and instruct. It was not a captive audience, for the children were always free to leave. But for several years the orphans were with them day and night, and through the constant teaching of the Word of God, rays of light began to dawn in hearts long darkened by Satan and his front, Asoná. One after another of the young people gave their lives to the Lord.

From the very first day that the Indians were with the missionaries, certain of the young people had seemed strangely drawn toward the white men and their wives. They would spend long hours just sitting near them, watching and listening, learning all they could of the strange ways of these curious folks. Dijere had been one of the two who first came to the house of Nicolás in El Encanto;

and when Harriet arrived to live in Zapocó, Dijere attached herself to her and seldom let her out of her sight.

She was in her late teens, of medium height, with a well-formed body and bright eyes. She smiled often, and her teeth shone white and even between full, thick lips. She wore only the traditional rough-woven skirt of the Ayoré women; and just above the knotted cord that held it in place her abdomen was deeply scarred from an old wound. When questioned about the scar, Dijere would blush and refuse to answer. But the orphans were not as inhibited. "She did that herself!" they chorused. "She cut herself with a knife!"

"But what on earth for!" Harriet demanded.

Tagaca, the oldest girl among the orphans, was ready with the explanation. "You see, we girls must do all of the courting," she began, in her soft, musical voice. "So when we are ready to marry, we cut ourselves in this way. When we can do it and not cry out in pain, everyone knows that we are now women and can bear children bravely!"

Dijere was giggling self-consciously in the background, but Bill pressed for further information. "Just how do the girls go about their courting?" he asked. "And do the men really consent to the girls taking the initiative, always?"

Tagaca continued to speak, and others of the orphans gathered around and filled in the story with bits of information of their own. Even Dijere lost some of her feigned bashfulness and interjected a word here and there. Bill learned a good deal that afternoon about the marriage customs of the Indians . . .

After cutting themselves on the abdomen, the girls are ready to look for a husband. This they do quite shamelessly, painting their faces and abdomens, singing and generally carrying on so as to attract the attention of the man of their choice. No matter how much he might care for one of the girls, a man must in no wise take the initiative. Usually, the unmarried women make their plans during the day while the young men are off in the woods, hunting. On the return, the girl meets the one of her choice on the trail, carries his pack into camp and prepares whatever food he might have brought in from the hunt. They eat together and spend the night together by her fire.

Bill Pencille's house (left) and church in Zapocó.

Left, some of the first Indians at Zapocó pause on the edge of the jungle. For a long time the Indians preferred to spend months hunting in the jungle rather than to settle permanently in Zapocó.

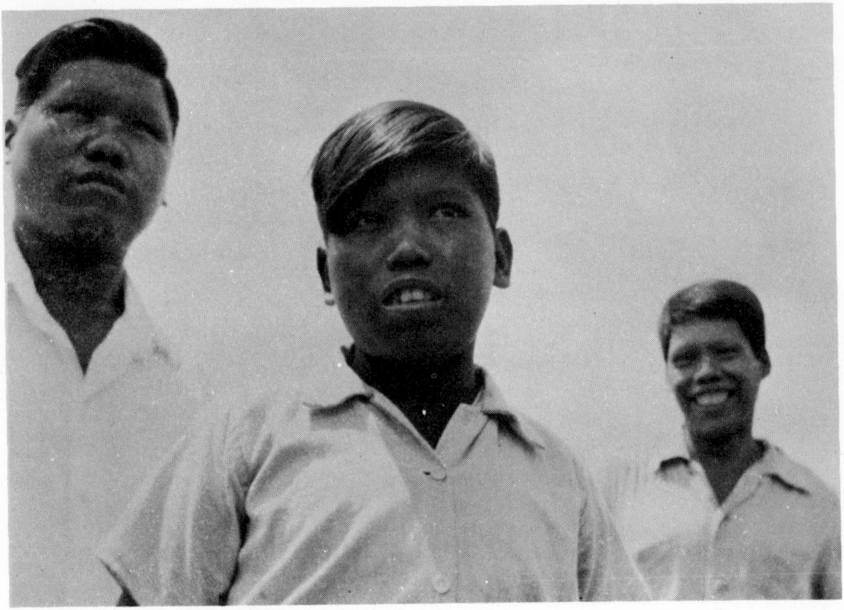

These are some of the first Christian Ayorés in Zapocó.

Often, at least for the first year or two, it becomes a trial and error type of marriage. When a child is born before the girl feels herself really in love with any particular boy, the baby is buried alive and she has no more responsibility. There is a social law in the tribe that says you are not married until you have a live child. So, of course, since you no longer have a living child, you are not married!

Bill soon found that these girls became most indignant when asked who their husband was. "I don't have a husband!" would be the response. "Can't you see I have no children? I'm not married!"

Tagaca went on to explain how they were finally married. "But when we really love someone, then we keep his child. In a few days it is named, and the whole family takes the baby's name. Then we are really married."

"Now I understand!" Bill exclaimed. "That's why Dajei is called Tarane now that they have a baby girl, Tara!"

"Yes," Tagaca went on. "And the mother is Taranate. The grandmother is Taranacode, and the grandfather, Taranaquide. They are all named after Tara."

Dijere was in the trial marriage stage. She was the most attractive girl in camp, and several of the young men were objects of her advances. On more than one occasion she practiced her coquetry on Bill. She had a quick temper, however. One day, furious with her husband-for-a-day, she began throwing his blanket, his bag, his honey gourd — all his possessions — into a bonfire. The Indians gathered round to see the fun, and the missionaries hearing the commotion ran up and tried to remonstrate with her. It was useless; she was wild with rage.

Angel Bravo had just ridden up after attending to the mission cattle. He dismounted, a small braided whip hanging from his wrist. Forcing his way through the crowd of wildly cheering Indians, he gave Dijere two light blows across the small of her back. It didn't even color the skin, but it certainly had the desired effect. She calmed down immediately, and sat sulking silently by her fire the remainder of the day.

When Angel's whip fell, an ominous murmur swept through the group of Indians. At that time, no one understood that the Ayorés believe that any blow will drive evil spirits into a person and cause sickness.

Months later, a growth appeared on Dijere's back. The missionaries tried in vain to cure it. Dijere was no longer her robust, buxom self. She became thin and emaciated. Eventually, however, the mysterious growth disappeared, leaving Dijere but a shadow of her old self.

A year passed, and a grippe epidemic swept through the camp. Some ninety Indians left Zapocó to escape the sickness. Dijere and her husband, Jemi, went with them. They traveled south toward San Miguel, a small Bolivian farming community. Several months later a traveler brought the news that a small boy had been cruelly murdered by the Indians. There was no question but that it was the work of the Ayorés. But why? After having had contact so long with the Gospel how could they have killed a boy in cold blood?

Weeks later, the group returned to Zapocó. Bill was in front of his house watching them as they came, one by one, up the path from the river. He looked for Dijere among the group, but did not see her. Finally her husband Jemi came, alone. Bill walked over to him and asked for Dijere.

The Indian was angry and sullen. With a scornful look he turned his back on Bill. "You ought to know!" he said.

Bill tried again. "Come on, where's Dijere?"

Jemi almost spat the words through clenched teeth. "She's dead!"

"Oh, I'm sorry!" Bill said.

"You big liar!" Jemi challenged, whirling around. "Angel killed her!"

"Why, Jemi, you know how much we all loved Dijere! How could that be? You —"

"Angel killed her! He whipped her! When we were in the jungle the spirits entered her back again — right where Angel drove in the sickness with his whip. She grew thin and died. If she had died here, I'd have killed Angel, and you, too! She died in the woods. But I got even — I killed the first white person I saw! It was a little boy gathering firewood. I got even!"

Angel had stepped on cultural toes, Bill mused, and it cost an innocent boy his life!

Some days later when Jemi was in a more communicative mood, Bill tried again to get information from him.

"Tell me, Jemi, how did Dijere die?"

"I already told you that. The lump came back on her back and killed her," he replied.

"I don't mean that. Did she ever talk of Dupade after she left here?" Bill persisted.

"Dupade!" Jemi spoke derisively. "That was *all* she talked about! Every day, she prayed to Him. Then, when she grew weak and couldn't talk very well, she made us pray to Him for her!"

Bill and Harriet were greatly encouraged. This was the second evidence of real fruit among the young people of the Ayorés. There was soon to be still further evidence of the working of the Holy Spirit.

The orphans had lived in the Pencille home for an entire year when Tagaca came to Bill and said, "I want to go under the water. I love the Lord Jesus."

She had witnessed baptisms of the Bolivian converts in the Zapocó river, and through the daily devotions that Harriet had with the orphans she had come to understand the Gospel. But Bill was filled with doubts. Could this savage girl, sweet-tempered and humble though she was, really understand the gospel message?

Months went by. Bill still had not consented to baptize Tagaca. Finally, the girl approached Harriet. She was sad and a bit indignant. "Don Guillermo doesn't believe me!"

"Why, of course he believes you, Tagaca! What do you mean?" asked Harriet.

"No, he doesn't," she replied, her eyes filled with tears. "I told him I loved the Lord Jesus, and wanted to be put under the water. But he won't believe me! He won't do it. He does not believe me."

When Harriet told Bill of her conversation with Tagaca, he was rebuked. If the girl had so openly confessed Christ as her Saviour, who was he to deny her baptism?

Bill sought out the girl. "Tagaca," he said, "I've been wrong in doubting your faith. Forgive me. If you want to be baptized, I am ready to do it."

They announced it in the camp, and went down to the river and put Tagaca "under the water." It wasn't long before others began to follow her example.

17.

A Hard Campaign

Another of the problems that arose when Bill tried to settle nomadic Indians in a fixed location was what to eat. For centuries, they had lived from the forest, traveling a little each day and eating whatever game, fruit and roots they could find nearby. To exist, the tribe had divided into small groups to facilitate hunting. When four hundred Indians settled in Zapocó, it wasn't long before there were no turtles or honey within miles of the camp. If they were to continue living there, some substitute would have to be found.

At first, Bill bought tools for them — axes, machetes, hoes — and encouraged them to farm for themselves. This was not too successful. For one thing, the cattle on the ranch were constantly breaking their makeshift fences and eating the crops. *How do you convince Indians to build a good fence?* Bill wondered.

From the beginning, it was felt wise not to give the Indians free food. They had to learn to work for whatever they received. This decision often made them angry, for they refused to understand why a person as "rich" as Bill wouldn't divide all he had among them! And to them, Bill *was* fabulously rich — anyone with one shirt was richer than an Ayoré who had none!

The Pencilles kept a "missionary barrel" of used clothing, and whenever an Indian wanted clothes, Bill would have him clean up the yard or bring firewood or do some other little job. Of course, the work he did wouldn't be worth a fraction of what he got in payment; but at least, he was learning to work.

For several years Bill struggled against the ideas of setting up a farm program in Zapocó. He felt it would weaken the spiritual side of his ministry. He wanted nothing to interfere with his primary aim — that of teaching the Indians about Jesus Christ. It took three years, until 1953, to realize that these early ideas were more idealistic than practical. He could not preach the Gospel to a congregation suffering from acute hunger pangs! Soon the game and honey around Zacopó were exhausted. The Indians harvested little from their garden plots and were unable to support their families. In short, there was nothing in Zapocó to hold the Indians long enough to preach the Gospel to them. They began to wander farther and farther afield in search of food.

One afternoon, Paoi came running down the road, through the camp and up to Bill's house. "Don Guillermo," he said breathlessly. "We are all going to Las Piedras to work! Don Daniel wants us to clear his land. He will give us trousers for our work."

Bill knew full well what would happen if the Indians moved to Las Piedras. They would clear don Daniel's land all right, but would never get paid. Daniel had never been one to pay his debts — especially when the creditor was an Indian!

The decision was made in a moment. "No," Bill said. "It would be better if you stayed here and farmed for me. I'll pay you for the work — and better than Daniel!"

The very first day of "farming" Bill learned a new lesson. He rounded up the able-bodied men and set them to felling trees. At noon he called a halt and told them to report back to work at 2:30. The hour came, he rang the work bell, and no one showed up! He went to the Indian camp to investigate and found Paoi seated by his fire making a new arrow.

"Come on, let's get to work," Bill said.

"Not us!"

"Why not?"

"You lied! You said you would pay us — we worked all morning and got no pay. We won't work any more!"

So Bill learned that the only way to keep things moving would be to pay them twice a day. He paid them at noon and again in the evening. Even so, he would have forty Indians working one day, and the next day not one would appear. They had all decided to go on a honey hunt!

Bill paid the workers with Bolivian money, in this way

teaching them its value. The Indians were intelligent and learned quickly, using their earnings to buy what they wanted at the mission store. They bought just enough food for one meal at a time. In the early days neighboring ranchers would take advantage of their ignorance and pay them any ridiculous price for a new axe or a new shirt that they had worked many days to earn. This was soon remedied under the new system. Once they knew the true value of money, no one could beat them at trading.

Even the old women who could not have learned to read or write, soon recognized the value of Bolivian currency. Inflation had long since put all coins out of circulation, and only paper money of large denomination was in use. Bills of five hundred and a thousand bolivianos were very common.

These numbers were often the first Spanish words that many of the Ayorés bothered to learn. One of the young women, undoubtedly trying to be sophisticated, used her new Spanish vocabulary to name her children. Her oldest boy was Quinientos (five hundred) and his little brother Doscientoscincuenta (two hundred fifty). Her name, of course, was Quinientosnate — "mother of five hundred"!

In spite of the obstacles, the land was finally cleared. With the first rains, Bill took the Indians out to plant corn. Everything had to be done by hand. The little holes were dug with a hoe and the kernels dropped in. The soil was pushed back in place with the side of the foot. Even though he was working in a field dotted with numerous half-burned stumps of fallen logs, Bill decided he would try to do things in an orderly fashion, and teach the Indians to plant in a straight row.

He chose the most intelligent of the budding farmers and said, "Do you see that dead tree over there? O.K., you keep your eye on it. Dig the hole about an arrow's length apart and keep heading for that tree. Don't go the right or to the left — straight ahead!"

The Indian laughed and said anyone could understand something that simple. Bill set him off and began instructing the next man. But by the time the third one had started, the first one was heading off to parts unknown and the second one had done a half-circle and was heading in the opposite direction. Finally, the holes were all dug in a not-too-straight line. They were ready to plant the corn.

"O.K., fellows," Bill said. "Four kernels to every hole!"

The Ayorés roared with laughter. "White men are more stupid than we thought! All this work and now he only wants a little corn to come up! Four kernels aren't enough — we will put handfuls in!"

Bill kept his patience. "Look, fellows. When you work for me, you have to do as I say. When you plant for yourselves, plant as much as you want. But I'm paying you to obey me — four kernels it is, and no arguments! If I don't get any corn, then laugh at me at harvest time!"

Grumbling, they set to work; and the ones Bill could watch put only four kernels in each hill. But the old men went off into the corners and threw in seed by the handfuls. When the day was ended, they had a good laugh — they had put one over on Bill! But they had forgotten that the corn would sprout some day. When it did, Bill took them back and made them pull it all up except four plants in each hill. After they had pulled it up, Bill said,

"All right, men. You disobeyed me and planted corn by the handfuls. Now you've pulled up the extra plants, but I won't pay you for this work. This was your own fault for disobeying."

They began to grumble again, but Bill continued, "You know, you thought you were putting something over on me. But you forgot one thing; you forgot that the corn was going to sprout one day! You see, when it came up I found out what you had done and you had to pull it up. You know, God is just like that. God says, 'Don't let anyone deceive you; no one can make God of no account. What is harvested is just like what is sown.' Everything you do in the darkness of your own houses — all of your wickednesses, your murders, your adulteries, your evil language — it's all going to meet you again some day, face to face, and you're going to have to pay for it to God, just like you paid for planting the handfuls of corn!"

If the Indians had laughed at Bill at planting time, their mirth at the first hoeing was unbounded. Bill's straggly four stalks to a hill looked miserable in comparison to the lush green growth that covered their thickly-planted corn plots. But when harvest came, it was all Bill could do to refrain from saying "I told you so!" Some of the ears of corn in his field were as big as his forearm, while those in the Indians' plots were more like their thumbs. The next year in every Indian corn plot were exactly four plants to a hill, well-spaced and planted neatly in rows!

The Ayorés were a proud people. They had their way of doing things which had worked for their forefathers and still worked, after a fashion, for them. Why change? Bill tried to teach them better farming methods, and they would respond angrily, "Don't teach us! We've been farming long before you were born!" It was all pointed up quite vividly one day when Bill had the men working in the little plaza between the houses. He tells the story of what occurred.

"There were about twenty of them, naked men and boys, working out in front of the house. When they work together like this, there is always a good deal of noise and friendly banter; and this day was no different. One poor fellow seemed to be bearing the brunt of their jokes. He was a natural bungler and nothing seemed to go right for him. They laughed uproariously at him, and called him *coñoi.* This means 'white man'! You see, they were equating a bungler with a white man!

"When I heard this, my blood really began to boil. I felt like telling them off for dragging down the vaunted white race in this way. After all, what right did these naked stone-age savages have to feel so high and mighty! But then, I realized just what it was — the pride of race which is in every one of us — and I had to chuckle at the thought of it.

"You soon come to realize how much like us they are. True, their language is different. Their skin is brown. Their customs are strange. But we all have the same father, and his name was Adam!

"This also brought me to realize that the only way I could ever teach them would be by example. Rather than just tell them how to do something, I would have to let them see it work and so realize that there were other and better ways of doing some things. They were all from Missouri — they would have to be shown!"

The farm program was highly successful, and thereafter there was always an abundance of food at Zapocó. But it never completely solved the problem of keeping the Indians at home. The old folks would come to Bill time and again, angry, and say, "We're leaving!"

"Why?" Bill would ask.

"There's no food here!"

"No food! There's all kinds of food! There's rice and corn and beans and sugar and squash and sweet potatoes and bananas! What do you want? You've got plenty here!"

"Liar! There's no food! We want honey!" To them, honey was synonymous with food. Off they would go to the woods, angry with Bill because there was no honey.

You can take an Indian out of the woods, but you cannot take the woods out of an Indian. Civilization could not easily cure their wanderlust and inbred nomadic instinct. At first, they would go back to the jungle to hunt. But they were always uncomfortable because of the insects. They soon found it easier to travel the roads from ranch to ranch, in spite of Bill's warnings.

"You liar," they would say to Bill. "All the white people are good to us! You just want to keep us here to work for you." And off they would go to visit the nearest ranch.

But they soon learned. The white ranchers put them to work but "forgot" to pay them. The white men bought their tools and weapons and cheated them on the prices. They stole their children to raise as household slaves. They seduced their wives and daughters. Colds and grippe would pass from the white people to the Indians, but no one would give them so much as an aspirin. Finally, the Indians began to learn that their life in Zapocó was not too bad, and that Bill and Harriet were their only real friends.

The greatest attraction of all was the railroad line, two hundred miles to the south. Their friends from Tobité who visited them made it out to be a land of milk and honey. "You can ride all day on the train, free, if you climb up on top of the coaches!" they explained to an enthralled audience. "There is plenty of work and good pay. People will give you five thousand bolivianos (forty cents) for one turtle."

They were easily convinced; the grass is always greener

on the other side of the fence! It was heartbreaking for Bill and Harriet to see their "children" go off to the railroad line. But they had to learn for themselves. Most of them came back after the novelty wore off. Some, however, never returned. Three girls of whom Harriet had been very fond, discovered that there was plenty of money to be had along the railroad line with no work at all involved. They took up the world's oldest profession, and by selling their bodies the three soon became wealthy, by Ayoré standards. They could buy make-up and brightly colored clothes. But they broke Harriet's heart. "What does it profit a man if he gains the whole world and loses or forfeits himself?"

There was a big exodus from Zapocó after the fire. One morning, Bill was awakened by a commotion in the camp. Everybody seemed to be running in and out of the houses and throwing their belongings into the plaza.

"What's the matter?" Bill shouted as he dashed toward the camp. Just then, he spotted a wisp of smoke coming from the thatched roof of one of the huts. Fire!

Fortunately, there was no wind and the dew had dampened the highly inflammable roofs somewhat. Bill called the Indians together and they started tearing the roofs off as many houses as possible. They saved all but six houses. The entire camp could easily have been reduced to a pile of ashes if prompt action hadn't been taken.

When things calmed down a bit and everyone was seated on the ground in the open plaza watching the smouldering ruins, Bill called Comai over and asked what had happened.

"Asidate and Nuidate got into an argument," he replied. "I've never seen two women so mad! But Nuidate was getting the best of the argument, so Asidate grabbed some fire and touched it to the roof of her house!"

"But Nuidate's house didn't burn!" Bill protested.

"No. I mean Asidate set fire to her *own* house!"

"To her *own* house! What in the world did she do that for?"

"To get revenge," replied Comai calmly, as if it were the most natural thing in the world to burn your own house down just because you are angry! Bill didn't push the point.

By then, he was accustomed to surprises. But later, he wrote:

"The houses were the least of the loss. They can be rebuilt with just hard work and material from the surrounding jungles. More serious is the fact that over half of the families here have left for the railroad line. They followed the lead of the offended chief whose wife was one of the guilty parties in the fight, and whose house was burned in the process . . . perhaps you can see just a bit more clearly now that our battle is really against Satan and his hordes, who will do everything in their power to keep these people from coming to a saving knowledge of Christ."

18.

The Eternal Triangle

One day, Tarane came to Bill with a delegation of Indians, and a formal request.

"We want you to come with us to kill the Guidaigosode!" he began. "You have guns, and if you will go along, we can make short work of them!"

"Who are these Guidaigosode, anyway?" Bill questioned.

"Oh, they are very, very bad Indians!" Tarane affirmed.

To this the entire delegation agreed loudly, and for a time Bill was not able to make sense of what they were saying, for all were talking at once. They trembled with anger as they recounted the misdeeds of the terrible Guidaigosode! Gradually the story became clear.

Until some fifty years ago, the whole Ayoré tribe had lived in a narrow belt in the southern part of the Bolivian Chaco, probably somewhere around the still-mysterious remains of San Ignacio de Zamuco. They were closed in by enemies on all sides. The Matacos pushed up from the south, the Terenas lived toward Brazil to the east, the Guarayos and the Sirionós to the west and north.

As the Ayorés began to increase in strength, they pushed their enemies back. Their territory expanded and gradually they became separated as a tribe. The Guidaigosode moved south, fighting the Matacos. The Direquedenagosode, the northern branch which was settled in Tobité and Zapocó, fought the Guarayos. But as they pushed on in opposite directions there grew a no-man's-land between the formerly united groups. Bad blood developed between them, and eventually they each turned against the other. A violent civil war exploded, with each sub-tribe confidently flexing its muscles after years of constant victory in war. The struggle went badly, however, for the northern groups. They were roundly defeated by the Guidaigosode. Hundreds of them were killed, and Guidaigosode raiding parties kept driving the others well up to the north of what is now the railroad line.

The resulting fear of the Guidaigosode was one reason why things went so well in the missionaries' contacts in Tobité and Zapocó. They looked to the white men and their guns for a measure of protection against their blood enemies. They never tired of urging the white men to go with them to do battle.

"God does not want us to kill our enemies, Tarane," Bill said. "We are to love them."

With a look of scorn, Tarane shot back, "You love them if you like! We won't! They didn't kill your father, or your mother, or your brother! We hate them!"

With heavy heart, Bill realized that the god of Asoná, who is a murderer from the beginning, was far from defeated.

Most of the immediate family groups of the northern branch of the tribe were now in Zapocó, but there were a few others, farther removed and more distantly related, who evidently would not come voluntarily to the mission. The largest of these groups lived along the Paragua River north of San Ignacio. Since the establishment of the Indians at Zapocó, the army and civil authorities of the region recognized that the evangelical missionaries had a special right to work with the Indians. Although this was advantageous in many ways, it also presented difficulties. Whenever the Indians attacked or killed in some outlying ranch or village, the sure reaction would be, "Look what *your* Indians did!" After a particularly bloody raid made by one of the groups along the Paragua River, Frank Pickering decided to try to contact these Indians and bring to a halt this bloodshed and plunder.

He consulted Bill and Ray Frazier, and it was decided that he take Indian guides from Zapocó. Bill also sent Comai to act as interpreter. Angel Bravo and John Hamm, a former automobile mechanic from Canada and new missionary, were eager to go. Jemi and Paoi, two of the young braves of Zapocó, completed the party. God blessed this expedition, guiding them in a few days to the Indian village. Paoi and Jemi, stripping off their clothes, easily made contact with the new group; and the Indians received Frank in a friendly manner.

The leader of this group was a most remarkable Ayoré named Cutaide. Tall, muscular, stoic, and with a slight deformity in his back, he maintained absolute authority in the tribe. It took Frank a long time to break through his hard, self-imposed shell, but once he did, Cutaide responded by making Frank chief in his place. In a dramatic jungle ceremony involving war cries, mock battles and the placing of a symbolic black necklace over Frank's head, power was transferred from the Indian to the missionary.

Although nearly paralyzed by fear throughout the ritual, Frank was able to maintain an outward calm with God's help. He accepted the position, then made the promise to protect the tribe from all enemies — Indian or white.

There were some seventy people in the group, and Cutaide said their tribal name was Nupedogosode. That night around the fire, Comai explained to Frank what the name meant.

"We are all Ayorés," he began, "These people have the same seven clans we have in Zapocó. The Guidaigosode are Ayorés, too. They also have only seven clans or families, in all of their group."

Frank interrupted. "But what does the word *gosode* have to do with it?"

"You see," continued Comai, "there is not enough food in the jungle to feed many Indians in one place. Another thing, we have so many chiefs who are jealous of their power, that they cannot live close to one another. So the Ayorés live in small groups scattered about all of the jungle. Each group has a name which usually tells something about them or the part of the forest they live in. Nupedogosode means 'people of the hole in the ground.' Guidaigosode means 'people of the village'."

"What are the folks in Zapocó?" Angel wanted to know.

"We are mostly Direquedenagosode, which means 'people of another day'."

"Say," Frank said, suddenly. "You saw how Cutaide made me a chief this afternoon. Is that the way they always make their chiefs?"

Comai laughed. "No," he replied. "That was special for

Chief Cutaide and his son.

An Ayoré man becomes a chief by killing either a jaguar or a man. The blond is Dick Pencille, Bill's oldest son.

An Ayoré youth makes a new kind of spear (pp. 166-167).
He wears a decorated clam shell (which shows he is unmarried), beads made from the seed of a water plant, and the traditional woven belt.

you, a white man. That would be too easy for an Ayoré! We have to kill a jaguar or a man before we have the right to lead others!"

Now it was Angel's turn. "How about the seven clans? What in the world are they?"

Comai was patient with their questioning. After all, white men were known to be quite ignorant of the ways of the forest . . .

"It's this way. There are only seven families, or last names, in all Ayoréland. I am a *Chiquenore.* Each of the clans has its own *edopasai.* Of course, you wouldn't know about them, either. They are animals and birds who protect us from Asoná, and give us what we need to live in the forest. When a girl begins to court a man, it must be some one from another clan with a different *edopasai.*"

The fire had burned down and a chill wind blew over the little camp. The Indians had long since fallen asleep, exhausted by the excitement of the day — the first friendly contact with white men! Frank and Angel tied their hammocks between the trees. Comai, Jemi, and Paoi simply rolled up in their blankets beside the glowing embers of the fire. Jemi noticed as he dropped off to sleep that *Edocarate,* the red star, was in mid-heavens. He must be careful to remember that these were the months in which the world was closed up!

Three months were to pass while Frank and Angel roamed the forest of the Paragua River, searching for a suitable location in which to settle the new Indians. Both Paoi and Jemi had wives back in Zapocó, and missed them greatly.

One day Cutaide's young daughter, Ajote, announced she was in love with Jemi, and that one of her girl friends had been attracted to Paoi. The whole affair called for a chief-to-chief conference, in which Cutaide asked Frank's permission for the marriage. Frank knew that for an Ayoré it was unthinkable that a man of their age be without a partner; so he thought it best not to interfere with the ceremony. Immediately, some of the men set to building an Indian-style shelter of palm branches. Jemi and Paoi then crawled into the hut and sat down. Then the men of the village picked up their weapons and set out on a hunting trip, in search of the day's food.

By now, the women had worked themselves up to a high pitch of excitement, and with much commotion and giggling took the two girls over to the palm shelter. The young ladies, probably not over twelve years of age, covered their mouths with their hands and looked at the ground in feigned bashfulness. They pretended they were being forced into marriage against their wills.

Actually, everyone knew full well that the girls, following Ayoré custom, had engineered the whole affair. They had fallen in love with the visitors at first sight. When they reached the shelter one of the girls sat down with Jemi and the other near Paoi.

The men returned late in the afternoon with their honey gourds overflowing and their packs filled with turtles. A wedding feast was in order. As night fell each of the brides kindled a fire in front of her husband, symbolically consummating the marriages. When the shadows darkened and the fires burned very low, the camp became still. The young lovers fell asleep in each others' arms.

Frank and the Indians scoured the area in search of a permanent camp site, but with no success. Finally, it was decided to take the Indians to Zapocó. Normally, they would never have agreed to such a move. Many years ago there had been a bloody quarrel and the two groups had separated and were sworn enemies. But Frank was chief; and no one questioned his wisdom or right to take them to Zapocó. They confidently expected him to protect them from their enemies. Could Frank have known what lay ahead, he might have searched longer for another campsite!

He sent John to Zapocó to get Bill. With Bill's jeep truck and Pickerings' power wagon, they began the move. They were well aware that the most difficult part of the trip would be the passage through the town of San Ignacio. Anything could happen in a town that had always been fanatically hostile toward the Protestants. Furthermore, many of the villagers had at one time or another sworn revenge on the *bárbaros* for past atrocities. When the motley crew of naked, stone-age Indians passed through on the trucks, there was more excitement in San Ignacio than during one of their frequent religious festivals. Fortunately, though, there was no trouble, and the group arrived intact in Zapocó.

Four months had gone by since Cutaide and his people abandoned their haunts on the Paragua River. They had been months of an uneasy peace between the rival groups settled in Zapocó. It was now October, the end of the dry season. Asoná had opened the world again, and the Ayorés had again paid her homage. Soon the rains would flood the rivers and make fishing impossible, so Cutaide took his group upstream on their last fishing trip of the season. They were camped three miles from Zapocó.

Each Saturday, Bill was accustomed to making the rounds of the camp, checking the tools against a written list. He had loaned the Indians axes and knives so they could clear their farms, but Indians easily "forgot" that the tools were loaned, not given, and they soon claimed them as their own unless frequently reminded otherwise! On this particular afternoon as Bill was setting out with Comai for the weekly check, Angel came galloping up. He had been assigned the job of caring for the mission cattle.

"They've stolen the wire!" he said as he slid from his horse.

"What wire?" Bill wanted to know.

"All the wire we had the corral tied together with! Now it's gone, the whole corral is falling to pieces. I can't be responsible for the damage the cattle will do to the Indians' crops." Angel was visibly upset.

Bill thought a moment, then said, "Thanks for the information. Let's check on it right now. We're heading for the camp."

Angel had been right. Without the wire ties, the corral had completely come apart.

The Indians were in an ugly mood, sitting or standing about in small groups, silent and sullen. Bill asked to see the tools, but no one made a move or said a word. They would answer no questions about the wire. Definitely, something was wrong. Bill knew them well enough to sense danger when it presented itself. Then he spotted a brand-new war lance leaning against the back of one of the huts!

The Indians had invented a new and more efficient type of weapon since living with the missionaries. They would knock the wooden handle off a machete and use the knife blade for the spear tip, which they inserted into a hardwood handle. Fifteen or twenty tightly-wrapped turns of wire held the knife securely in place. As Bill went from house to house, he found no machetes. But he did find dozens of new war lances — all tied together with the wire from the corral!

Bill continued asking questions here and there. He realized that trouble was afoot, and he intended to discover what it was. Little by little the Indians admitted they had made plans for war. They would leave the next morning at sun-up and massacre Cutaide and his people.

What to do now? Once again the missionaries were thrown back completely on the mercy of God. Humanly speaking, it would be impossible to prevent a civil war; but try they must! With Comai interpreting when necessary, they talked to the Indians until midnight; talking, arguing, praying, cajoling — anything to get them to change their minds, and call off the impending battle.

Finally, the warriors' mood softened. The chiefs sat down with Bill for a pow-wow. They admitted that the missionaries were right and agreed not to go to war. Cutaide and his people could live. They would even make good the loss of the machetes and the wire! Worn out but rejoicing, the missionaries that night slept the sleep of utter exhaustion.

The day was breaking when John Hamm stepped outside his house. Things at the Indian camp seemed strangely quiet. As he stood looking in that direction trying to figure out what could be wrong, an Ayoré woman came up to him. "They've gone!" she said.

"Who has gone?" John asked.

"The men. They have gone to kill Cutaide!"

"But last night they promised they wouldn't go!" John protested.

"After the missionaries left, the women began ridiculing the men. They nagged them all night long, saying they were cowards, and afraid to fight! Now they have gone to kill!"

As the woman broke the news to John, a little boy standing nearby ran down the stony path toward the river where Bill was watering his vegetable garden. John followed him on the run. By the time he got there, Bill had dropped his watering can and was running toward his house.

"They've gone to fight!" John yelled after him.

"I know it! Let's get moving!"

They raced toward the jeep, calling to Comai on the way. Bill jumped into the driver's seat, but before John could climb in beside him, he said, "Wait a minute! I'm going to get some guns!"

This was without a doubt the most dangerous situation the missionaries had faced since the initial contacts. What would it be like to stand between two bands of fierce savages intent on murder?

Bill returned with the guns and started the motor. Suddenly John exclaimed, "Bill, we don't have enough gas! I forgot to fill the tank last night — I'm not sure we have enough to reach the other side of the camp!"

Bill made a lightning decision. "We can't do anything about that now! Let's get going and take our chances. If the Lord wants us to get there, He'll make sure the gas holds out!"

The jeep was off with a roar and a cloud of dust. They overtook the war party halfway to Cutaide's camp. Their bodies were painted completely black. Each man wore all the feathers he owned, and the neck feathers were ominously pointing straight up in the sign of war. They had smeared their chests and abdomens with bees' wax in which countless tiny white feathers were stuck. Each man was armed with three or four weapons. This was war!

Bill revved the jeep up to full speed as they roared past. They wanted to reach Cutaide's camp first and warn him. As they passed, the Indians shouted for them to stop. Bill drove another half mile or so before coming to a halt. He needed time to think. Up to this point, everything had been done almost by instinct without time to plan or figure out their next move. All he could do was play it by ear and trust in God.

Bill and John each got out of his side of the jeep and left the doors open, with their guns inside within easy reach. There they waited as the sweating Ayorés came running up the trail towards them. They had no idea what they would do.

The chief was in the lead. "Where are you going?" he called out as he drew near.

"We're going to warn and defend the others!" Bill replied in a harsh voice. His face was grim and set. "You know better than to go through with this crazy plan!" Both Bill and John were braced for action, ready for the first arrow to fly through the air towards them.

But the chief's mood seemed to change. "Well, what do you want us to do?"

"I told you last night what I wanted you to do!" Bill replied in the same determined voice.

"It's not my fault!" the chief started to excuse himself. "Five men swore to kill Cutaide. But if you will give them each a blanket they will call the war off!"

Bill felt that five blankets was a cheap enough price in exchange for what could be scores of lives! The bargain was made.

The jeep looked like some pre-historic porcupine as it pulled up in front of the Pencille's house. Every Indian who could possibly get inside or on top was there, squatting down with his war spears sticking up. Bill recalls, "What a picture it would have made! And I almost lost my life trying to take it. When I went for my camera, tempers flared. I learned that there are times when you just do not take pictures of the Ayorés! This was one of those times!"

When the Indians got down and walked over to their camp, John got back into the jeep and stepped on the starter. The engine sputtered and stopped. Out of gas!

One problem was momentarily solved, but how about Cutaide and his people? Had word of the intended assault reached them? Would he and his Indians still be in their camp? Or had they fled in terror into the forest?

Bill had to find out. That same afternoon, he packed food and medicine into his army rucksack and set out on foot for Cutaide's camp, Comai at his side. Too much time and effort had been spent on Cutaide and his group to lose contact with them now. These were souls for whom Christ died, and they needed to know of Him. Bill could give Harriet no idea as to when he would return.

These partings, when it became necessary for Bill to travel with the Indians, were never easy for Harriet and their children. Now, with all the danger and uncertainty involved it was especially difficult. But He who said, "My grace is sufficient for thee," also said, "As thy days, so shall thy strength be." Somehow, somewhere, there was always strength enough to go through with it when the time came.

The fishing camp by the riverbank was deserted when Bill and Comai arrived. It was obvious that the Indians had fled in confusion, and it was difficult for even an expert tracker to pick up the trail. The entire afternoon was spent in fruitlessly following one path after another, only to discover that the savages had taken special pains to cover their trail. Even Comai was confused and at his wits' end.

Just before sundown, however, they were able to pick up the main trail. Before long, they were in the midst of a confused, terror-stricken mass of Indians. They accepted Bill and Comai without question, and listened quietly as Bill told them what had occurred. When he finished, Cutaide arose and said, "Tomorrow, we will leave at daylight. We shall return to our old hunting grounds!"

There is no radio in Ayoréland, no television, no newspapers. All of the current news as well as the history and lore of the tribe is passed on by storytellers around the evening campfires. That night, around one of these fires, Bill and Comai learned the answer to the question that was plaguing them — what had caused this civil war?

It proved to be nothing less than the proverbial love-triangle. Jemi, before going with Frank in search of Cutaide's group, was already married to the daughter of one of Zapocó's witch doctors. Then, while he was in the woods to the north he was remarried, this time to Cutaide's daughter. Predictably, the two girls did not get along together in Zapocó. Then the in-laws got into the quarrel and the result was war! Cutaide announced that he had put a curse on the father of the other girl. In retaliation, the girl's father persuaded his group to "beat their machetes into war spears!" He was saying in effect, "Let's see how strong this impostor's curse is against weapons like these!"

Bill wrote later, "They say it's love that makes the world go round . . . well, it makes it go, anyway!"

Bill tried to convince the Indians to either return to Zapocó or to settle down somewhere else with the missionaries — anything but return to the jungle. Cutaide and his men loved Bill, but would have no part of this suggestion. Their lives had been threatened by a superior force, and precipitous flight was the only means they knew of protecting themselves.

Unable to bring himself to abandon them, Bill continued to travel with them as they fled. They readily accepted and appreciated his presence. One night, in a deserted ranch called Santa Elena, Bill was awakened by a weird noise. In the bright moonlight he could make out the hunchbacked form of Cutaide, performing some sort of ritual. He seemed to be in agony. Bill caught a few of the words he was chanting, especially the repetition of the name for God, "Dupade."

It was apparent that the event must have some sort of religious significance, but Bill couldn't make out what was going on. When it was over, Comai stole over to Bill's hammock and whispered, "Cutaide just had a vision! He saw God! God told him that He didn't have to be afraid any more. His enemies in Zapocó won't do him any harm!"

"Do you think he believed it?" Bill asked.

"All Ayorés believe their visions," Comai assured him.

"Let's talk to him," Bill said, rolling out of his hammock. They walked over to the chief who obviously was still in the throes of a tremendous emotional crisis.

"Cutaide," said Bill, "did you see God?"

The flickering firelight illuminated Cutaide's raised eyebrows.

"What was He like?"

"God is good! He loves the Ayorés! He will protect us!" intoned the chief, impressively.

"Cutaide, would you like to please God?" asked Bill.

"God is good to Cutaide. Cutaide will be good to God!"

"Then, Cutaide, you should become a child of God! God wants to be your Father. You know what it means to confess your sins and to trust in Jesus to forgive you, don't you?" Bill had explained the Gospel to him countless times.

The chief raised his eyebrows affirmatively, looking straight at Bill.

"Will you turn your life over to God and become one of His sons right now?"

"I want God to be my Father! I am a bad man, but I love Jesus! I want God to forgive me my sins, and I want to obey Him!"

Cutaide's experience with Dupade was the turning point in Bill's dealings with the frightened group; and the next morning they agreed to make permanent camp at the next suitable spot. After walking for about six miles, they found good water and fertile soil. The first little palm-leafed shelters that took shape there formed the humble beginning of the second station of the South America Indian Mission among the Ayorés. They named it Bella Vista, or "Beautiful View." It was eighteen miles up-river from Zapocó.

19.

A Little Leaven

THE SITUATION in Bella Vista was tense. Under the constant fear of surprise attack by the Zapocó Indians, Cutaide and his people lived in a depressing atmosphere of suspicion and hostility. On several occasions they fled back into the forest; and had it not been for Cutaide's determination mixed with his growing faith in God, the contact would have been irreparably broken.

Angel Bravo was the logical man to take charge of the new camp, but he was on vacation at the time, attending the annual Bible Conference in Santiago. Until his return, Bill and John Hamm took turns living at Bella Vista. This caused real hardship, for they themselves could hardly be spared from their duties in Zapocó.

Cutaide's influence on his people was strong, and one day when John was in Bella Vista, the power of the Holy Spirit manifested itself in an unusual way. Cutaide and some twenty others openly confessed their sins and expressed their desire to know Jesus Christ better, and to serve Him.

When Angel returned, he was anxious to move to Bella Vista and take charge of the Indians. It was a heavy responsibility to place on the shoulders of this young Bolivian pastor; but he was able, and his faith was strong. The Ayorés were overjoyed at seeing their old friend once again. He was the only Bolivian Christian capable of handling such a job, and no missionary was free at the time to help him.

Angel was delighted to learn of Cutaide's faith in Dupade, and rejoiced that the Indians were beginning to show an interest in spiritual things. He embraced the chief, and listened to his testimony as he told how he he had given up witchcraft and superstitions. But that same night, Angel was awakened by a strange disturbance among the Indians. The whole tribe was gathered around a small campfire, and Cutaide was in their midst.

"What is it?" Angel whispered to his wife who was now awake and had come to his side.

"I don't know," she said. "Is he going to start his witch doctor tricks again? Several of the Indians are sick."

"It looks like it, but let's wait a minute and see what happens. He told me just today that he was through with that kind of thing!"

Shortly, the general commotion seemed to die down. Cutaide thrust his spear in the ground. Leaning forward on it and swaying back and forth, he began a weird-sounding chant.

"What's he saying?" Julia murmured.

"I can't get too much of it," Angel responded. "I can understand a little, though — be quiet!" They strained to catch the strange words.

After two or three minutes, Angel grasped Julia's arm. "Why, Cutaide *is* through with witch doctoring — he's praying that Dupade will heal the sick Indians!"

As the days and weeks passed, it became more and more evident to the missionaries that Angel, with his wife Julia, were God's choice for Bella Vista. Daily he learned more of the Indian language. His experience on his father's farm and cattle ranch stood him in good stead as he taught these wild jungle nomads the first rudiments of agriculture, enabling them to grow their own food. He was architect and builder of all the houses. He was police chief with the responsibility of settling their endless quarrels. He was doctor, curing their ills as best he could. He was pastor with a genuine burden for the salvation of Ayoré souls. He was a living fulfillment of the Pauline example of "all things to all men." And the Indians loved him like a brother.

Bella Vista was founded in November, too late in the season to clear land for planting. During that long first year, all food supplies had to be carried up-river from Zapocó. It was not too difficult during the dry season, when the river was low. Although the river cut across the trail no less than ten times in as many miles, it could easily be forded. The last six miles of trail led right up the river bed itself.

When the spring rains began, however, supplying Bella Vista became a major problem. Pack oxen and horses were used for a while, but by February the river was 100 yards wide and twenty feet deep! The rains were heavy that year, and for a month it rained every day. Bill was extremely concerned. He wrote: "What were Angel and Julia eating? Had sickness struck since last we heard from them? How could we get food to them? These were just a few of the questions that forced themselves upon my troubled mind."

Bill decided that the only possible way to get supplies to Bella Vista at that time would be to carry them on their backs! It would be a difficult, dangerous task, and Bill never asked his people to do what he himself would not do. He asked for volunteers to go with him. Manuel the cowboy offered to go, as did ten of the Indians. They made small packs of only about thirty pounds, and each one carried a rubberized bag. When they reached the river, they would put their packs in the bags, tie them up at the mouth, and float them across the water. But at the first little tributary, really nothing more than a creek, normally, they were amazed to see it swollen to fifty yards in width and flowing swiftly. They had to swim across, dragging their rubber bags along behind them. At this point half of the Ayorés turned back — why should they risk their lives for their enemies in Bella Vista, they said! This meant that Bill and the others who remained were forced to carry double packs.

Bill tells the story of the trip: "Most of the next two days we spent in the water. The widest and deepest crossing meant a swim of a hundred yards. One of the Indian women had gone along with her husband to help carry the load. But when she saw that swirling water, she decided that it was just too much; she sat down at the edge of the river and refused to budge.

"Then we figured out how we could get her across, and she agreed to try. Tying all of our ropes together, we had one long enough to reach the other bank. Manuel took one end in his teeth and swam to the far side of the river. I tied a loop in our end and told Taranate to hold on to it for dear life. Then we both jumped in. I was swimming against the current to keep her from being washed downstream, and Manuel on the other end was pulling mightily.

"All went well until the full strength of the current caught us in midstream. Then Taranate panicked. With a scream, she let go of the rope and grabbed me around the neck! Swimming was impossible, and I was hard put to just keep both our heads above the water. The current carried us around a wide bend in the river, and right into the branches of a huge fallen tree which had become lodged among rocks in the river bed. While the Indians on the bank doubled with laughter, we made our way to shore on the branches and trunk of the tree!"

Since that day, the name of this river crossing has been *Taranate Batigai* — The Place Where Taranate Nearly Drowned!

Bill continues, "With our bodies a mass of painful cuts from the sharp swamp grass, and thoroughly soaked from head to foot, we trudged up the path from the river to Angel's little grass-roofed house. It had taken us three days to traverse the eighteen miles! We were indeed a bedraggled group, but a most welcome one. Julia had prepared the last of the food for the noon meal, and that afternoon had wept tears of bitter discouragement. Angel, to keep her spirits up, had sung hymns and choruses. As we approached they ran out and hugged us warmly. 'God certainly brought you to us at the right moment!' they said."

As time went on, several more of the Indians became Christians under Angel's ministry, and learned to pray publicly. But at no time was life easy in Bella Vista. A flu epidemic prostrated the entire tribe and three Ayorés died. When the rest had recuperated somewhat, they told Angel that they were going on a hunting trip. They asked him to watch over the things they were leaving in bags in their houses.

Weeks dragged into a month, and still they did not return. Angel became suspicious, and sent a messenger to Bill in Zapocó. He came immediately with Aside, the Zapocó witch doctor. When they reached Bella Vista, Aside's intuition told him that all was not well. He walked over to the abandoned houses and began looking around.

"They've gone for good!" he shouted as he ran back across the clearing. "They aren't even thinking of coming back!

"Look!" he said, as he dumped out the contents of one of the bags he had found in the Ayoré houses. Four or five large stones tumbled to the ground at the missionary's feet.

"So *this* is what they asked me to take care of!" Angel exclaimed with a mixture of anger and embarrassment in his voice. "Now what are we going to do, Bill? They have a thirty-day head start on us!"

The matter was something that needed careful thought. If the savages had left with a grudge, blaming the deaths on the missionaries, things might go very badly for the next white man they got their hands on. This was one of those decisions requiring more than mere human wisdom. In order to be sure of God's will, they decided to "put out the fleece," and ask God for a sign.

"We'll need two guides from Zapocó to make the trip," Bill said. "And there's no telling whether any of them will feel like helping look for their enemies. But if Tarane and Sirine, who are excellent in the woods, will go with us, let's take it as a sign that God wants us to go after Cutaide and his group!"

It seemed unlikely that the two Indians would go. When Bill returned to Zapocó he found that the Indians had all gone on a fishing trip; and moreover, they were half-sick with colds. To make matters worse, the Zapocó witch doctor announced he had just had a vision: "If anyone goes to search for the Bella Vista group, he will never return! He will be murdered in cold blood!"

In spite of all these obstacles, when Tarane and Sirine heard of the projected trip they accepted Bill's invitation to accompany him. God had given the sign. They went to Bella Vista and then headed out into the bush, following the faint footprints of the fleeing Indians.

Once on the trail the four made excellent time, and since Cutaide's group was traveling slowly, foraging for food as they went, it soon became apparent that they would have no trouble in catching up. Tarane and Sirine followed the almost invisible trail with the same ease with which

Bill would have found his way through the halls of Moody Bible Institute. They stopped for lunch in one of the camp sites that the fleeing party had abandoned many days since. As Bill and Angel were preparing dinner the two Ayorés had a look around.

"Come here!" Sirine suddenly yelled from a spot a few yards up the trail. "A jaguar ate a woman here!"

Bill and Angel were instantly at his side. The evidence was only too clear. A torn cloth which was once a skirt, and the bleached bones with scraps of dried flesh and matted hair still clinging to them, gave mute testimony to the tragedy!

Bill reflected on the sad scene. A few days before she had been a live woman, a human being who laughed and ate and played and cried and argued and scolded. She was also a woman who had sinned, and for whom Christ had died.

From his years of experience in the jungle, Bill could well visualize what had happened. The woman had taken sick and couldn't keep up with the group. A year ago her relatives would have simply buried her alive; but now they had absorbed enough Christian teaching not to resort to that. They wouldn't bury her alive; but at the same time, she would be too much of a burden to carry. When they broke camp in the morning there was a general agreement . . . if she was too ill to walk, she would have to remain behind and fare for herself! The Indians, as they left, didn't bother to glance back. Soon their voices faded in the distance, and they were gone.

The poor woman was too weak to stand, but began to inch her way down the trail, following the people she loved. Before long, her strength gave out and she lay back on the damp earth. That night, she heard the jaguar! The grass rustled as he circled round and round, closer and closer, until he was sure she couldn't defend herself. Then a leap . . . a scream . . . a roar . . . and once again . . . silence, broken only by the rhythmical crunching of bones between the cat's powerful jaws . . .

But her soul? Bill was certain that she had heard the Gospel. He could only hope that she was one of those who had received Jesus Christ as her Saviour! As he and Angel buried the remains, they were filled even more with the urgency of reaching Cutaide and convincing him to return to Bella Vista!

A few days more, and they heard the toc-toc-toc of an axe against a hollow tree. Cutaide's group was nearby!

The Ayoré guides stopped, sat down, and began checking their weapons minutely, to make sure the blades on their lances were tight. They increased the tension of their bowstrings. Fear and uncertainty was written on their faces. They knew how Ayorés greeted uninvited and unwanted visitors! If God would protect them, well and good; if not, they were going to be ready for the worst. They recalled that, before he left Zapocó, Bill made sure that his revolver was clean and well-oiled.

"You're a Christian, Tarane," Bill said. "Wouldn't you like to pray with us?"

Tarane agreed.

"And you, Sirine?"

Sirine stared at the ground and worked the bowstring nervously between his fingers. He had not as yet received Christ as his Saviour, although he freely admitted that he should — someday. Nevertheless, he closed his eyes as Angel led in prayer in the Ayoré language, committing them all to the Lord's care.

A short distance more and they found themselves in the midst of Cutaide's camp. They were not greeted with the anticipated war cries and volley of arrows. Instead, joyous shouts of welcome rang through the forest. God had truly answered prayer and prepared the way for them. Cutaide himself came walking up the trail with a broad smile on his face. Tarane and Sirine looked at each other incredulously. Then Sirine turned to Bill, "Dupade is good!" Shortly after, he made a public testimony of his faith in Christ.

Someone has said of Christian workers, "Few men run well to the end." The Apostle Paul recognized the danger even in his own life when he said, "But I keep under my body, and bring it into subjection; lest by any means when I have preached to others, I myself should be a castaway!" Unfortunately, all missionary work isn't a success story — and Angel Bravo ended his career at Bella Vista a castaway.

Like many Latins, hot-blooded Angel failed to keep his passions under control. Word of the scandal spread in the two Indian camps like fire in a thatched-roof house. Bill and Frank were crushed by the situation, and attempted to counsel Angel, but in vain. Bill spent long hours with him, trying to help him in the Lord. But Angel's heart was hard and he showed no sign of repentance. Reluctantly, they placed him under church discipline, and he was forbidden to partake of the Lord's Supper or participate in the church leadership. Not being able to reach Angel's heart, the missionaries were thrown back on prayer.

And prayer, it seemed, began to be answered. Ten Indians in Zapocó had asked to be baptized, and all were required to testify publicly of their faith in Christ before they entered the water. One of them prayed and said, "Dear Lord, now that I am dead to sin and am entering a new life with Thee, help me to live better than don Angel!"

When word of this reached Angel in Bella Vista he seemed to be shamed into better conduct, but it was only temporary.

Bill Pencille said, "Many of us gave of our time and prayers and love to try to restore and help our brother; but to no avail. Months passed, and he showed no change or desire to change. Finally, I had no alternative but to ask him to leave Bella Vista with his family. The Indians were furious and blamed me bitterly for sending away their friend and leader. Of course, they were all only too happy to have this type of man over them. Sin likes company. His actions gave them license for theirs. During those days, three of the Indian families in Bella Vista broke up due to the unfaithfulness of the husbands — a thing almost unheard of in married Ayoré couples! One of the young mothers, heartbroken over the loss of her husband, buried their lovely little baby alive!"

"A little leaven leaveneth the whole lump."

Frank was still chief of the tribe; and although he jeopardized his authority by so doing, he convinced the Bella Vista Indians that they should again move to Zapocó. As they gathered up their possessions, Frank rented three large oxcarts from a nearby ranch. Bill, in Zapocó, consulted with most of the leading men there regarding the move and found them willing to receive Cutaide and his people.

The Zapocó Indian men were not in camp when the oxcarts arrived. Bill had taken them out to clear farm land. But as the carts lumbered into Zapocó, the women gathered around them amicably — at first. The newcomers piled out onto the grass in front of the Pencille house. Perpetually hungry, they began to kindle little fires and prepare food. "As soon as Bill arrives," they said, "he will show us where to build our houses."

Some of the Zapocó women, however, did not seem as willing as their men to forgive old scores, and began to shout insults at the new group. The missionaries did their best to keep order, but things were obviously getting out of hand; so Ray quickly saddled a horse and galloped off to get Bill. He was the only one who might prevent the situation from developing into something more serious.

Bill rode back on the horse, ahead of the men; at the sight of him the women quickly fell silent. The men were not slow in following Bill back to camp, and went directly to the Pencille house where the group of newly-arrived Indians was still gathered. They seemed ready and willing to forget and forgive old insults and hatreds, and live together now as Christians.

One of the men, however, had gone to his house unnoticed by Bill and the others, before joining the group. Now he emerged with his war spear in his hand. Curiously enough, it was Bajode, always one of the quietest and most humble men in the whole camp! But Bajode's eyes glittered with hatred as he walked into the midst of the group and faced chief Cutaide, who was talking to Harriet and his wife as he reclined against the wheel of an oxcart. The others sensed the explosiveness of the moment and drew back, leaving Bajode and Cutaide alone in a large semicircle.

"You killed my father!" shouted the young brave. "And now I will kill you!" With the speed of a toad's tongue capturing a fly, he threw his spear straight at Cutaide's heart!

Cutaide was an old and seasoned warrior. As casually as Bill might play a game of catch with his boys, he raised his right hand and caught the tip of the spear. The weapon pierced through his hand and blood gushed out in great spurts. The Ayoré chief pulled out the spear and, ignoring his bleeding hand, snatched up his bow and arrows to retaliate.

Bill sprang into action and placed himself squarely between the two Indians. That in itself was a supreme act of courage; for to a maddened savage no life, whether it be that of a white man or of one of his own race, is worth anything. Pandemonium broke loose around them; but miraculously, the missionaries were able to prevent further bloodshed. In a quick aside, Bill told Harriet to get Bajode into their house where he could do no more harm. Meanwhile, Tarane and others of the leading men apologized to Cutaide for what the young brave had done, and urged him to remain in Zapocó. They promised to help and protect him and his people. Appalled by what had occurred, several of the Christian Ayoré women hastened to their own camp fires and returned with gifts of food for the other group.

But Cutaide was wise in the ways of his people. He heard them out as Bill dressed his wound, and then said: "No, it is better that we not stay. Sooner or later, there will again be bloodshed. And then we might not be able to avoid a massacre. I will return to Bella Vista with my people!"

Within half an hour, the three big oxcarts were on their way back upriver.

Failing to protect Cutaide from his enemies as he had promised, Frank was no longer regarded as the tribe's chief. From that day, the Bella Vista group has been a dispirited group of Indians; sullen, disillusioned and spiritually frigid. Finally, in 1960, those that were left returned to the jungle. The Bella Vista station was permanently closed.

20.

Stepping on Cultural Toes

As August of 1954 drew near, Bill and Harriet sought for some substitute they could offer the Christians to take the place of the coming festival to Asoná. They decided to try a week-long Bible school. Let the unbelievers go off to worship Asoná — the Christians could stay behind for their special Bible school!

But it didn't turn out that way. The unbelievers were so curious about the Bible school that they postponed their trip and they, too, remained for the week of Bible teaching, flannelgraph stories, memory work, handicraft and reading lessons. Then, when it was over, they all went into the woods, anyhow! The Christians said they were going just to hunt — they wouldn't participate in the worship of Asoná. Nothing the missionaries could say would keep them in Zapocó.

Alone in the silent camp, the Pencilles spent much time in prayer for the Indians they loved so dearly. They felt they understood Job's emotions as he prayed for his children, gathered in one of their houses for a big feast. "Oh, God, keep Thy children from sin!" they prayed.

When the Indians returned many of the Christians were radiant with joy in the knowledge that they had remained faithful to God. Dupade, and not Asoná, was the Ruler of their lives! Some who had taken part in the bird worship had guilty consciences and confessed their sin. Others, however, had returned to the ways of their forefathers.

"Some seeds fell by the way side . . .
Some fell upon stony places . . .
Some fell among thorns . . .
But other fell into good ground and brought forth fruit."

Now that there were faithful, baptized believers, it became necessary to begin regular worship services. Up until this time, the meetings had been held in camp around the Indian fires, and were most informal. But where to hold the services? The only available place was Pencilles' large front porch.

A worship service, in Bill's thinking, meant an uninterrupted hour of hymn-singing, prayer and preaching. Customarily, it is identified with order, quiet and a peaceful atmosphere. Bound by custom, Bill could not imagine God's being pleased with anything less. The Indians had to be taught all of this, however, as order and quiet are completely foreign to them.

The first communion service on the porch came a long way from measuring up to Bill's standards. Few of the communicants wore clothing, and each had brought his children and his dogs along. Ignoring the noise, things went relatively smoothly until the time came to partake of the bread and wine. At that moment a dog barked, and a dozen others joined in the chorus. A lone rider came cantering up the trail.

"Someone's coming!" shouted the congregation, tumbling over the benches and vaulting the porch rail to see who the visitor might be. When they had found out what his name was and had shaken hands with him, they filed back and sat down again, ready to continue with the communion service!

Bill says, "I came to realize that actually I was the only one who was 'getting out of the Spirit' by the bedlam! In their camp, their leaders might be carrying on singing or telling a story while the women weave, the children play, and the men talk in little groups by themselves. Indians seem to be perfectly capable of carrying on a conversation and listening at the same time. There's always a low roar in the camp, and still they miss absolutely nothing that their leaders say!"

Bill was uneasy, though, when he received word that a representative of the British and Foreign Bible Society would visit Zapocó accompanied by the Bolivian agent, Tom Hudspith. He had never met the man, but was quite anxious that he not be there over Sunday! Knowing nothing of the background of the Indians, the Englishman undoubtedly would think the whole situation outrageously sacrilegious.

"I wouldn't say whether it was an answer to prayer," Bill admits, "but at least, the visitor (whom we enjoyed very much, by the way,) didn't stay over Sunday, and we were quite relieved!"

Singing, for an Ayoré woman, is directly related to seeking a husband. The girls who are actively courting may sing, and they do so; but once a woman is married, singing would brand her as immoral! For this reason, they could never get the married women to sing in church. Roots of culture are not easily pulled up.

It took years before the Christian Ayorés began to understand that they, too, have the responsibility of telling others about their faith. A missionary never feels that he has accomplished his aim until he sees his converts becoming missionaries themselves. One of the most encouraging moments came when Comai, by now a young man, returned from a trip to the railroad line.

"Don Guillermo," he said, "one day, I met a man sitting beside the road, and he had his head bowed in his hands. I asked him if he was sick, and he said no, just sad and frightened."

"What was wrong?" Bill questioned.

"He said he had just heard that the train had been traveling one day toward Roboré. Suddenly, a woman having the appearance of the Virgin Mary appeared on the tracks ahead, carrying a small suitcase. The train stopped and they invited her to get aboard. She did so, but when they tried to lift her suitcase they found it was so heavy they could not budge it. When they asked her what it contained she answered. 'Three bottles: of wind, of fire, and of judgment, which are soon to come upon the world!' The man said that this really had him worried!"

"And what did you do, Comai?" Bill asked, intensely interested.

"I sat down beside him and told him that it was true that judgment was coming. But that Christ Jesus had come to offer salvation and escape to any and all that would accept it!"

Is there ever a real work of God begun without an almost

immediate counterattack of Satan? Were not the tares sown the very night after the wheat was put in the ground?

Angel Ortíz* and his young son had come to Zapocó to saw lumber. The huge cedar logs had to be laboriously sawed by hand with a ripsaw, and Ortíz spent several months working in Zapocó. Bill was not there at the time, and Ray Frazier told him the story on his return.

"Ortíz and his son were out here sawing cedar boards for the church building. He sawed some of those over there," Ray pointed to the new church building.

"He was in my house after supper and then left, saying he was going to change clothes for prayer meeting. Not ten minutes later, an excited uproar from the direction of the Indian camp told me something was wrong. I started in that direction to investigate when someone spotted me and yelled, 'They've killed Ortíz!'

"I ran up, and there was a bloody trail leading from the door of his little house to where he lay about fifty feet away. He was dead before I arrived. When we looked him over we saw that the murderer had struck him on the back of the head with the blunt end of an ax, then, as he fell, had hit him again with the sharp edge across the bridge of the nose! The cut went clear down through his palate and even split his tongue."

Bill was silent for a moment. "Do you have any idea of who did it?" he asked.

"Well, not for sure. We have some suspicions. John Depue loaded the body in the jeep that same night and took it to the family in Tucumán. Man, what a job! Think of getting Ortíz' wife and children out of bed in the middle of the night to turn the body over to them!"

"I'm glad I didn't have to do it!" Bill said.

"Then John went to town and brought out the police. The lieutenant from the army was here all day asking questions of everyone. He didn't accomplish much, though. He was sure, of course, that an Indian had done it. He asked Ortíz' son if his dad had any enemies among the Indians. The boy told him that Omi was his enemy; but Omi wasn't even in camp at the time!"

Bill was thoughtful as he walked slowly home across the

---

*Not to be confused with don Angel Bravo.

moonlit plaza. Who could have done such a terrible deed! Knowing as he did the Indian inability to keep a secret, he decided to bide his time, hoping to discover the answer.

Not too many days later, he was conversing with some Indians around their campfire. They were in a communicative mood.

"Ray and John don't know who killed Ortíz," one man said. "We didn't want to tell them. But we want you to know; it was Gaturai!"

Too shocked to even register anger, Bill exclaimed, "But whatever for? Ortíz never did any harm to Gaturai!"

"Yes, he did! He borrowed three thousand bolivianos (25 cents) from him, and wouldn't pay it back! So Gaturai got even with him. He stole John's ax and made a new handle for it. Then he killed Angel with it. When the police came, his mother hid the bloody clothes under his bed!"

Angel Ortíz had stepped on cultural toes, and it cost him his life!

One of Bill's narrowest escapes came one night as he was trying to be a Good Samaritan. A group of Ayorés had been out for a few weeks hunting. On their way back to Zapocó they became ill, and sent a messenger to ask Bill to come out with the jeep truck and carry the women and children home. It was late afternoon when Bill received the message, and he was weary after a long day's work; but he agreed to go. They knew he would never refuse a plea for help.

The Indians had made a camp about eighteen miles west of Zapocó. It was dark when Bill arrived, and they were waiting by the trail. He turned his jeep around, ate a bit of the honey they offered him, and then told them to get in the jeep. There was always the problem of too many piling in the back of the vehicle — the Ayorés had no concept of overloaded springs. Bill didn't want to carry too heavy a load over the rough trail, and checked the springs with a flashlight. As he was stooping over, a skinny black dog arose from his bed in the ashes and without warning took a solid bite out of Bill's right thigh! He tore his pants and drew a good bit of blood. As Bill jumped to his feet, the dog walked nonchalantly back to the fire and lay down again.

Bill angrily grabbed a stick of firewood lying by the side of the jeep and threw it at the mongrel. Unfortunately for Bill, his aim was excellent. He hit the dog squarely on the side of the head. It yelped once, rolled over, kicked a moment, and then lay still. Blood streamed from its nose and mouth. The enraged Indians thought Bill had killed the dog. So did Bill.

Somebody yelled, "The white man has killed our dog! Kill him!" and they ran for their weapons.

Bill says, "I had a revolver in the truck on the seat, but I knew if I'd turned my back for even an instant it would have been the end. My only hope was to keep looking at them and stall for time. If I'd turned my back they'd have speared me in a moment — I wouldn't have had a chance! So I stepped quickly over to a big tree and sat down with my back to it so no one could get at me from behind. Then I said, 'Your dog bit me!'

" 'Liar! Liar! Liar!' Of course, when they are angry, they won't let you say a word, you know. I thought this was it! They had me completely surrounded, five deep, shouting and threatening. 'We'll kill him!' they roared. 'Then we'll go to the railroad line. We have had enough of him, anyhow! Let's kill him and wreck his truck!'

"I said, 'All right, you can kill me. But don't forget I'm your best friend! You have no one else among the whites that is a friend like I am. Really, when you think of it, I've never harmed you in any way, have I?'

"I was doing plenty of praying! It was difficult to keep my voice level. An Indian admires courage and I didn't want them to sense the fear that was in my heart. I admit I was stalling for time.

"Just then the dog rolled over, got up and walked away. It wasn't dead, it had just been stunned. It walked off, sort of wobbly-like, into the woods. The Indians, watching it, lowered their weapons and said, 'The dog did not die, after all! We'll let him live — we won't kill him this time.' "

Bill likes to philosophize about the implications of this almost fatal case of stepping on cultural toes. He says, "Well, the jokers! I know what Bill Pencille would have liked to have done! He would have liked to have put them all off the jeep and made them walk home! But so many times, you have to. . .

"You know, I'm not the One that said that I wasn't willing that any should perish! God is the One who said that, and not I. There are numberless times in working with savages that I lost all patience with them. But then, God moved in and shed His love in my heart, and I could love them in spite of what they were. I often think I must have been infinitely hateful in the eyes of a holy God, but He loves me!

"So I merely said to them, 'All right, let's go home!' They piled into the truck and we drove back to Zapocó!"

21.

Toward the South

During the years that Comai was growing up in the Pencille household, his older brother was living near the railroad line to the south. Natui had become the war chief of his group, and although he had made a profession of following Christ, he was swayed by two passions that often took precedence over his Lord. He was proud and covetous of power in the tribe and he hated the Guidaigosode.

Word came flashing to Zapocó one day on the portable radio transmitter-receiver that Natui had left with a group of armed Indians to make war with his enemies to the south. His destination was the Salt Lake near the border of Paraguay, where he knew the Guidaigosode would come for salt during the dry season. Comai was heartsick, and much prayer was offered that God would thwart the efforts of his brother. Natui and his gang, however, were back in a few months with five captive women from the Guidaigosode and glowing reports of fifteen killed — shot in the back as they fled from their guns!

At one time, such news would have caused great rejoicing in Zapocó. A profound change was taking place in Indian hearts and lives, however. Now the news brought sorrow, for many of the Indians were Christians and were meeting weekly for prayer. The men and women met separately, the men with Bill and the women with Harriet. Bill tells of these meetings:

"We held them on Friday nights, and they became the social event of the week. Everyone attended, Christians or not. But only the Christians prayed. Here is where I would find out how effective my teaching had been! They would always pray back to me my latest sermon.

I recall the time I tried to teach them about God as a Trinity; Father, Son and Holy Spirit. One God, but three Persons. I was not at all certain that I had been able to really get anything over to them. But in prayer meeting that week, one of the men prayed to God and thanked Him for living in his heart by the Holy Spirit; and finished with the words, 'Father, I ask you these things in Your Name of Jesus!'

"Naturally reserved and retiring, no Indian has ever come to me directly to tell me he is a Christian. But in the privacy of a prayer meeting they would confess their faith in the Son of God!"

Here, too, they first began to pray for their enemies, the Guidaigosode. Though they still feared them, they were at least willing that they should share heaven with them. When Jurugai escaped from the Guidaigosode who had held him captive for years, Bill learned where the nearest of their villages was located. After the corn was hoed that year, he took a group of the older men to see if they could make contact with them. They were only able to go some sixty miles in the jeep truck and then continued on foot. The rainy season was long overdue, and the risk of getting the jeep stuck for six months was too great. After ten days or so of fruitless search, they came unexpectedly upon a narrow road that threaded its way through the jungle. It wasn't too long before a party of Bolivian cattlemen, on horseback, came trotting down the road.

"Looking for Indians?" asked the bearded leader of the group. "I'd sure like to find them, too! They just killed an old man down in Puerto Céspedes. You sure it wasn't one of these fellows that did it?"

"Three or four years ago, maybe," Bill said, "but I live with three hundred Ayorés all the time and *they* don't kill anyone! These are friends of mine. We've just come down from Palmarito."

"If you find them, I hope you slaughter the whole lot of them!" was the grim response as they cantered off.

The road was almost impassable, and to reach Puerto Céspedes meant walking for days through ankle-deep mud. But they couldn't let this opportunity slip by. They headed toward the town, sixty miles to the south.

When they arrived, the people said, "The Indians came out and killed an old man who was hoeing his corn. Not only that, but the same day another group stole corn from the Japanese colony!"

"Where's the Japanese colony?" asked Bill.

"Nine miles south on the river!" They were on the banks of the sluggish, winding Rio Grande, the largest river in eastern Bolivia, and a tributary of the Amazon.

"When did they kill the man?"

"Ten days ago."

"And when did they steal the corn?"

"The same day!"

It was obvious that there were two separate groups. "Didn't you do anything about it?" Bill questioned further.

"The day after we found the body, we followed the *bárbaros* into the woods. But a boy we had with us got nervous. When he heard the Indians ahead he fired his rifle in their general direction and scared them off. If he hadn't been so nervous we might have killed them all! But we took everything they had left in their camp when they fled."

"Where are the things?" Bill asked quickly.

"The colonel just left for Santa Cruz yesterday and took everything back with him. He's the one they sent out to investigate."

"What kind of things were they?"

"Oh, feathers, bags, arrows, bows, gourds, axes —wait a moment! I kept an ax myself for a souvenir. Here it is!"

The Ayorés with Bill took one look at the ax and their brown faces turned a sickly gray. "This is from the Guidaigosode!" they whispered. They knew instantly by the way the wire was wound around the ax head. It was as clear to them as if the Guidaigosode had left an engraved calling card.

Bill had prayed for years for the Guidaigosode, and now at last there seemed to be a chance of meeting them! He asked his companions if they would be willing to try to catch up with them. They agreed only on the condition that they take more guns. Bill's .22 was not enough to face these fierce warriors, they said. Three armed Japanese left their farm work to accompany them. Thus encouraged, the Indians were willing to go on.

From the cornfield of the Japanese colonists the trail led into the forest to the south. Before they had gone far, Bill was indelibly impressed with the ingenuity and cruelty of the Guidaigosode. Had they been running in pursuit, they would have been severely wounded. The wily Indians had planted a razor-sharp spear in the ground in the middle of the trail, camouflaged with leaves. Virtually invisible and bellyhigh, it would have inflicted an agonizing wound in anyone running up the trail. Fortunately, they located the spear in time, and later found several others like it.

Farther on they were surprised when the narrow trail they were following became a yard-wide "super highway." It took a turn to the left, but about one hundred yards away came to a dead-end in a ravine. They searched everywhere but couldn't pick up the trail beyond the ravine. Returning to where the trail had widened, they soon saw that the wide trail was but a ruse to give time for defense. The Guidaigosode had slept just beyond the lost trail, and had set up an ambuscade of leaves and branches from which to attack their pursuers, thrown off guard by the sudden ending of the trail. They intended to surprise them from behind, let fly a volley of deadly arrows and then melt back into the jungle. No wonder Bill's companions trembled in fear! Bill himself felt a healthy respect for them as warriors and strategists.

Three days later, the search party came out of the forest along the railroad line. The Guidaigosode were only three days ahead of them, when they were halted by a torrential downpour. Wet, hungry and afraid, Bill's companions refused to go on. It was one thing to meet a small group of Guidaigosode in friendly territory; it was quite another to invade their homeland in the south! Nothing doing! Bill finally was able to persuade one of them to accompany him to their next camp beyond the railroad and leave gifts as a proof of their friendship; but the Indians refused to venture further. Thus ended the first Guidaigosode expedition.

Almost two years passed before Bill was able to return to check on the gifts he had left. This time, the expedition was better organized. Instead of older men he selected seven of the younger and, he hoped, the more courageous braves. Most of them were Christians, and had prayed publicly for the Guidaigosode. Comai was included as well as Genaro Moreno, a Bolivian believer.

By this time John Depue had arrived in Bolivia and had completed his Spanish study. A tall, broad-shouldered, muscular farm boy from Pennsylvania, he and his wife Phoebe were destined to play a strategic part in the future Ayoré work. Bill did not hesitate to invite John to accompany him on the trip.

Just before leaving, Bill wrote to a friend in the States:

> Among the unsaved Indians there is little joy over this trip. Today, they came and offered to give me a gift if I would not go to the Guidaigosode. If you knew their extreme poverty, you would better understand what this means. I still don't know whether it was for fear of danger to me or just not wanting their enemies to hear of Christ. Many of them, I fear, have Jonah's attitude toward the Ninevites. But this is a real matter of prayer, for there is liable to be considerable unrest here when I go. And some of them are likely to leave Zapocó. Let us pray together that Satan will be put to flight, and that the peace of God will reign in their hearts as we take this step forward. Of course, what they need is the love of God in their hearts toward their old enemies.

Bill found the gifts still in the campsite just as he had left them. The Guidaigosode had not returned. It would have been too tedious to try to follow their grown-over trail, so they decided to follow it only far enough to discover its general direction and then strike out through the jungle. After twelve grueling days of battling with thorns and thirst they came out on a well-worn Guidaigosode trail. It headed straight south and most certainly would lead to one of their main villages.

The missionaries were excited and anxious to push on to their goal. But the Ayorés began to have second thoughts. Perhaps they had thought when they agreed to go with Bill that they would never really reach the Guidaigosode. They wanted to have a ride on the airplane and the train, and enjoy a good camping trip! But with real, live Guidaigosode just a few days down the trail, the picture changed considerably!

That evening, the Indians complained of being sick. They were sure they had fever and grippe. Bill took their temperatures and found them normal. There was nothing organically wrong. But they really *were* sick — sick with fear! As they sat morosely around the campfire, Bill told them the story of Gideon and his three hundred. He said, "Look, there are only ten of us, but we don't have to fear! The God of Gideon is with us!" They were somewhat encouraged when they went to sleep, but next morning were hesitant to break camp and push on.

The trail they had been following was heavily overgrown. Bill picked up a machete and took the lead, clearing the trail. The rest began catching up a couple of hours later, and Bill stepped off to one side of the trail. He counted them as they filed past. Two were missing.

"Where are Jurugai and Jecuresi?" he asked.

"They've gone back!" one of the braves responded in a tremulous voice.

That was the turning point. For the next two hours, almost every step was a struggle — three white men trying to urge five reluctant Indians along. If they were *that* frightened many days walk from their old enemies, what would they be like in an actual contact with the Guidaigosode? Bill realized that he would have to force a showdown. He called a halt and the group sat down to rest. After a few minutes he arose and walked a few paces down the trail.

"All right, men," he said. "This is it! God has called us to reach the Guidaigosode. He has promised to help and protect us. You fellows prayed for the Guidaigosode back in Zapocó. What are you going to do about it, now? Will you be cowards and go with Jurugai and Jecuresi? Or will you go with us to the Guidaigosode? If you're with me, come over here! If not, now's the time to turn back!"

John and Genaro stood to their feet and went over beside Bill. Four of the Indians fitted their pack straps over their foreheads and silently headed back along the trail. Only Comai hesitated. Then he picked up his bag and took a few steps after the rest. Bill stood watching him, wordlessly. Suddenly, Comai stopped, turned, and walked straight back to where Bill stood.

"I'm sorry I even had the idea of going back!" he confessed bravely. "I'm with you, don Guillermo!"

But there was no hope now of going on. The four of them sat there a few minutes, each engrossed in his own thoughts. When would they ever reach the Guidaigosode? Could they never depend on the Ayorés for help? As they headed back along the trail, they had ample reason to feel discouraged.

The only bright spot was that one of the Indians who had turned back waited for them on the trail. It was Egarede, one of the finest young men in the group. He had realized that he was disobeying God, and after a tremendous struggle with himself had decided to go on to the Guidaigosode, come what may! But it was too late.

The missionaries arrived first in Zapocó, and after a few more days the Indians began to come in. They had traveled more slowly, hunting along the way. They were a bedraggled lot, sick with grippe that they had contracted. Jemi went directly to Bill's house. It was already late at night.

"Egarede needs you!" he told Bill.

"What's wrong? Where is he?"

"He's out on the trail, sick. For two days he has not spoken — he just seems to sleep and moan!"

Bill immediately went out to the pasture and caught his horse. He fixed the saddle and his medicine kit, and prepared to leave when the moon was up to see what he could do for his friend. But before he left another Indian arrived.

"Egarede's dead!" he announced.

"How did he die?" Bill asked, saddened by the news.

"Egarede was unconscious for two days. We took care of him. But last night he awoke, sat up and looked at us. His eyes were very clear — we thought he had gotten well! Then he spoke. He said, 'Brothers, come with me on the narrow way. Leave the wide way; the narrow way is lovely, beautiful! The narrow way is Jesus Christ! Come with me!' Then he breathed very hard, lay back, and was dead! We buried him there."

Weeks before, Bill had told the Indians the story of the wide way and the narrow way. Egarede had learned well.

22.

Soul Conflict

COMAI NEVER COULD BRING himself to call Bill *"Yapa,"* father. He was always *don Guillermo,* Bill. But in every other way, their relationship was as father and son. And even more than this, for Comai was Bill's spiritual son as well. Just as Bill taught his own sons, he taught Comai God's standards for Christian living. Comai accepted Bill's admonitions and counsel, and his desire was to serve his God.

But his was not an easy life. He was constantly torn between the strict, Christian atmosphere of Bill's home and the pagan, immoral standards of the Indians. Bill encouraged him to spend as much time as possible with his own people, so that he would learn well their language and customs. His progress in the Ayoré language was always a matter of constant admiration to Bill. His vocabulary and grasp of legends and customs was a fountain of information that never seemed to dry up. But he was growing up, with all the drives and passions of a normal teen-age boy. Each time he would sit down among his people in the camp, their immoral talk and actions would flood upon him, contradicting and combating all he had learned from Bill.

And so the inner conflict grew into a raging flame.

It was again time for the festival of Asoná, and Bill and Harriet held the special Vacation Bible School mentioned previously. After the week of classes the entire camp moved out into the woods. The young folks stayed behind for a day or two after the older ones had gone, but finally they, too, succumbed to the lure of the jungle.

They promised Bill that they wouldn't worship the bird — they just wanted to "hunt honey." There was nothing the missionaries could do or say to change their minds, and off they went.

"Are you going, too?" Bill asked Comai while the young people prepared to leave.

"No," he replied. "I'm staying with you and Harriet."

After the Ayorés had gone, the oppressive silence that settled on the camp made Zapocó seem like a tomb. With three or four hundred Indians there, a constant hubbub of laughter, talking, singing and squabbling filled the air. But now, the silence was almost unbearable, and even Bill and Harriet found it depressing. If the missionaries reacted in this way, how much more Comai! In spite of his years in Bill's house, Comai was and always would be an Ayoré. The "honey hunt" was calling! For two or three days he remained, but finally loneliness overcame him.

When he told Bill he was going after his people, he could not meet Bill's gaze. "Comai," Bill told him with an affectionate pat on his shoulder. "You're old enough to make your own decisions. If you want to go it's up to you. I won't stop you. But remember — God will be with you in the woods even as He is right here. Don't do anything to displease Him. I'll be praying for you!"

Ten days later, the teen-aged girls were the first to arrive back in Zapocó. They came on the run, screaming and laughing, all trying to be the first to shout the news. Bill and Harriet were on the porch to greet them, but couldn't make out at first what it was they were shouting.

Finally one of them made herself clear. *"Uapede e chisa Comai!"* The missionaries looked at each other, sick at heart. The girl had said, "Uapede married Comai!"

Uapede was only thirteen, and the last girl in camp Bill or Harriet would have chosen as a wife for their "son." Stubborn, taciturn, incompetent, difficult to manage, they could only wish he had made a better choice. If love is really blind, they felt, here was living proof!

Bill didn't mention the matter to Comai immediately. But the following day he took a walk with him and said, "Comai, the Indians are saying that Uapede became your wife out on the honey hunt. Is it true?"

Comai hung his head and was silent.

"Well, how about it," Bill persisted, gently.

Finally, his eyebrows lifted in affirmation.

"You surely remember what I've told you about this. In

God's sight, you're married! Uapede is your wife. God frowns on the trial marriage the Ayorés practice."

Comai was humble and repentant. "I know it," he said.

"I'll help you build a house," Bill went on, "Where do you want it to be?"

"As close to yours as I can, don Guillermo." Perhaps he hoped to draw strength from the physical nearness to the man he loved and respected; perhaps he wanted to be as far away as possible from the temptations and sins of his own people.

At any rate, they walked back toward the house and chose a site to the west near the Pencille's garage. Comai cut the timber and Bill hauled it with the truck. When he had the pole frame up, they brought in several loads of *motacú* palm leaves for the roof. Bill hauled the dirt for the mud and wattle walls, and it wasn't many days before Comai had a sturdy little house.

But this house was never to be a home. Comai's first year of married life was a complete failure. Not that Uapede was contentious or nagging or unfaithful — it was worse than that! Day after day, she would just sit motionless and silent in the corner of the house with a blank expression on her face.

Harriet tried to counsel her, but met with complete indifference. Comai worked hard in the fields or at the translation table all morning with Bill, but never did he find food prepared at noon. Uapede would be in her dark corner of the one-room house with her back to the door. The fire would be out, no wood or water in the house, no food, no clothes washed or mended. Comai would patiently go to the mission store and buy food, draw water, light the fire, cook his own pot of rice for lunch, all the time trying in vain to draw her into a conversation. He would buy more food and leave it in the house for her to prepare for supper. But when he returned at night, exhausted after a day's work in the broiling sun, it was the same story. He was miserably unhappy, but made a manful attempt to rise above the situation.

He continued to read his Bible. He helped in the preaching. Sensing the situation but unable to help, Harriet always saw that he never left her house hungry when he worked with Bill on translation problems. But finally, after an especially trying week with no sign of change in his wife, he broke under the pressure of his own emotions. A group of Ayorés was leaving for the railroad line, and Comai went with them, leaving Uapede behind. Bill was sorry to see him go — no telling what might happen to him down there — but he couldn't really blame Comai. He wondered what he would have done, but for God's grace, under like circumstances! He breathed fervent thanks to God for his own wife — wonderful in every way!

Comai was gone for several months when the news came back that he had married Dago, Nuine's daughter. With an aching heart, Bill knew that this meant that Comai would have to be disciplined by the church. He could see no other way. Loving him as they did, the decision was heartbreaking to the missionary couple.

Comai was no stranger to church discipline, for he had been with Bill when Angel Bravo had been sent away from Bella Vista, and had explained the proceedings and the reason for it to the Indians there. All of this affected Comai deeply. He instinctively knew that his relationship with Uapede was not real marriage, and that his new and satisfying life with Dago was. But he was stricken with guilt, knowing what Bill would think. The grapevine brought him news that he was under discipline by the church in Zapocó, and although he knew this would be the consequence of his act, still it sank him deeper into despair. He began to wonder if he was even a Christian! Soon a little boy was born to brighten his life with Dago, but he himself had no peace in his heart. For a number of years he lived in defeat, out of fellowship with the Lord and His people.

Comai's older brother, Natui, had become war chief of Tobité. Until the time of his death in a train wreck in 1962, no one could be certain whether or not Natui was really born again. If he was, he had never allowed the Holy Spirit to remove his passionate hatred and desire for revenge on the Guidaigosode. To defeat his enemies was the driving force in Natui's life. He often made trouble, and was a source of heartache to the missionaries in Tobité.

When they reprimanded him for his murder of the fifteen Guidaigosode, he became angry and left Tobité in a rage.

He sought out his brother, Comai, and suggested that together they call the Indians from Zapocó and Tobité, and establish their own village. If Bill Pencille and Howard Morarie (a New Tribes missionary in charge of Tobité) could run Indian camps, so could they! Natui would be chief and Comai his first lieutenant. The brothers were confident that they would soon have all the Indians of both missions under their command. Their camp could then be used as a base for operations against the Guidaigosode. With ten or fifteen guns they would be able to wipe out their old enemies, and there wouldn't be any missionaries around to stop them or tell them that they were disobeying God!

They chose as their location Los Aceites, on the railroad line and a comfortable 150 miles from either Tobité or Zapocó. This was going to be the Ayorés promised land!

They got off to a good start. They cleared many acres of farmland, and a little village of comfortable huts soon sprang up. Natui was exuberant! After they sold their harvest and bought more guns, they could invade the south again!

Then disaster struck! The Indians in Zapoco came down with the measles. From Zapocó the disease spread to Los Aceites. Twelve Indians died in the first wave of sickness, and the rest evacuated the village. Natui learned that he might not need the missionaries, but he did need their medicine!

Comai moved his little family to a ranch called El Cerro. The Bolivian owner encouraged the Ayorés to stay, and gave them what work he could. He was one of the few nationals who really had the welfare of the Indians at heart. Several Ayoré families settled there, living mostly by hunting, but working for the rancher from time to time when they needed money. It was a miserable existence for Comai. He and Dago had little to eat and became thin and emaciated. They had long since sold all of their possessions to buy food, and were reduced to poverty. Dago kept only her cooking pot and Comai his machete. He still had the .22 rifle he had bought from Bill just before leaving Zapocó. One of his dreams in leaving Zapocó was to become rich, working along the railroad. God had never removed His hand from His servant, however; and like the prodigal son of old, he found himself instead of rich, reduced to abject poverty.

Often, he longed to return to Zapocó! Bill and Harriet were there again after a much-needed furlough. But — how about the church discipline? Would Bill and Harriet want him any more? How he missed their love and counsel! Comai didn't know what to do. He was bitter and spiritually defeated. His pride held him back from making the move that his heart told him he must make.

Things went from bad to worse. The ranch owner failed to pay them for their work. They had absolutely no money and no food. Then Comai's little baby, already weak and undernourished, fell sick with the flu. There was no medicine and no money with which to buy it. The baby was very ill. It seemed probable that he would not live through another night.

That evening at dusk Comai, driven by desperation and unrest, wandered aimlessly down the path toward the garden. He carried the rifle, more from habit than with any clear purpose in mind. Halfway through one of the cornfields he sat down on a log. He was at the end of his tether. The bitterness and rebellion of the past three years seemed to melt away with the fading light of the dying day. He knew he must turn his life back over to God, come what may. It was his supreme moment of surrender after which he could say, "For me to live is Christ!"

It would mean returning to Zapocó. It would mean facing Bill. It would mean a confession of sin in the church. It would mean humiliation and shame. It would require all of his courage. But it was the only way. For the first time in months, Comai prayed and opened his heart to God. As he finished, he said brokenly, "And Lord, if it is Thy will, please, please save my baby!"

His eyes were filled with hot tears as he finally raised his head. It was nearly dark. Long night shadows were creeping halfway across the cornfield. He brushed the tears from his eyes. What was that dark object there? Over against the wall of jungle on the other side of the cornfield — was it a deer? Comai rubbed his eyes again as he looked intently at the object. It moved slightly! Might as well take a chance. He slipped the safety off his rifle and took quick aim. It would be an almost impossible shot. He could barely see the front sight of the gun. He fired!

By the time he reached the other side of the clearing, the buck had stopped kicking. It had fallen in its tracks with the bullet in his heart. Comai wasn't *that* good a shot — he realized that God Himself must have guided the bullet!

By selling half the meat, he got money for the medicine he needed for his baby. The other half went into the stew pot. When he and Dago had regained their strength, they began the long trip back to Zapocó.

Bill Pencille was up at daybreak, and went over to his little study in the rear of the church. The grass was wet under foot, and there were puddles in the path. It had rained during the night, but the clouds seemed to be breaking up under the heat of the rising sun. Bill sat down at his desk and began to read his Bible. It was difficult to concentrate that morning, for his heart was heavy. Comai was again in his thoughts. He tried to pray, but was not too successful in that, either. He did ask for another opportunity to see Comai.

After breakfast, there was a flat tire to fix before taking the Indians to work. This was the one job he liked least — changing tires. Halfway through the task he was startled to hear a shout from camp: *"Ayoré quiiiiii!"* "Ayorés are coming!"

He looked up in time to see Comai and Dago walking slowly down the road. A little boy was riding piggy-back on his mother's pack.

Dropping his tire irons, Bill ran to meet them. He hugged Comai warmly, and took them over to his house. Harriet always had a pot of coffee on the stove, and soon they were having a belated breakfast. It was the first time in months that Comai had enjoyed bread and coffee for breakfast. He seemed relieved that Bill had received him back, but they were surrounded by Indians welcoming their friend home, and there was no chance to talk.

Later in the day, Comai sought Bill out. He wanted to talk to him alone. He related to him the story of his return to God and the deer incident. Bill realized that this amounted to an Ayoré confession of sin, and told him how much he had missed him. Before they were finished, tears

Right, Comai with his wife Dago and small son. *Below top,* Comai and this Chiquitano Indian were ordained to the ministry on the same day. *Bottom,* the ordination service in which the author (in glasses and white shirt) took part.

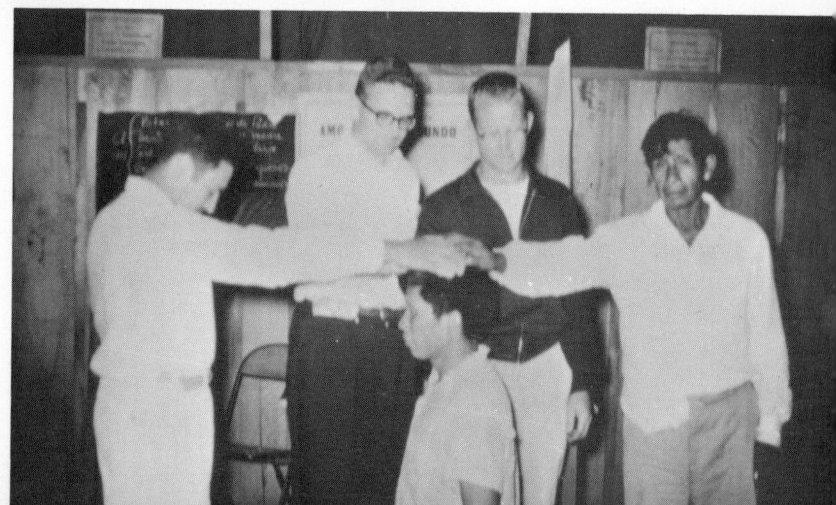

were coursing down both their cheeks. The story of the Prodigal Son was again re-enacted in real life.

Bill says, "I have never again mentioned Comai's first wife to him. I see now that it had been a case of teen-age fornication; I don't believe I should have insisted on the marriage. Uapede has subsequently turned out to be absolutely no good — she's one of the harlots of the railroad line. In fact, for months no one knew where she was. Apparently she was never really a Christian."

Comai had been through the fire. He has been faithful ever since, and has had a consistent testimony for Christ. In 1961, he was ordained in Zapocó and became one of the first Ayoré ministers of the Gospel.

Bill went on to say, "This ordination has had a tremendous effect on Comai. All of my contact with him since that time has been on another level. Before, he would become extremely discouraged, as we all do. But he has changed. Again and again, he has mentioned the laying on of hands and the gift he received at that time. He knew that his responsibility now as an ordained minister of the Gospel was to be faithful to his Lord!"

23.

Sword of the Spirit

YOU CAN NEVER have a strong, indigenous church until at least its leaders are able to read the Bible in their own tongue."

Bill could no longer remember where he had read the words, but he could not erase them from his mind. The growth of the infant church among the Ayorés pointed up the need for the Scriptures in their own language.

Many of the Indians now professed to believe in Jesus as their Saviour, and many of them manifested much fruit in their lives. The younger generation seemed to have lost completely its fear of Asoná, and the witch doctors were not as frequently at their arts and incantations. Aside remarked to Bill one afternoon:

"I don't have nearly the power I used to have as a witch doctor! I used to be able to kill my enemies by simply putting a curse on them!"

"Why do you suppose that is?" Bill wanted to know.

"Oh, that is quite simple. There is just too much Jesus around here!"

But if the Christians were to grow, they needed the Word of God in their own tongue, and they must be taught to read it. Comai had become completely bi-lingual, as much at home in Spanish as he was in his own tongue. He read the Spanish Bible fluently and with good understanding. But what about Jecuresi? Or Taguide? Or a dozen other young men who were potential spiritual leaders of their people? Rough translations had already been made of many of the story-portions of both Old and New Testament. Simple reading primers were written, using, often, the very phrases lifted from these Bible portions. With these primers as beginning readers, school was begun in Zapocó. Through the years Janet Briggs, a cheerful auburn-haired school teacher has ably carried this important phase of the work.

The lessons were of necessity as simple as possible, introducing just a few new words each day.

God made everything
God made the sun
God made the moon
God made the stars
God made Asoná
God made Ayorés

Even with this extreme simplicity, it was a problem to capture their interest. It is not true that the Indian is inferior in mental capacity. But this capacity has lain dormant for so many generations that it is difficult to awaken. While Janet labored patiently at the blackboard drilling the simple words over and over, the boys' minds would be far away following some turtle's tracks to his hidden cave, or tracking the honeybee in flight to his sweet, succulent nest in some hollow tree. Not until they became truly Christians, with a desire to learn more of God through His Word, was the desire to read awakened in them. Obviously, they had to have more to read than the simple stories which were in print in their little primers.

Some five years after the first Indians arrived in Zapocó, Bill and Comai began the first serious Bible translation work. They chose the gospel of Mark for their first efforts. What often seemed, on the surface, to be an easy task proved to be a job of many weary months. There was nothing in Mark that could not be said in Ayoré, but the question was, how to say it!

Soon after Bill began the task, he came across a quotation from Martin Luther which made him feel as if he were in good company:

> Good heavens — how hard it is to make the Hebrew writers speak German! They resist our efforts. They don't want to give up their native tongue for a barbarous idiom. Just as the nightingale would not want to change her sweet song to imitate the monotonous cuckoo.

Things hadn't changed much in four hundred years!

Since the pagan, animistic Ayorés had no words for Christian theological terms like repentance, baptism, forgiveness, etc., an expansion often had to be coined in order to communicate the idea to them. When Bill came to the fourth verse of Mark 1, he scratched his head, perplexed. "John did baptize in the wilderness, and preach the baptism of repentance for the remission of sins." After days of struggling over this passage, it finally came out, "John, who put their faces under the water, arrived in the uninhabited place and taught them that they should change their minds about sin and be put under the water for the blotting out of sins."

Many things that Bill thought would be easy to translate proved to be most difficult. For example, the story of the paralytic in Mark 2 did not seem to pose any problems. And it did go well, at first: they couldn't get near the house — they took off the roof and let the man down — Jesus healed him — he picked up his bed and walked — all the way down to the very end of the story. But the comment of the people was, "We never saw it on this fashion." Bill asked Comai to translate it.

Comai was silent.

Bill repeated, "Translate: they said, 'We have never seen it on this fashion.' "

Comai said, "I don't understand. Are they lying? How could they say they'd never seen it if they just got through seeing it?"

Bill realized that Comai was a born literalist, and patiently explained that what they meant was that it was the first time they had ever seen anything like that. The problem was solved.

Satan appears on the scene in the first chapter of Mark. One would think that a people so given over to the works of the devil would have all kinds of concepts of him! But not so. They knew something of a supreme being, but had no idea of who Satan was. It appears as if one of the tactics of this wicked one who so dominates their lives has been to keep his own identity hidden from them. When Bill found the word *dicore* he thought it might refer to Satan. But since there was a plural to the word he concluded that *dicore* must be demon. The Spanish *Satanás* had no meaning for them at all. Finally, though, it was deemed best to use this name and by teaching, fill it with the Biblical concept of Satan.

The familiar story of the feeding of the five thousand presented a serious problem when Bill came to the part where the disciples said to Jesus, "Shall we go and buy two hundred pennyworth of bread?" How do you explain that amount of money to a people who, until a short while ago, knew nothing of money? The obvious solution would be to go to a Bible dictionary, find out the value of a "pennyworth," change it into Bolivian currency values and multiply it by two hundred. But the Bolivian economy was in a spiraling inflation at the time and within six months this value of money would be cut in half. The price of bread was changing from week to week.

Bill said, "I finally ended up with what I thought was a very good translation of it. I had Philip saying, 'Lord, shall we go and spend all the money we have in the bag to buy bread?' and I sent it off to the Bible Society. My reasoning was that Philip knew exactly how much money was in the bag when he suggested this. Well, Dr. Nida of the Bible Society didn't like this at all! He said, "How do you know that was all the money there was? That's interpretation, not translation!" Then he came up with a simple and logical solution that I should have thought of. A penny was a day's wage in Bible times, and what Philip really said was, 'Lord, shall we go and spend all the money that a man could earn by two hundred days of labor and buy bread?'

"This, of course, was the answer. As the money inflates the wages also increase, and the comparison would remain more or less meaningful."

At first Bill skipped over the parable of the sower in chapter four. In the midst of the poverty of a wild Indian tribe, how could one ever translate the meaning of the thorns that grew up and choked the plants? Jesus interpreted them to mean "the deceitfulness of riches and the cares of this life." But when riches are comparatively unknown, how can you describe their deceitfulness?

Finally, when he returned to the passage and discussed it with Comai the answer was quite simple. Comai said, "Well, we know all about that, don Guillermo. We've got fellows in our tribe who are so anxious to get rich that they're always trading. They trade a lance for a bag and the bag for something nicer and they're always trying to get the best of a deal. They don't have time to hunt for honey or turtles for their families because they're so anxious to get rich!"

Once again, Bill realized that the Bible is a Book of the heart rather than of the intellect, capable of being received and understood by people everywhere!

At last the job was completed and approved by the Bible Society. In the ensuing years other books of the Bible were translated, and used mainly by the missionaries in their teaching and preaching. Strange as it might seem, one of the most thorny problems from the outset was the decision as to the best alphabet to use in writing Ayoré. The first one used proved to be so complicated that few of the Indians could read it. Only in the past few years had a simplified one been adopted which makes reading easier.

As time passed, Bill was ever learning more of the Ayoré language, and it became clear that his first translation of Mark was in need of revision to better give the true meaning.

In translating the passage which speaks of the disciples following Jesus, Comai gave the obvious word to follow, *ajna.* Later knowledge showed that *ajna* meant "to follow" all right — but only to follow some animal or enemy with the purpose of killing him! The passage which speaks of Joseph "knowing" his wife, Comai insisted could be translated just as the English and Spanish had it. He insisted on using the word *imo,* to know. When Bill questioned this, he refused to change it. You see, if Spanish people could say it that way, his language was not a whit inferior! The Ayorés could say it that way, too, he affirmed. Now Bill knows that the word *imo,* to know, can never have the significance of the consummation of the marriage relationship. The idea can be expressed in Ayoré, but not by the verb *imo.*

The most immediate, tangible evidence of blessing from the endless hours spent at the translation table was the growth in Comai's spiritual life. As Bill poured over the Scriptures with him day after day, explaining, illustrating, phrase by phrase, word by word, Comai became imbued with the very Spirit of the Word of God! This spiritual growth was none too soon.

Comai's father-in-law had been chief for many years. Now he wanted to pass on the task to someone younger. The unanimous choice of the tribe was Comai! This was a great honor. Comai was still a young man, and not immune to feelings of pride and vanity. As soon as he knew of the decision of the tribe, he came to Bill for advice.

"Do you think you can take on the duties of a chief and not compromise your stand as a Christian and preacher?" questioned Bill.

Deeply troubled, Comai hesitated. He knew how intimately the pipe and tobacco were involved in all the decision-making of the chiefs. He knew the stand that the evangelical church in Bolivia took on tobacco. Although Bill had not actively opposed tobacco in the case of the old men of the tribe, lest he destroy the Ayore chain of authority and end up with anarchy, he had made the Bible's position clear — "Know ye not that your bodies are the temple of the Holy Ghost!"

Finally, with a wistful smile, Comai said, "No, I cannot be a chief and a Christian. I am going to continue to serve God!"

24.

Total Commitment

SELDOM NOW was the name of Asoná heard in Zapocó. Hymns of praise to God, prayers, the busy hum of children bent over their school books, the hard work of productive farms had supplanted her in the lives and hearts of the Ayorés. The red star still rose at sundown in the month of May. The dry season still followed harvest. The little birds and animals still hid themselves until the first rains of spring brought the forest back to life. The *cuyavo* still sang at the full moon of August. But now the Ayorés understood that that was the way things were because God had made them so. They knew that sin in their hearts and lives was what would condemn them, and not the careless breaking of endless taboos.

But among the Guidaigosode, living around the Salt Lake in the south, Asoná still reigned unchallenged. Bill, along with the new Ayoré Christians, could not escape the feeling of urgency to seek a way to bring them the message of the Gospel which alone could free them from the bird god's hard bondage.

Humanly speaking, going into the jungles around the Salt Lake to look for the Guidaigosode was the most foolish decision of Bill Pencille's life. When he announced his intentions to mobilize a total effort for a contact, objections and criticisms began to pour in from all sides — from his Bolivian neighbors, from his friends in the States, and even from fellow missionaries. Bill had some misgivings himself, and it was not an easy decision to make. The conflict raged in his soul — innumerable voices clamoring to be heard . . .

Don't be foolish, Bill! You've done enough. To reach the Guidaigosode will mean leaving Zapocó and your comfortable house that you worked so many years to build and furnish! You don't want to go back to the jungle! The bugs, the thirst, the boredom, the heat, the uncomfortable jungle hammock . . .

Jesus Christ was "comfortable" in heaven, too. But He left the ivory palace and willingly came into this world of woe!

Look what opportunities you have with the Ayorés here in Zapocó! You've given your life to these people! Don't abandon them. They need you right here!

But God called me to reach *all* the Ayorés! The Guidaigosode are part of the tribe. I can't teach these Ayorés to be faithful to God's call if I myself am not!

Remember Cornelius Isaak! Remember the five New Tribes fellows! The Guidaigosode are not like these Indians here. They're not going to come to you for refuge like these did. They're afraid of no one. And furthermore, they're insanely angry at Natui for killing their women! They'd just as soon kill you to get even with him!*

But Jesus Christ counted not His life as dear unto Himself!

Maybe not your life, but how about Harriet? How about Dick? And Bruce? And Jeanne? And little Stevie? You have a responsibility to your family.

If any man come to Me and hate not his father, and mother, and wife, and children, and brethren and sister, yea, and his own life also, he cannot be My disciple!

How about the younger missionaries? There's Chuck Ramsey; there's John Depue; there's Russ Beuchler; there's Howie Morarie — let them go this time! You're old enough to take it a bit easy!

But God didn't tell me He was calling my brother — He called me! It's my responsibility — and no one else's.

Do you realize that every trip will cost you over $200? You don't have money like that! Where's it all to come from?

My God shall supply all your need according to His riches in glory by Christ Jesus!

---

*A Mennonite missionary who tried to reach the Ayorés in Paraguay in the summer of 1958, but died of a spear wound he received on his first contact with them.

As the battle of "voices" raged in his mind, Bill realized that the objections were not valid excuses for inaction. The obstacles in the way of reaching the Guidaigosode were great, but there were favorable considerations, also. He knew the Ayoré language — but would he get a chance to use it? He also knew their customs and would not be so likely to "step on cultural toes" — but would just his appearance be enough to provoke an arrow or a lance thrust? He could take friendly Indians with him as guides — but they trembled at the very name "Guidaigosode"; and Bill had learned that even the Christians might suddenly desert and leave him stranded in the jungle. Then again, if he reached the Guidaigosode in the company of northern Ayorés, they might take him for their ally — an enemy that must be exterminated.

To all these doubts and objections Bill finally said, "Get thee behind me, Satan!" His mind was made up. Harriet was in perfect agreement and gave him every encouragement. On August 3, 1959, Bill wrote: "Now it seems that God has truly opened the door and we are ready to go forward. The road is open from Roboré 210 miles south to the Salt Lake, and the Army colonel in Roboré reports that on an aerial survey he saw a large Indian village in that area. I plan to leave Zapocó in two weeks, buy some kind of vehicle in Santa Cruz, take it to Roboré on the train and from there attempt to penetrate Guidaigosode territory."

But there were to be still other obstacles to be hurdled. Shortly before the date set to leave, Bill drove to Concepción and brought a new missionary out to Zapocó in the jeep. The young fellow had kept his .22 loaded and under the seat, ready in case they ran across any game along the way. When they arrived in Zapocó Bill was unloading the jeep, all the while chatting with Harriet and the Indians. He picked up the rifle by the barrel to pull it out along with the supplies he had brought.

BANG! The gun went off! The young missionary had forgotten to unload his rifle!

Bill doubled over and fell against the car, his face writhing in pain. "This would be an ignominious way to die!" he thought wryly, leaning against the jeep in the darkness.

Harriet remained calm — at least outwardly — and directed the men in getting her husband into the house and on the bed. The Indians were not so calm, however, and ran for their weapons. They knew whose gun was responsible, and wanted to murder its owner. It was all Harriet could do to restrain them, and only when Comai and a picked delegation of Ayorés were allowed to enter the bedroom where Bill was lying, and see for themselves that he was alive, did they grudgingly consent not to kill the new missionary! Even so, they said, if Bill were to die —

Although Bill was alive and conscious, he was white and shaking and gasping for breath. Harriet quickly covered him warmly and sent an Indian running to summon Chuck Ramsey. Chuck, who was destined to take over the station in Zapocó, was a good missionary "doctor." He found that the bullet had gone through Bill's right shoulder. He soon had the wound dressed and Bill was resting more or less comfortably. But the accident proved even more serious than they thought at first, and they had to take the risk of transporting Bill over the rough road to Concepción in order to fly him to Santa Cruz.

At the commercial airport in Santa Cruz Jonathan Tamplin, the tall slender World Gospel Mission pilot was taxiing his Cessna 180 to a stop, when he heard over his earphones the summons to Concepción to pick up an emergency case. He radioed the tower that he would take the assignment, and in less than an hour was in Concepción. Jonathan was shocked to find that the pain-racked form on the stretcher they hurriedly brought out to the plane was that of his friend Bill!

At the hospital Bill was placed on the critical list, and was operated on immediately. Good medical care eventually restored him to his usual robust health.

When Harriet saw her husband so close to death and contemplated the possibility of becoming a widow with four children, she was forced to rethink the Guidaigosode project. Was she *really* willing to let her husband risk his life to save the souls of those savage Indians? She knew Jean and Dorothy Dye, and Audrey Bacon, whose husbands had perished at the hands of the savages! Through them, she had come to understand some of the feelings of a widow's heart. It was not easy, but Harriet's indecision was short-lived. She could not be disobedient to the heavenly vision and prevent her husband from doing what he knew to be right.

Bill shook off the effects of the accident and even before his bullet wound was completely healed he made the exploratory trip to the Salt Lake in September. He took his pickup truck as far as San Ramón, and with two other missionaries trekked over 250 miles along the Guidaigosode trails, exploring the region and looking for the Indians. Before they left, Bill knew the area well enough to lay definite plans for the next dry season.

Just north of the Paraguayan border he pinpointed the exact location of the large Salt Lakes. In the rainy season they would become marshy lakes of thick brine. But in the dry season they hardened and formed glistening white expanses of crystal salt. All of the Ayoré tribes including those in the north, visited the area every year or so during the dry season, to carry away their year's supply of salt. The Salt Lakes were so flat and hard that an airplane could easily land on them in an emergency.

Midway between these Salt Lakes was San Ramón, an abandoned army outpost with some fairly serviceable buildings. Its most important feature, however, was the water hole. Dug centuries ago by the ancient Jesuits, it fills with water during the January-February rains. Covered by water lilies which impede evaporation, it seldom dries up. Bill knew that San Ramón would make an excellent base for the Guidaigosode advance. They found no Indians that September as they had all come for salt a month or so previously. But when the next dry season began, they would be back. Bill planned to be there to meet them.

The abandoned army outpost of San Ramón (below) became Bill Pencille's base for reaching the Guidaigosode Ayorés. He and Comai and four others worked six days a week for three months to clear enough jungle for an 800-yard landing strip. *Above*, Bill works with a native hoe-shovel.

Bill Pencille's son Bruce examines Ayoré clan marks at the Salt Lakes. (See pp. 98, 162, 221.)

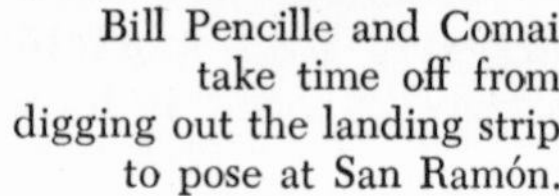

Bill Pencille and Comai take time off from digging out the landing strip to pose at San Ramón.

Jonathan Tamplin, bush pilot of the World Gospel Mission, was the group's first visitor in three months at San Ramón (p. 221).

25.

New Conquests

THE FOLLOWING APRIL in the old jeep truck, Bill headed south from Roboré once more. Destination: San Ramón and the Salt Lakes. Comai was with him, as well as four others — two Bolivian Christians and two Ayoré Christians. This time, they carried a little portable radio transmitter-receiver set. They were to need it long before they had expected!

Seventy miles south of the railroad, the jeep suddenly clattered to a stop one morning, and refused to budge. The clutch plate had simply disintegrated. There was nothing to do but walk back to an Army post and hire oxen to pull the jeep back there! The whole situation would have been much more serious had it not been for the radio. They were able to contact Santa Cruz immediately and order a new clutch on the next airline flight to Roboré. One of the men rode back to Roboré on a borrowed horse to pick it up, and in a week they were on their way again. Bill could not help but think this was a rather inglorious beginning of a noble missionary venture! "Were we out of the will of God?" he asked himself. No. Rather, he felt that this was one more attempt of the god of Asoná to keep them from reaching the Guidaigosode!

It was slow going, for the road had become badly overgrown since their last trip. The last twenty miles of road to the Salt Lakes had to be reopened completely. Many years had passed since any kind of vehicle had used this section of the road, and it took a whole week to advance those few miles.

San Ramón was still four miles from the Salt Lakes where they hoped to reach the Indians. But here they stopped because of the fresh water. The previous October when Bill had passed through San Ramón, the water hole had been dry. They had only secured water to drink by digging in the mud in the center of the hole and drinking the thick, stinking water that seeped out of the mud. Now the hole was filled with clear, sweet water from the rains of the last rainy season. San Ramón was to be home for the next six months.

Like an army consolidating its newly-won positions, they spent the first week reconnoitering the whole area, ranging north fifteen miles, beyond the northernmost Salt Lake. They explored with special care the main Salt Lake to the south, where it seemed probable that the Indians would arrive first. Although it was still early in the season and no salt was yet available because of the amount of water in the lakes, there were already footprints in the soft sand of the beaches. Around the southern Salt Lake they found four well-worn Indian trails, used on the yearly visits for salt. On each of these trails Bill left gifts of machetes, axes and clothing. The Ayorés who were with him carefully painted their clan signs in charcoal on trees from which the bark had been peeled. Then they settled down in San Ramón to wait.

Bill knew that the narrow margin between death and life, should the Indians attack them, would be the ability to call in the airplane. Jonathan Tamplin of the World Gospel Mission had promised to help in any way possible, and was on constant radio alert in case of trouble in San Ramón. With the compass, Bill calculated the best direction for the antenna, and for the airstrip. While they waited for the Indians to make their appearance, they busied themselves digging out an airstrip by hand, fighting the jungle for every square yard they were able to wrest from its control. They worked from daylight until dark six days a week. It took three months! "We could have done a far better job in a couple of afternoons with a small bulldozer," Bill mused.

April passed into May. June came and went. Twice a week, someone would walk to the Salt Lake to examine the gifts and the sand on the beaches. But there were never fresh signs of the Guidaigosode.

The men were working every day on the airstrip, to the point of exhaustion. Food was scarce. It was often too cold to sleep at night. There were no indications that the Indians were anywhere in the vicinity. Bill asked himself more than once if it was worth it all! With so many villages up north wide open to the Gospel, was he justified in spending so much time and money and effort on a project that might never be successful? Time after time, he was thrown back on the sure knowledge that God had led him to San Ramón. Whatever the outcome, he must rest in the knowledge that he was in God's will!

It was a great day when they were finally able to call Jonathan Tamplin and tell him the airstrip was ready. Just the sight of the Cessna 180 gliding to a perfect landing and taxiing up to the dilapidated house which they called "home" was a tremendous boost to their morale. Now that they were airborne their whole perspective changed.

"Sometimes we felt as though we would lose our minds," Bill said, "closed in day after day by the oppressive wall of the jungle! What a change now that we could fly over it instead of laboriously fighting our way through it! On one of the flights we saw smoke rising through the carpet of green below us and knew that the Guidaigosode were down there, even though we couldn't see them through the inpenetrable green roof of the forest. It was easier to wait, though, now that we knew they were nearby!"

July ninth began just like any other of the hundred days Bill had waited in San Ramón. Jonathan had given a few instructions for improvements on the airstrip, and after a breakfast of black coffee and bread, Bill led the men to work. Comai, as usual, took the .22 rifle to hunt meat for the noon meal. Small brown turkeys abounded in the region, and there was often fat turkey meat in the rice pot.

Only two days before, the men had reported all quiet at the Salt Lakes. Strangely, though, this day Bill's mind was filled with premonitions. He could not escape the feeling, as he worked with the others putting the final touches to the airstrip, that they should go immediately to the Salt Lakes. He tried to dismiss the idea from his mind, arguing with himself that they had been there only two days ago! Still, some inner voice seemed to urge him, "Go to the Salt Lakes!"

Over plates of boiled rice and turkey, Bill proposed

that they all stop work in the afternoon and drive down for another look around. The idea met with instant approval if for no other reason than that it offered release from the backbreaking work of digging stumps from the approaches to the airstrip!

As the jeep crept slowly through the deep sand and around the last curve before the Salt Lake, Comai began to beat furiously on the cab. "Don Guillermo!" he shouted. "They've been here! The machete is gone!" Sure enough, the knife was gone, and in its place hung a string of beads and some feathers!

The men jumped to the ground before the jeep fully stopped. The road up from the beach and the ground surrounding the gifts were deeply imprinted with footprints of the Guidaigosode. Some had been barefooted. Others had worn the typical oblong sandals made from slabs of wood. The footprints were so confused there was no way of guessing how many Indians had been there.

"How old are these footprints, Comai?"

"They were here yesterday!" was the response.

Where were the Indians now? Wasn't there danger that they might at this moment be sacking the camp in San Ramón? Bill made a hurried decision. "Comai, you and Cuchacarataide follow their trail to see which direction they have gone! I will take the two Bolivians back to San Ramón to guard the camp, and to pick up a gun or two. Then I'll catch up with you. Wait for me once you know which direction the Guidaigosode have taken!"

"That's a good idea!" Comai agreed. Turning to his companion he said, "Come on, let's go!"

The Bolivian men were nervous at being left alone, so Bill told them to barricade themselves in the house. He left a gun for each of them to quell their fears, and went roaring back to the Salt Lake in the jeep. The road ended at the edge of the beach, and from there Bill went on foot, half running, following the trail of the Guidaigosode, and more recently, the footprints of Comai and his companion. The footprints were deeply etched in the soft sand, and there was no difficulty in following them. From the depth of the trail, Bill surmised that there must have been forty or more Guidaigosode in the party!

The trail led southward for some seven or eight miles, following the shore of the Salt Lake. Then it turned abruptly west into the thick, thorny brush which grew right to the edge of the beach.

Bill stopped for breath before plunging into the bush. He had still seen nothing of his friends. In their enthusiasm they had gone ahead, eager to catch up with those for whom they had prayed so long. As he rested, breathing heavily from the exertion of half-running through the deep sand, Bill suddenly heard shouts and screams in the distance. He was instantly on his feet, his .30-.30 grasped firmly in his sweaty hand. He started swiftly up the trail into the brush in the direction of the voices ahead. A thousand thoughts filled his mind . . . had the Guidaigosode killed his friends? . . . What if some returning hunter should hear him in his noisy passage through the brush, and ambush him from behind? . . . What did the confused shouting up ahead mean?

The shouts grew ever louder until they were only a hundred yards away. Bill stopped momentarily to catch his breath and breathed a prayer to God, then shouted at the top of his lungs. He did not want to come upon the Indians unawares. He would be better able to defend himself if they had to come to him, rather than his walking unannounced, into their midst!

In a moment he was surrounded by sweating, grinning savages. They were shouting, almost in unison, *"Omi yoque!"* "We are pretty! We mean you no harm!" Comai and Cuchacarataide were in their midst, safe but nearly naked. They had given their clothes to their new-found friends in token of their friendship.

Although the young warriors of the group were jubilant, many of the older men were sullen and watchful. Bill could hear them muttering under their breath, "This is a trick! No white man is good!"

The sun was rapidly sinking behind the treetops in the west. Bill felt it would be unwise to sleep with the Indians. Why give them a chance to murder you in your sleep? he reasoned. He asked for volunteers to return with him to San Ramón, and the captain chose ten young braves to accompany him.

There was enough daylight left to reach the edge of the

Above, suspicion fills the eyes of Guidaigosode Indians who have never before seen a white man. *Below,* this friendly Guidaigosode warrior was one of the first that Bill met. He took a gift machete to Chief Uejai (p. 226).

Salt Lake; but from there they walked on in complete darkness. A cold south wind blew, and the Guidaigosode, completely naked, trembled with cold. Bill asked Comai about the contact, and what had happened when they met the Indians.

"We got to within a hundred yards or so of their camp and I shouted to warn them of our presence," he answered. "Immediately, about forty of them surrounded us. They were heavily armed. But I showed them our guns and told them not to come closer. I had come in peace, I assured them, and wanted to talk to them."

"Did they attempt to attack you?"

"No; but the chief said, 'If you're so peaceful, what have you got guns for? Put down your guns and we'll talk of peace!' I told him he should be able to see that we are peaceful because we shouted first instead of shooting. Then he said he hadn't thought of that, and he came forward and gave me his spear. We took off most of our clothes and gave them to the men. That's about when you arrived!"

It was nearly ten o'clock at night when they arrived back in San Ramón. The poor Bolivians were nearly paralyzed with fear. They were sure that Bill and his companions had been massacred, and neither of them knew how to run the radio to call for help. Never, perhaps, had Bill been welcomed with more enthusiasm!

He was exhausted, and soon dropped off to sleep in his hammock. But not Comai! He stayed up most of the night, telling his new friends of Dupade. He started with creation and finished with the crucifixion. They listened with rapt attention.

Next morning, Bill began to question them about their tribe. "Who is your chief?" he asked.

"Uejai."

"Who are the other chiefs?" Bill held his ubiquitous pad and pencil.

"There are many other chiefs. But Uejai is the big chief!"

"How many other chiefs are under Uejai?"

The Indians started counting, and before they had finished they had used up the fingers and toes of one man and were on the third toe of another! Thirty-three subchiefs under one leader! No centralized authority like that ever existed up north. Uejai must be tremendously powerful, thought Bill. He estimated that there were perhaps 1,000 Ayorés under his command! The ten men were actually from Uejai's own village. Bill realized that the key man to the future of the Guidaigosode work would be Uejai!

The warriors also told Bill that an epidemic had recently passed through the tribe and that many of the old chiefs and witch doctors had died. This placed a good deal of the tribal power in the hands of the younger men who were quite eager to make friends with the civilized people. "If you had arrived a year ago," they said, "you would probably have been killed!"

Toward noon, some of the visitors picked up their bags and said they were going to return to their camp. A few told Bill they wanted to stay with him and go to the railroad line, but he refused to take them. He felt it would be much more profitable if they would spread the news of the contact through the jungle and perhaps open the way for a meeting with Uejai himself. Finally, they agreed and Bill gave them all parting gifts and sent his best machete as a special gift to Uejai.

As they went down the trail their parting words were, "We will come back — with our families! We cannot tell you just when it will be. Maybe Uejai will send us back quickly so we can learn more about the white people. Or perhaps he will gather all the Guidaigosode and return with hundreds of men. Many may not be friendly at first. Some may even want to kill you. But we will protect you, for we are now your friends!"

26.

Uejai — King of the South

It was just a week after this contact, as Bill and his companions were relaxing in their hammocks in San Ramón, that they heard shouts coming from the direction of the Salt Lake. They were on their feet instantly, and in a few moments nine Indians appeared at the edge of the jungle on the far side of the landing strip. There were three women among them — the first women courageous enough to come to San Ramón. They were unarmed, and the men waved their empty hands above their heads to prove it. Neither Comai nor Bill recognized any of them as having been in the first group.

Bill walked toward them. He was unarmed, and went very slowly, not wanting to frighten them by any false moves. Comai was at his side. They reached the men and tried to talk with them; but the Indians were so frightened they could not speak coherently. Even so, Bill marveled at their courage in coming out the way they did. He knew the inbred fear of whites that was in their hearts.

Gradually they became more composed and Bill invited them over to his camp. Comai sat down with them in the shade of a huge, thorny *cupesi* tree, while one of the Bolivians prepared a pot of beans for them. When they had eaten and were more at ease, Bill asked, "Who is your chief?"

"Uejai is our chief!"

"Why did you come?"

"Uejai sent us. He wants to know if the white man is still here."

"Where is Uejai now?"

"He is nearby — just beyond the Salt Lakes!"

"Will he come to my camp?" Bill tried to hide his eagerness.

"Uejai will come."

At dusk, three of the men left to bear the news to Uejai, leaving the other six, three men and three women, in San Ramón. Each night, Bill gathered them around him and told them of the Gospel. One day, twelve more Guidaigosode appeared and the group swelled to eighteen. One man in this new group was extremely hostile and caused Bill some very anxious moments. By this time, he knew the Indians well enough to read their feelings in their facial expressions. Like small children, they are incapable of disguising emotion. Every one of the new arrivals would look at Bill with an open and frank expression and return his smiles — except this one. When Bill glanced his way, he invariably glared at the missionary with a baleful look, then under Bill's steady gaze he would turn away. "Here's a troublemaker!" thought Bill.

Before long, Bill noticed that the warrior was following him wherever he went. "What's the matter with this fellow?" the missionary asked the other Guidaigosode.

"He does not trust the white man," was the response. "He says you are a spy and want to tell Natui where we are! Then Natui will come with the noise sticks! He says no white man can be good, and he does not like white men!"

Bill went out of his way to be friendly to the warrior. Once he put his hand on his shoulder and said, "You know, I really like you!" When he passed out gifts, he made a very great show of including the sullen Indian, although he probably expected to have been left out. Indians give gifts only to friends, and he was no friend.

For two more days the hostility continued. Then, on the morning of the third day the Indian walked up to Bill and said, "I like you!" A friendly smile lighted his round, brown face. From that time on, he became one of Bill's dearest friends.

At last the long-awaited day arrived, and Uejai came to San Ramón. It was a Sunday morning. The sun had not fully risen and Bill was still half-asleep. Suddenly, over one hundred naked savages came pouring out of the jungle with a mighty shout. There was pandemonium as the other Guidaigosode ran out to welcome the newcomers. Uejai walked fearlessly, unarmed, into the camp and met Bill, chief to chief. It was one of the most thrilling moments in

Bill's missionary career; he knew at once that he had never before met an Indian like Uejai!

About Bill's height, he was the best formed Ayoré warrior Bill had ever seen — a perfect physical specimen. Apparently in his forties, he was one of the few Indians with a high forehead, slightly bald. His black hair was wavy and his features unusually fine. His dark eyes expressed alternate amusement or displeasure beneath their lashless lids, but his manner was most dignified. From head to toe Uejai was a chief. The Indians called him *Ayoré-pisi,* "The Ayoré!"

From that moment there was a continuous uproar in the camp. Bill insisted the Indians must have slept in relays, for the noise continued twenty-four hours a day. There were almost one hundred and fifty Indians in San Ramón!

With so many of the Guidaigosode as his guests, Bill had his share of problems. The most urgent was the fact that they couldn't seem to understand why he wasn't interested in an interim wife! The fact that he insisted he had a perfectly good one back home didn't impress them in the least! Bill tells the story:

"You see, no Indian ever lives for anything but *now.* A man's wife might die today, and tomorrow if there is an eligible woman in camp he is married to her. It does not mean that he did not love his first wife. They simply live for today, for there may not be a tomorrow. When they find plenty of honey, they eat it all immediately, never thinking that they might go hungry for the next several days.

"They just couldn't understand why I was not interested in another wife, and a number of girls offered themselves as a solution to the problem. I realized that the only answer would be to crank up the radio and ask Harriet if she would fly down for a month. I hated to bring her into a situation like this . . . the dirt, the stinking water, the heat, the lack of privacy, the crush of wild, sweaty, noisy Indians! But she jumped at the chance to come, and Jonathan Tamplin flew her and five-year-old Steve down the next day. She was with me a month, and I suppose we taught them more of God's ideal for a family by that month of living among them than we would have done in a thousand sermons!"

Uejai himself had four wives, and Bill says that during the

This Indian thought a Corn Flakes box would make a good hat. Harriet Pencille had sent Bill some cookies in it.

Uejai, Chief of the Ayorés

many months he lived in close association with him, he never was conscious of any discord or rancor either among the wives themselves or between Uejai and his wives. The chief explained the situation to Bill as their solution to a surplus of women living in a completely closed society. The Guidaigosode had always been warlike and the death of so many warriors had resulted in a surplus of women. By allowing the chiefs to take plural wives, chaos was avoided in the marital life of the tribe!

The thrilling thing about this contact with Uejai and his group was the ability to preach the Gospel to the Guidaigosode from the very first day. In Zapocó, in the early days, it had taken years to learn enough of the language to make them understand spiritual truths. Now, however, both Bill and Comai were constantly with them, taking advantage of every opportunity to preach to them and teach them about the things of God. Harriet had a constant following of women and children, and they listened most attentively as she would teach them Bible truths.

The Guidaigosode proved very open and receptive to the Gospel, and Bill had great hopes that there soon would be a group of Christians among them.

One afternoon the honey hunters came in and excitedly spread the news that they had come across the trail of another group of Indians! The witch doctors and chiefs began their ceremonies and incantations that night, trying to stir up the tribe's emotions to a fighting pitch. They were planning to kill the other group in the morning!

"Why not just talk to them and bring them here?" suggested Bill.

"Bring them here! They are our enemies! We are going to kill them!" was the fierce response.

Next morning, about forty of the young braves, their spears sharpened and their bodies painted black, started up the trail on the run. Nothing Bill could say would deter them in their deadly plans.

At noon they were back with a roar, their arms filled with the spoils of victory. They had found the camp of the other group, but only three women were there. All the rest were hunting in the forest. They tried to get these women to come back and live with them, but they declared themselves faithful to their own husbands. So they murdered them and brought back everything they could carry from the camp.

One of the things they brought was a partially woven skirt which they gave to Harriet as a gift. Harriet could plainly see where the last stitch had been taken before its owner had fallen victim to a fatal spear thrust! As she thought of the terrible death and eternal destiny of the woman, a tear fell onto the skirt — when would the love of God penetrate into these savage hearts!

That evening the men who had done the killing blackened their bodies once more, and did the *tarigai* dance. In this way they were supposedly free from all danger from their victims' spirits. They made a small clearing and then chanted and stomped the ground around its perimeter. They stomped the spirits into the ground. By morning the whole affair was forgotten. Life is cheap in Ayoréland!

This incident brought Bill to the abrupt realization that the Guidaigosode were still a long way from understanding the truth of God's Word! Neither Asoná nor Sidi ever taught them any moral truths by which to govern their lives. When Bill first began to teach them about sin they would invariably respond, "We're not bad! The white men are bad, they kill us. Our enemies are bad, but not us! We are good!" Fornication bad? Murder evil? They had never thought of such things! After all, you only murder in self defense . . . those who hate you, or would kill you if they got a chance, or had put a curse on you! Selfishness and anger, however, were evil; for they would quickly disrupt the close-knit life of the tribe.

Is sin relative after all? Of course we know it isn't! We make it so by making some sins more sinful than others. But the Word of God is the answer to all sin, and the Son of God became sin — that we might become the righteousness of God! Bill now shifted his emphasis in preaching from the love of God to the law of God.

"Do you want to know more of what God has told us?" he asked them.

"Oh, yes; we do! Tell us more!" they chorused.

"Well, many years ago, God gave us His law. He said that we must not have other gods except Him. We must not kill one another; we must not be adulterers; we must not steal; if anyone does these things, God will surely punish him!"

That afternoon no one said that he wanted to believe. "By the law is the knowledge of sin." And by the preaching of the law their hearts were being laid open, wounded, and made ready for the healing balm of the Gospel.

Harriet felt flattered when Uejai assigned four of his fiercest-looking warriors as her personal bodyguard. "You will not leave the white woman; protect her from harm!" he ordered them, brusquely. They obeyed his orders implicitly. But the royal service had its difficulties, too. There had never been much privacy in San Ramón, since the Indians had arrived. Now for Harriet there was none, ever! She partially solved the problem by sleeping in her clothes and not changing them for the entire six days that Uejai was with them! Nothing Harriet could do or say would get rid of these four men. Uejai had spoken and they were to obey!

During the time they were together, Bill became very friendly with Uejai. From the beginning there was a strong mutual respect. He fully accepted Bill as a chief and his equal, including him in his council meetings and asking for and acting upon Bill's suggestions as to the handling of daily problems.

Bill says, "Uejai was the biggest miracle of all! I had had plenty of advice as to how we would have to handle him. The tame Indians maintained that we would have to kill him with guns before we could ever hope to do anything with his people. The whites often suggested handling the whole Indian problem by catching one of them, giving him smallpox and sending him back to expose the entire tribe! God, however, had His own way of dealing with Uejai; He had been working in his heart preparing him for this meeting."

Before long, the young men began to put great pressure on Bill to take them to the railroad line. This Bill was not willing to do. After the heartbreaking experience in Zapocó fighting a losing battle with disease, Bill now hoped it might be possible to live with the Guidaigosode in their own villages, far from civilization, until they had slowly built up a resistance to disease. When he explained the plan and his reasons to Uejai, the chief immediately saw the wisdom of it.

"What shall we do, then?" Bill asked the chief.

Uejai was thoughtful for a time. Then he looked up with a serious, sad expression and said, "You go home. I will take my people to a new water hole two weeks' walk from here. There we shall build a new village and plant our crops. We will celebrate the festival of Asoná on the way. Then, in three moons you return here. I will personally meet you and take you to the new village. Then you can live with us, and my people will be saved from the ravages of white man's diseases!"

For Bill, it was the hardest parting he had ever experienced. As he bade good-by to his new friends and headed back toward Roboré in the jeep truck, he wondered if things would really work out this way! "Three months is a long time!" he reasoned to himself. "Especially when it concerns stone-age Indians!"

27.

Peace at Last

Bill sold his jeep truck in Roboré and went back to Zapocó. If Uejai moved fourteen days' journey back into the jungle, the jeep would be useless in reaching him. For future trips he would depend on Jonathan Tamplin and his airplane. Back in Zapocó, he carefully laid plans for following up the contact with Uejai.

Above all, he wanted to prevent the Guidaigosode from coming out to the railroad line. There they would scatter, sickness would kill many of them, and they would become corrupted by civilized life before they understood the Gospel. Bill planned to live with them in the woods for as long as necessary. It might be months or even years. He planned to make an airstrip at their new village. At least, in this way he would be reasonably certain that they had heard and understood the Gospel before becoming civilized.

Bill had been back in Zapocó only a few weeks when the transmitter crackled to life one morning: "CPL 7G. CPL 7G. This is Tobité calling CPL 7G. Over!" It was Howie Morarie from Tobité, calling Bill.

"This is CPL 7G," Bill answered into the microphone. "Reading you fine, Howie. What's new in Tobité? Over to 7A."

"Bad news, 7G," came Howard's matter-of-fact voice. "It looks like Natui is up to his old tricks. They held a council of war all night, and this morning about eighty of them headed down to wipe out the Guidaigosode! I tried to stop them, but Natui told me they were just going to make peace! Ha! Over to 7G."

"Have they any guns, Howie? Over."

"Plenty! A dozen or so that I know of, maybe more.

They wanted to buy a box of shells from me! How's that for brass? Over to 7G."

"Shells-for-peace program, huh?" Bill responded. "Look, do you know if they're all from Tobité? Over."

"I believe so. Maybe there are some others. They're sending word to Zapocó and along the railroad line for the others to join them. Over."

"Roger, Howie. I'll have to do something about it. Thanks for the news. Anything more? Over to 7A."

"Nothing at the moment. Let me know what you are planning to do. This will be CPL 7A!"

On the same radio contact, Bill was able to get in touch with Jonathan. He was in the midst of their annual mission conference, but readily agreed to fly Bill to San Ramón the next day. Time was important. If Natui took food supplies and didn't have to waste time by hunting along the way, he might make it to the Guidaigosode village in ten days or two weeks. Bill had never been to the new village and he wondered if he could make much better time from San Ramón through unfamiliar country. But he had to beat Natui! He was the only one who would have a chance of stopping the slaughter.

Bill knew that another war would make it difficult if not impossible to ever work again with the Guidaigosode. Uejai would surely think that Bill had been a spy. He would be certain that he had given reports of the Guidaigosode location and strength and had sent Natui down to kill them. The Guidaigosode had not been softened by civilization, and had the reputation of being one of the most powerful of all the Amazon tribes. Guns or no, they would give Natui a battle he would never forget!

Jonathan was delayed and didn't get to Zapocó until late afternoon. They had time to fly only as far as San José before dark, and continued their trip to San Ramón the next day. Comai and Cuchacarataide were with Bill. He kept a diary of the trip.

Nov. 12, 1960. Left 8:30. 40 minute flight to Salt Lake. Didn't see Natui's group. Found Guidaigosode and I dropped them my shirt . . . . Right brake went out in San Ramón landing but made it OK. Nice group of Indians here, arrived yesterday. Soldiers are here to hunt, but one of the Indians killed their pack-ox.

From the Stone Age to the Space Age – the World Gospel Mission Cessna 180 lands for the first time in the jungle where Ayoré Indians can inspect it.

Holding a hand-cranked generator between his legs and his homemade spear in his hand, an Ayoré warrior eyes the whole radio transmitter outfit with caution. It was a sharp spear like this that killed Cornelius Isaak (p. 213).

When the Ayoré men are not hunting, or relating their hunting adventures (above), they play games to keep their muscles in fighting trim. This one (below) is their favorite, a game of Touch or Tag.

I forgot to take the generator crank out of the plane, so I had to make one of wood. I'm not sure it will work well enough to get on the air.

Every place I go here is full of memories of Harriet and Stevie's having been here! How I miss them! May God give me the grace and courage I need for this job.

Uejai and some 100 arrived in the afternoon and told me it was their young warriors who had stolen the soldiers' stuff and killed their ox. Uejai was angry at all the young fellows because of it. I decided it best to keep quiet, and told him I would not mention it to the soldiers.

Nov. 13. Finally got the crank fixed out of wood and got on the air. The Indians are nervous over the killing of the ox and began to leave shortly after noon. I told Uejai I'd come tomorrow. But he was reticent to leave without me, and so about 4:30 we packed and left. Slept with them three miles out. Found water I had known of.

Nov. 14. Broke camp by moonlight about 4 A.M. Headed north. My being with them, instead of them with me, has its advantages! They take complete care of us and are carrying our packs. The life of Riley!

Stopped for 7:30 radio contact, but the man carrying the generator didn't catch up with us in time. Began to rain at 8:30. Arrived soaked at their camp north of the Salt Lake. Many, many Indians here whom we have not previously seen. Some 300 in all. Not an unfriendly face in the group. At 4:30 talked with Zapocó on the radio.

Moved to new camp in the evening. Cold! Getting by on honey and *saó* (palm heart), plus a little rice and coffee we have brought along. Still waiting for Natui and his gang. Talked to group of young people at night. A pretty young girl wanted Comai. We did not try to have a regular meeting as there was too much noise. Their village is four days from here, west.

Nov. 15. Cold! ! ! . . . Had a good meeting at night — almost a command performance by order of Uejai. Good attention. There are five men who have been praying since we first told them of the Saviour in San Ramón last September. Uejai put on a good show after the meeting. He sucked a comb from my foot (which, by the way, hasn't bothered me down here.) *

---

*Bill had hurt his foot in San Ramón, but it was on the mend. However, because Bill was limping, Uejai offered to "cure" the foot by "sucking" out the trouble. This was accompanied by a great deal of ceremony and ritual.

The young women wanted Cuchacarataide last night, but I don't think anything came of it.

Nov. 16. Time drags slowly in a place like this with nothing to do! I have already read everything I have with me. We had a good meeting in the evening. One of the hardest things of all is to pray and read the Word. Privacy is impossible as they follow me everywhere.

Nov. 17. All four witch doctors finally got to work on Comai — really worked him over. What a picture this makes, as four of them go to work on a prone figure while one hundred or more Indians look on!**

I don't believe I have ever in my life seen such absolutely loose living! Very few seem to sleep with the same partner on two successive nights.

Nov. 18. We moved about a mile west to another water-hole. These holes have all been dug, for there are high banks of earth around them. But the trees seem too large — the water holes could not have been dug just twenty-five years ago during the Chaco War. Perhaps they are relics of the old Jesuits.

I washed some clothes today. This proved to be quite an operation. I stripped to my shorts and was immediately surrounded by a mixed crowd that insisted I take them off, too! They were not too convinced even yet that I am of the male sex. I didn't feel in the mood to oblige them.

Slept early. My hammock is almost in the center of the camp. We wouldn't last fifteen seconds if they would turn against us.

Nov. 19. In the evening meeting passed from resurrection to case of Jesus' raising Lazarus from the dead. Fair attention. Young men not too interested, though. Every night is one great party between them and the women. Jonathan has gone on vacation and I'll have no way out of here unless I walk.

Nov. 21. This is paganism without any trappings of culture at all! What a dirty, smelly place this camp is after four days! The forest is clean and pure until man arrives. Only man is vile! I think I can understand what camp life with Moses must have been like. I have tried to get Comai to witness more to the Indians personally.

Nov. 22. Uejai has ordered a move west to the village, but no one has moved as yet. They are reticent to go. I don't know why. It probably just lacks someone to lead off. We

---

**Comai's trouble was stomach pains. The witch doctors all worked at "sucking" out the assorted causes.

finally got off at 11, and went until nearly one o'clock, to another waterhole. Have upset stomach and am not eating *saó* to see if that helps! The Indians are sick with colds, and I am thankful there is still no fever. They say it is the spirit of the ox they killed in San Ramón that has made them ill. Uejai is still angry at the young men over the killing.

Am praying much for Comai and Cuchacarataide. I am sure they are under tremendous temptation. They were all carrying on last night until past one. (The Guidaigosode) have an interesting and I think a good custom, by the way. When either a man or woman leaves his partner for someone else, the rest of the tribe have the right to carry off everything he or she owns, and there is no reclaim. A good punishment for adultery, but I don't see that it has much effect here.

Nov. 23. Was able to have a good time in the Word with them at sundown. It is most interesting. At first, when we mentioned the Gospel and the love of God, many said they would believe. Of late, we have been dealing with sin and the law — we don't hear much any more about believing!

Nov. 24. Thanksgiving! And how much I have to be thankful for, though this is not quite turkey and trimmings. Palm heart and honey water for breakfast. But I am happy just the same to be here, for my Lord has sent me. And I wouldn't be any other place in the world.

We had quite a time getting space cleared to put up the antenna. 116 feet in a straight line is a long way in this brush!

One does not feel especially hungry here once you are out of the habit of three regular meals a day. Thirst is worse. A terrifically hot night. I'm sure I can't be as thirsty as I feel! It must be the knowledge that all day tomorrow and most of the next will be waterless!

Nov. 25. Beautiful rain just before daylight until about 9. My watch has stopped. Filled everything including ourselves with water. Our Heavenly Father is indeed never too late, only my faith is faulty.

Ducubaide wailed again last night. The other Indians who came into camp brought word of the death of his son among the many who died in the sickness they got from the oil folks in Paraguay. I know of nothing that cuts me to the heart like this death wail in the middle of the night! And I am sure now we will have to more or less live with them in a more accessible place. Otherwise, they will soon die off.

Nov. 26. My foot has been bothering me, and we squeezed a good bit of matter from it last night.

Nov. 27. Walked at least six miles south and are approaching the village. Met some of the women out this way hunting. Was our dog, Canela, ever glad to see us! She is fat as butter. We gave her to them last September, but she still remembers us.

Arrived in the village at about 2 P.M. My stomach is acting up and I feel generally ill. No doubt it is the sun. I have never known it to be hotter! What a sight this village is! There must be nearly four hundred Indians here. Many very old men and women and a host of children. The village is well laid out on an oblong plan, with a sort-of plaza in the center. They have some squash so perhaps we won't fare too badly.

Nov. 28. Looked around for suitable landing strip, and think we can make one here. Will perhaps start tomorrow. Indians are quite bad off with colds and sore eyes, but so far no grippe or pneumonia.

Difficult to preach to them. During the day the heat is such that they are all scattered under whatever shade they can find. At night the witch doctors are usually carrying on. But I think I found the answer last night — just sitting down with a small group and talking the Word of God to them.

Last night, they killed and buried a baby just like you might kill an unwanted puppy, with a club! Oh, God! How great is the darkness! Might it not overwhelm me! Give me of Thy light and of Thy grace and I will shine for Thee! I am Thy bondslave, Lord Jesus, and a debtor for these people, for Thy sake.

Bill had been in the jungle living an Indian's life for twenty-two days. Natui and his hostile group should be arriving most any day if they had gone through with their plan. Tension was building up. Every able-bodied Guidaigosode man had made a good supply of arrows and had sharpened his lance to a razor-edge. All weapons had been placed in strategic positions, ready for any emergency, and a guard had been posted.

Bill oftened wondered what he would do when Natui actually arrived. He hoped his presence wouldn't be a surprise to the war chief! To avoid this, he and Comai had left a note at a spot a couple of days up the trail. He knew that some of Natui's men had learned to read in the mission schools. Chances were that Natui wouldn't attempt a surprise attack — he would announce his presence, temperatures would rise, and a free-for-all would result. Bill might well find himself right in the midst of it all. If he did, it certainly would go bad for him.

Of course, there was always the possibility that Natui had become discouraged and turned back. But in daily radio contact with Tobité, Bill knew that Natui had not returned home. Only a sick couple had gone back, but they said that Natui was determined to follow through and defeat Uejai once and for all. Bill figured that his chances of stopping the war were slim. But God could do it! He could only pray that peace could be made after generations of hatred and inter-tribal warfare.

Bill was talking to a group of five men about the work on the airstrip one hot December morning at about 8:30 when suddenly the air was penetrated with the shrill cry that all had been expecting and dreading.

"*Ayoré quiiiiii!* Ayorés are coming!"

Mothers rushed to gather their children together and ran with them into the forest. The warriors snatched up spears, bows and warclubs, and prepared for a stand to the death.

Bill quickly grasped his revolver in his right hand and ran up the trail, alone, to confront Natui. If they were going to fight the Guidaigosode, Bill had determined that they were going to fight him first!

The big chief, rifle in hand, was in the lead. They were all painted black and their war feathers were up in the fighting position. Bill noted several other guns in the crowd. One well-placed bullet would end everything.

When he saw Bill, Natui called a sudden halt. Bill must have looked as fierce as any Indian with his three-week beard, tattered clothing and revolver drawn and ready in his hand. His eyes flashed as he approached Natui. The Indian chief spoke first.

"*Omi yoque!*" he called out. "We are pretty! We want peace!"

"All of you?" Bill shouted back, grimly.

"All of us!"

Bill walked up to Natui. They knew one another well, and there was a mutual respect between them. But there had never been any close bond of friendship. Natui had little use for missionaries, and he didn't care who knew it; but Bill commanded his respect.

Bill spoke quietly, but firmly. "Natui, I want it understood that if there is any trouble, I'm going to defend my new friends! You know better than to kill. If you want war, you might as well fight me first!"

"We are not going to fight!" insisted Natui.

"Did you find my note?"

The burly war chief raised his eyebrows in assent.

Bill turned his back and walked into the village. The Guidaigosode warriors had lined up on the far side of the little plaza with their weapons ready. Uejai was out in front. Comai stood over on the right side, a .30-.30 rifle in his hands. Bill wondered, as he took his place next to Uejai, how Comai would react to his brother's arrival. Would he remain loyal to Bill? A glance at his set face reassured him.

Natui had seventy-five men with him. They formed parallel lines with the Guidaigosode, on the opposite sides of the open square. Everyone was tense and watchful.

Suddenly, the clearing reverberated with infernal shouts. Natui took one step forward and let out a blood-curdling war cry. He stomped the ground and raised his rifle over his head! A murmur went up in the crowd of Indians around Bill. Uejai answered with his even more fierce, gutteral cry. Bill's heart nearly stopped beating. What if someone should fire a gun or loose an arrow? He had promised to defend the Guidaigosode. This would be a battle to the death. Should he — could he — shoot to kill? A vision of George Haight crossed his mind. "If you have to use your gun, do it!" George had said.

So many thoughts seemed to race through his mind in a moment of time. Why should he suddenly remember the words of a prominent psychoanalyst? "The mark of the immature man is that he wants to die nobly for a cause; while the mark of the mature man is that he wants to live humbly for one!" Bill was conscious of a deep desire to live.

But there was no time to think or rationalize. Things were happening too fast. War cries and threats were being hurled from each side, and the very jungle echoed and re-echoed with the sound. Tempers were as taut as the

Above, a group of Ayoré braves, dressed for war, emerge from the jungle. Later, with civil war averted, the chiefs sat down to smoke the peace pipe (*left*). Chief Uejai (in front of the jaguar-hatted Ayoré) has the pipe.

Comai poses with two Guidaigosode braves who might have turned out to be less friendly (pp. 221-226). In moments of excitement or rage an Ayoré man will slash himself to demonstrate courage. The man on the left has chest scars.

strings on their bows. One arrow or one bullet would have lit the fuse and the camp would have exploded like a bomb.

Suddenly, a Guidaigosode brave dashed out from the group into no-man's-land between them. He raised his lance and slashed himself across the forehead, opening a long, crimson gash. Blood spurted from the wound and streamed down his face, as he shouted and screamed insults at the enemies from the north! Things seemed to be getting out of hand. Bill prayed silently for a miracle.

Then, as suddenly as the shouting had begun, it ceased. Apparently the whole thing had been a show, a face-saving ritual, important for both sides, a primitive Geneva peace conference! The commotion died down, and Bill breathed a little easier. Only then did he notice that his sore foot was throbbing.

Natui's warriors stopped their threats and calmly walked over to their estranged relatives' firesides. They sat down to chat with them as if they had been practicing that sort of savage "brinkmanship" every day!

That afternoon Natui, Uejai and two or three of the main sub-chiefs from either side gathered in a circle in front of Uejai's house. The pipes were lighted and passed around. As the smoke, the spirit of Sidi, went up and dissipated into the atmosphere, so the hostility of decades was broken down. The pipe was a pipe of peace. Neither Natui nor Uejai had lost face.

That night after the camp had become quiet, Uejai sought Bill out in his hammock. "Now you've saved me three times, don Guillermo! You saved me from the white men and their sickness; you saved me from the anger of the soldiers when my warriors killed their ox; and now you've saved me from Natui!"

Bill silently prayed that there would be a fourth time, when Uejai accepted Christ as his Saviour and Lord!

He knew that the real struggle was not between two savage chieftains! It was a spiritual struggle, a struggle in which once again God had demonstrated His power over the powers of darkness. Perhaps now the light of the Gospel would begin to penetrate into the darkened hearts of the Guidaigosode!

28.

Defeat of Asoná

ONE AFTERNOON some weeks before Natui had arrived, Bill had been walking out in the bush and through some tangled branches saw a tiny form on the ground beside a few glowing embers of fire. Going closer he made out the form of a little girl lying half dead on the ground. The entire right side of her head was terribly burned. The corner of her eye was drawn up and the top of an ear was gone. The burn was covered with a hard crust of ashes and dirt, and matter oozed out around the edges. Even at the distance of several paces, the stench was nauseating. The child was in excruciating pain and was unspeakably filthy. Obviously, the Indians had thrown her away.

Bill strode angrily to Uejai and asked, "Why have you thrown that child away?"

The chief fixed Bill with a stony stare. "What girl do you mean?" he said, with feigned ignorance. Bill knew very well that he was the one who must have given the order to banish her from the camp.

"You know who I mean!" Bill answered, his face as grim as the chief's. "The little girl over there behind the houses."

There was silence for a long moment, then the chief spoke slowly. "Oh — you mean Simatague?"

"I don't know her name, but if that's the girl with the burn, then that's the one I mean!"

The chief straightened his back and spoke with authority. "Simatague must die! I can do nothing. You cannot help her. The witch doctors have done all they can for her. But she will never recover. Asoná has cursed her!"

"What did she do to offend Asoná?" Bill inquired.

"She woke up Asoná!"

Bill understood instantly what that meant. It was *the* unpardonable sin for an Ayoré. When the world was "closed up," she had been walking through some dry leaves and happened to kick a hibernating *cuyavo*. The bird fluttered away into the woods, but poor Simatague was doomed from that moment on. Later, she had had a nightmare and rolled into the fire, burning the whole side of her head. No one doubted why this had happened. "Asoná!" they exclaimed. "Asoná pushed her into the fire!" There was nothing to do but to throw her away.

This was Bill's opportunity. He said, "I know your bird has power. But I've been telling you about Dupade, who is much stronger than Asoná!"

The Indians were interested so Bill went a step further. "Bring the girl here!" he ordered. The chief nodded his approval.

They carried Simatague back into camp, and Bill knelt beside her in the sand. Her little chest was sunken and her ribs protruded in parallel ridges. Bill placed his hand lightly on her little head as he prayed to Dupade in the Ayoré tongue, asking him to heal her. "Oh Dupade, show your power over this wicked Asoná!"

As they listened in awed silence to the prayer, in their innermost hearts the Indians hoped that Dupade would answer! They were well aware that Asoná held them in her unrelenting grip. They would gladly worship a stronger spirit who was good, instead of the wicked and vengeful bird god! But — would it be safe to do so?

Then Bill opened his medical kit. "I sent a little boy down to the waterhole," he wrote later, "with the coffee can I used to cook squash in. He brought back some water. All the things in my medical kit were magic to them — all of those bottles and things, and of course, they considered it all witchcraft. I don't purposely deceive them, but neither can I explain to a savage within a few months after I meet him, how an antibiotic works! So I don't try to explain. I let them draw their own conclusions. And the conclusion is that just as their witch doctors have power over the spirits, so this great spirit, Dupade, who sent me, has bestowed his power on me.

"I picked up a little bottle, opened it, and took out a tiny black pill. I dropped the pill into the can of water. The water turned blood red! Potassium permanganate was all it was — a disinfectant. But of course, it was magic — it turned a can of water blood red! They oh'd and ah'd at that. Then, with a piece of cotton I dripped the potassium permanganate on her head until the ashes and dirt softened and sloughed off and I got down to the burned, raw flesh.

"I took out a couple of other white lumps, ground them to powder and sprinkled this powder carefully on the wound. The powder was nothing but a sulfa drug, of course.

"Then I took out of my kit what to them were just two pieces of glass. Lo and behold, one of them fit right inside the other! I took a piece of wire with a hole through it and fitted it right on the end of the glass. I opened a bottle, and they all spit on the ground. Alcohol was what was in the bottle, but they didn't like the odor and spat to show their disgust. As I washed her arm with this, they had quite a gagging time of it. Then, with all the magic of sterilizing a syringe and boiling it and putting it together and washing the top of a bottle and sticking a needle in and filling the syringe with penicillin — you can imagine how that would impress a raw savage! And then as they gasped, I plunged this thing into her arm!

"By the end of my month in Uejai's village new flesh was beginning to appear. You could see the old wound drying up around the edges."

When it was clear to all that Simatague was getting well, Uejai became very thoughtful. His savage mind understood nothing of science or medicine. To him the month-long healing process was a bitter struggle between the two most powerful supernatural forces he knew — Dupade and Asoná. Instinctively Uejai knew what many modern day sophisticates deny: that "we wrestle not against flesh and blood, but against powers, against the rulers of the darkness of this world, against spiritual wickedness in high places." The little girl had awakened Asoná, and Asoná had struck back with bitter revenge. But Bill Pencille had invoked the power of Dupade, and for the first time in his life Uejai saw that the wicked curse of the bird god could be challenged and conquered.

One evening after Bill had cleansed and dressed Simatague's head, Uejai arose from his place by the fire and walked over to him. He placed his rough hand on Bill's shoulder and said, "Dupade has defeated Asoná. Ayorés will follow Dupade."

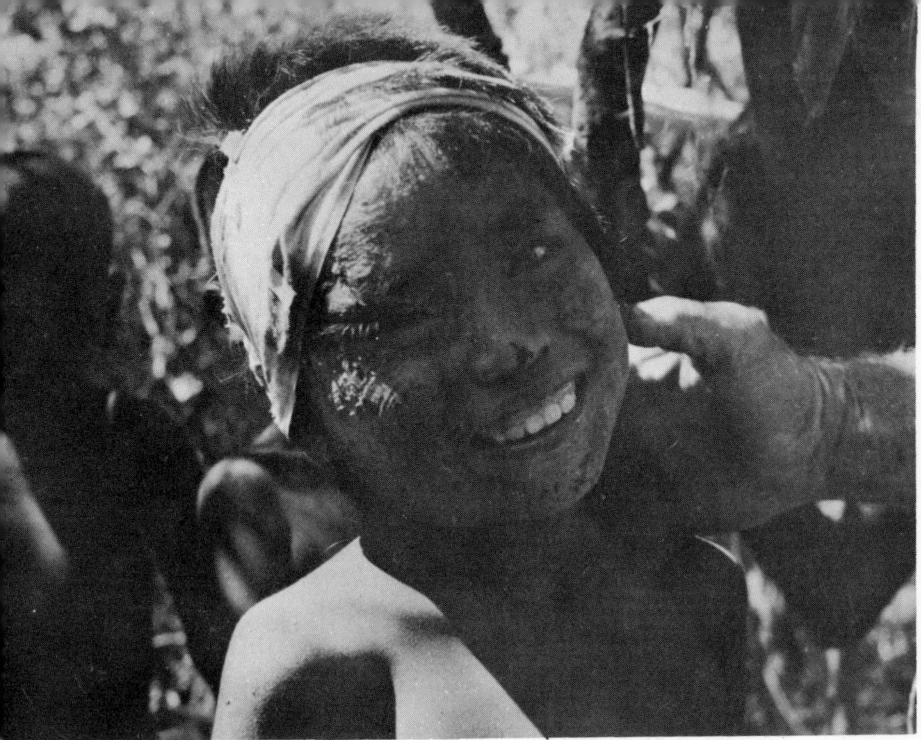

(Above) The Indians threw her into the jungle because they said the bird god had made her fall in the fire. But through little Simatague, Bill Pencille was able to prove that God is more powerful than the bird.

(Below) When his baby died, this man threw a shovel full of hot coals on himself in order to share some of his son's pain.

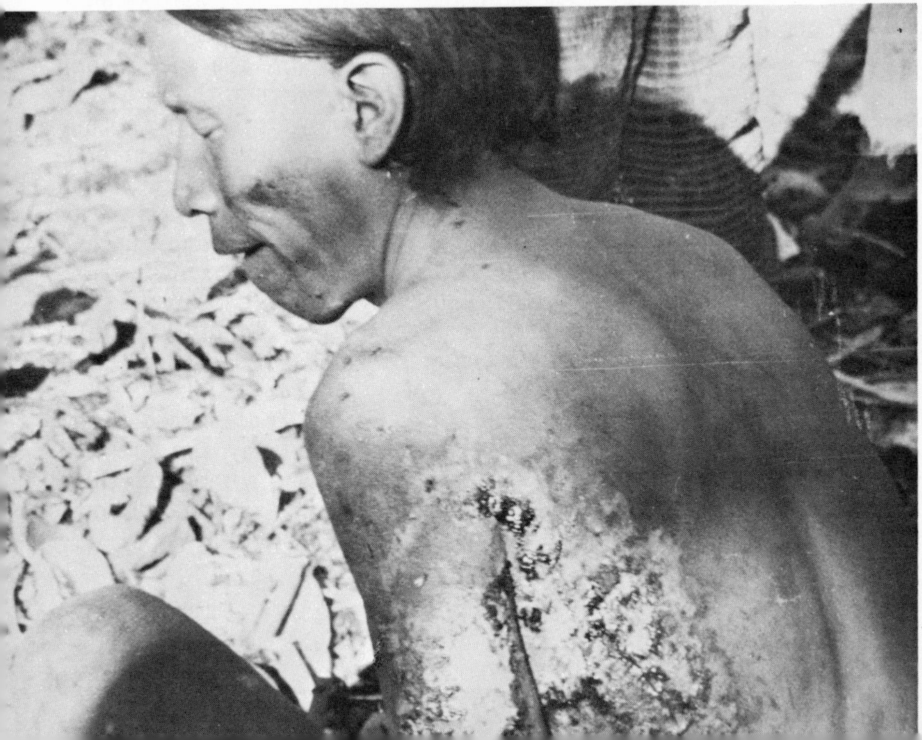

Epilogue

UNABLE TO KILL UEJAI and his people, Natui and his braves changed their tactics. They now urged the warriors to return with them to the railroad line, promising them tools, clothing and food. Some seventy accepted the invitation.

Uejai was brokenhearted. He was wise enough to see that this exodus was but a presage of the breaking up of his power. He called Bill to his campfire that night and said, "Bill, you don't love me!"

"Why do you say that, Uejai?" Bill queried, perplexed.

"If you really loved me, you'd take me to the railroad."

"O.K., if that's what you want, let's go!" There was no alternative.

Three months later, the first of the Guidaigosode arrived at the railroad line. There were over seventy of them. The rest were strung out behind them along the Quimome River. Then three things happened in rapid succession.

The Indians from Natui's group broke their treaty with Uejai and shot three of the Guidaigosode in the back.

A Bolivian rancher lost his nerve on seeing so many naked savages, and fired four shots at them. His hand trembled so, that he missed. But the Indians were infuriated, and killed three pigs and a horse in retaliation — one for each shot.

A strong epidemic of grippe raced through the area, and the Indians began to cough.

The chief came to Bill one morning and announced that the group was going south into the forest for a few days to hunt. Bill accused him of hiding his true purpose, and said that they probably did not plan to return. But when the chief gave assurance that they would be back in a few days, Bill consented to their going.

A month passed, and when they did not return, Bill, along with John Depue and a few Christian Ayorés, went in search of them. It was a sad trail they had to follow. It soon became evident that the grippe had struck in full force, and after several days of walking the party began to come upon little groups of stragglers, sick and unable to travel, lying in little leaf shelters by the side of the trail. Quickly treating each one with medicine, they pressed on. They found where the little group that fled had contacted the larger groups still working their way northward, and contaminated them with their sickness. Then all had turned and fled together. They found other groups of stragglers, too weak to walk. And they found twenty-six bodies, skeletons, and fresh graves.

Many miles south of the railroad line the trail ended in a vast, dry wasteland. Bill could go no further. Gathering up the thirty or so stragglers, he brought them back with him to the railroad and nursed them back to health. Eventually, they were settled along with some one hundred others in a new mission station which John Depue founded and named Yoquidai ("our village"). The few of the Guidaigosode who have stayed in the missions have proven exceptionally receptive to the Gospel, and nearly all of them have professed faith in Jesus Christ.

But the majority of the Guidaigosode still roam the vast forests surrounding the Salt Lake of Bolivia. They are part of the still unfinished task — the bringing of the Gospel to the lost tribes of the Amazon.

Key to pronunciation of Ayoré names (approximate)

Ajaronate	ah HA row nah tay
Ajote	ah hoe TAY
Asidate	ah SEE day tay
Aside	ah SEE day
Asona	ah so NAH
Ayore	ah yo RAY
Bajode	bah ho DAY
Chiquenore	chee KAY no ray
Comai	koh MY
Cucaratedo	coo kah RAH tay doe
Cuchacarataide	coo cha ca ra TIE day
Cutaide	coo TIE day
Dago	dah GO
Dajusui	dah who SU ee
Dajei	da HAY
Deguide	day GOO ee day
Dijere	dee HAY re
Diraidaquide	dee rye DAH key day
Direquedenagosode	dee reh keh DEH nah go SO day
Ducubaide	do COO bye day
Dupade	do PAH day
Ebiadate	EH bee ah dah TAY
Egarede	egg are EH day
Enune	eh NEW nay
Gaturai	ga TOO rye

Goane	go AH nay
Guede	gay DAY
Guedoside	gay doe SEE day
Gueodeuechai	GAY oh day WAYCH eye
Guidaigosode	gee die go So day
Idaide	ee DIE day
Igarede	ee gah RAY day
Jara	ha RAH
Jecuresi	hay coo ray SEE
Jemi	hay Me
Jururgai	who RUE guy
Naramia	nah rah ME ah
Naropie	NAH row pee aye
Natui	nah TOO ee
Natuinacode	nah TOO ee nah koh day
Natuinate	nah TOO ee nah tay
Natuine	nah TOO ee nay
Noraine	no RYE nay
Nuidate	NEW ee dah tay
Nuine	NEW ee nay
Nupedogosode	new pay DOE go so day
Ojidaquide	oh HE DAH key day
Omi	oh ME
Pajei	pa HAY
Paoi	pa OI
Sidi	see DEE
Simatague	see mah TAH gay
Sirine	see REE nay
Tagaca	tah GA kah
Taguide	tah GOO ee day
Tara	tah RAH
Tarane	tah rah NAY
Taranate	tah rah nah TAY
Uapede	WAH pay day
Uejai	way HI

Glossary of Plants and Foods

Spanish

arroz — rice

cardo — rather broadly used of several species of thorny plants, growing both on the ground and in trees.

curupau — a hardwood tree with smooth gray bark and red heart. Widely used as firewood and as a source of tannin.

motacú — a palm of medium height with broad fronds. Widely used in roofing. The heart is edible.

saó — the needle palm

toborochi — the bottle tree

Ayoré

chicore (chee KOH ray) — the sipoy

cupesi (coo PAY see) — the Spanish *algarroba,* a leguminous tree with an edible seed pod. Most of the tribes living in the Chaco of Paraguay, northern Argentina, and S.E. Bolivia make extensive use of this pod for food.

doria (doe REE ah) — very similar to the *doriaquedena,* but with an edible heart. It is not suitable for fiber.

doriaquedena (doe REE ah kay DEH nah) — Spanish: *caraguatá*; the wild pineapple, used as a source of fiber for weaving by the Ayorés.

dutuhe (do too AYE) — summer squash

guenai (gay NIGH) — corn